Ethical Hacking Essential Concepts

1st Edition

https://ipspecialist.net/

Document Control

Proposal Name	:	Ethical Hacking Essential Concepts
Document Edition	:	1st Edition
Document Release Date	:	14th April 2025
Reference	:	CEH
Exam Code	:	312-50
IPS Product Code	:	20250204010501

Scan Me

Feedback:

If you have any comments regarding the quality of this book or otherwise alter it to suit your needs better, you can contact us through email at info@ipspecialist.net

Please include the book's title and ISBN in your message.

Understanding IPSpecialist Paperback vs. eBook Versions

At IPSpecialist, we strive to provide high-quality learning resources tailored to different learning preferences and needs. Whether you prefer a concise and focused study experience or a comprehensive deep dive into the subject matter, we offer two distinct formats:

1. Paperback Version – Concise & Structured Learning

Our paperback books are designed to be precise, structured, and exam-focused, ensuring that learners get all the essential information required according to the book's title and certification objectives. The concise format helps professionals, students, and exam candidates quickly grasp core concepts.

Key Features of the Paperback Version:

- Focused content with only the most relevant information necessary for the certification or subject.

- Optimized for quick reading and last-minute exam preparation.

- Covers core topics with clear explanations, key points, and essential study notes.

- Additional in-depth resources and expanded explanations are available through our GitHub repository.

Access More Detailed Content Online:

Since the paperback edition is concise, IPSpecialist provides exclusive access to supplementary materials, hands-on labs, and expanded concepts on our GitHub repository. This allows learners to delve deeper into topics as needed while keeping the book streamlined for efficient learning.

2. Kindle eBook Version – In-Depth & Extensive Coverage

For learners who prefer an extremely detailed and comprehensive approach, our Kindle eBook version provides **all**-inclusive coverage of the subject matter. This format is ideal for those who want to explore every aspect of the certification.

Key Features of the eBook Version:

- Extensive and detailed explanations covering all concepts in the domain.
- Rich with examples, case studies, and practical scenarios
- Includes online resources, additional references, and interactive links.
- Regular updates ensure you always have the latest information.

About IPSpecialist

IPSPECIALIST LTD. IS COMMITTED TO EXCELLENCE AND DEDICATED TO YOUR SUCCESS.

At IPSpecialist, we are passionate about empowering individuals to excel in the ever-evolving world of technology. As a leading provider of Cloud Computing, Cybersecurity, Networking, DevOps, Artificial Intelligence, and other emerging technologies, we strive to equip our students with the knowledge and skills they need to succeed in these dynamic fields.

Course Features:

❖ Self-Paced Learning
   • Learn at your own pace and in your own time
❖ Covers Complete Exam Blueprint
   • Prep-up for the exam with confidence
❖ Case Study Based Learning
   • Relate the content with real-life scenarios
❖ Subscriptions that Suits You
   • Get more and pay less with IPS subscriptions
❖ Practice Questions
   • Practice questions to measure your preparation standards
❖ On Request Digital Certification
   • On request digital certification from IPSpecialist LTD.

Free Resources:

For Free Resources: Please visit our website and register to access your desired Resources Or contact us at: helpdesk@ipspecialist.net

IPS Personalized Technical Support for Customers: Good customer service means helping customers efficiently and in a friendly manner. It is essential to be able to handle issues for customers and do your best to ensure they are satisfied. Providing good service is one of the most important things that can set our business apart from others of its kind.

Excellent customer service will attract more customers and attain maximum customer retention.

IPS offers personalized TECH support to its customers to provide better value for money. If you have any queries related to technology and labs, you can simply ask our technical team for assistance via Live Chat or Email.

About the Authors:

This book has been compiled with the help of multiple professional engineers. These engineers specialize in different fields, e.g., Networking, Security, Cloud, Big Data, IoT, etc. Each engineer develops content in their specialized field that is compiled to form a comprehensive certification guide.

About the Technical Reviewers:

Nouman Ahmed Khan

AWS/Azure/GCP-Architect, CCDE, CCIEx5 (R&S, SP, Security, DC, Wireless), CISSP, CISA, CISM, CRISC, ISO27K-LA is a Solution Architect working with a global telecommunication provider. He works with enterprises, mega-projects, and service providers to help them select the best-fit technology solutions. He also works as a consultant to understand customer business processes and helps select an appropriate technology strategy to support business goals. He has more than eighteen years of experience working with global clients. One of his notable experiences was his tenure with a large managed security services provider, where he was responsible for managing the complete MSSP product portfolio. With his extensive knowledge and expertise in various areas of technology, including cloud computing, network infrastructure, security, and risk management, Nouman has become a trusted advisor for his clients.

Abubakar Saeed

Having started from the grassroots level as an engineer and contributed to the Introduction of Internet in Pakistan and elsewhere, a professional journey of over twenty-nine years in various organizations, national and international. Experienced in leading businesses with a focus on Innovation and Transformation.

He is also experienced in Managing, Consulting, Designing, and implementing projects. Heading Operations, Solutions Design, and Integration. Emphasizing on adhering to Project timelines and delivering as per customer expectations, advocate for adopting technology to simplify operations and enhance efficiency.

Dr. Fahad Abdali

Dr. Fahad Abdali is a seasoned leader with extensive experience in managing diverse businesses. With an impressive twenty years track record, Dr. Abdali brings a wealth of expertise to the table. Holding a bachelor's degree from the NED University of Engineers & Technology and Ph.D. from the University of Karachi, he has consistently demonstrated a deep commitment to academic excellence and professional growth. Driven by a passion for innovation and a keen understanding of industry dynamics, he has successfully navigated complex challenges, driving growth and fostering organizational success.

Mehwish Jawed

Mehwish Jawed is a Senior Research Analyst with a strong background in Telecommunication Engineering and expertise in cybersecurity, artificial intelligence (AI), cloud computing, and databases. She holds a Master's and Bachelor's degree from NED University, with published research on TWDM Passive Optical Networks (PON). Her experience spans roles as a Project Engineer and Product Lead, and she has deep technical knowledge of AWS, GCP, Oracle Cloud, Microsoft Azure, and Microsoft technologies. Mehwish's skillset in AI and databases enhances her ability to deliver secure and efficient solutions across diverse platforms.

Mohammad Usman Khan

Muhammad Usman Khan is a Technical Content Developer. He holds a Bachelor's Degree in Telecommunication Engineering from Sir Syed University of Engineering & Technology. He holds the First Position in Telecommunication Engineering and received two Gold Medals, the first from Sir Syed University of Engineering & Technology and the second from the Institute of Engineers Pakistan (IEP). He worked on many Deep Learning projects. He is a Cisco Certified Network Associate (CCNA). He is also certified by the National Center of Artificial Intelligence (NCAI), which is a research institute of the Government of Pakistan in the field of Artificial Intelligence. He is also certified by the Nvidia Deep Learning Institute in Deep Learning with Computer Vision.

Tooba Nisar

Tooba Nisar is a cybersecurity professional with experience in network security, and penetration testing. She has extensive knowledge in domains including SSCP, GIAC

GSEC, CompTIA Security+, CompTIA CYSA+, CEH, CCNA, and Linux for Penetration Testing. She holds a degree in Telecommunications Engineering from NED University of Engineering & Technology. She is currently pursuing post-graduation in Information Security from NED University. She also has experience with Fortinet solutions such as Fortinet FortiGate and FortiGate Operator. With more than 2+ years in reviewing and validating technical content, she ensures its accuracy and relevance. She translates complex cybersecurity concepts into clear, actionable insights for professionals and enthusiasts in the field.

Rafia Bilal

Rafia Bilal is a technical content creator specializing in cloud computing (AWS and Azure Cloud), networking, and cybersecurity. She has authored and contributed to multiple books, including AWS certification guides, cybersecurity, and networking resources. At IPSpecialist, her expertise extends to scripting, video creation, and voiceovers for technical training materials. Rafia holds a degree in Telecommunications Engineering from NED University of Engineering and Technology. Passionate about making complex tech concepts accessible, she helps professionals and learners navigate the evolving cloud and cybersecurity landscape.

Our Products

Study Guides

IPSpecialist Study Guides are the ideal guides to developing the hands-on skills necessary to pass the exam. Our workbooks cover the official exam blueprint and explain the technology with real-life case study-based labs. The content covered in each workbook consists of individually focused technology topics presented in an easy-to-follow, goal-oriented, step-by-step approach. Every scenario features detailed breakdowns and thorough verifications to help you completely understand the task and associated technology.

We extensively used mind maps in our workbooks to visually explain the technology. Our workbooks have become a widely used tool to learn and remember information effectively.

Practice Questions

IPSpecialists' Practice Questions are dedicatedly designed from a certification exam perspective. The collection of these questions from our Study Guides is prepared to keep the exam blueprint in mind, covering not only important but necessary topics. It is an ideal document to practice and revise your certification.

Exam Cram

Our Exam Cram notes are a concise bundling of condensed notes of the complete exam blueprint. It is an ideal and handy document to help you remember the most important technology concepts related to the certification exam.

Hands-on Labs

IPSpecialist Hands-on Labs are the fastest and easiest way to learn real-world use cases. These labs are carefully designed to prepare you for the certification exams and your next job role. Whether you are starting to learn a technology or solving a real-world scenario, our labs will help you learn the core concepts in no time.

IPSpecialist self-paced labs are designed by subject matter experts and provide an opportunity to use products in a variety of pre-designed scenarios and common use cases, giving you hands-on practice in a simulated environment to help you gain confidence. You have the flexibility to choose from topics and products about which you want to learn more.

Companion Guide

Companion Guides are portable desk guides for the IPSpecialist course materials that users (students, professionals, and experts) can access at any time and from any location. Companion Guides are intended to supplement online course material by assisting users in concentrating on key ideas and planning their study time for quizzes and examinations.

Study Cards

IPSpecialist Study Cards offer concise, to-the-point notes designed for efficient memorization of key exam concepts. Aligned with the exam blueprint, each card covers essential technology topics with clear explanations and real-world examples.

Content at a Glance

Table of Contents

About CEHv13 Course

This course offers a comprehensive and practical approach to mastering the skills required to pass the Certified Ethical Hacking (CEHv13) 312-50 exam. Developed by IPSpecialist, this course is designed not only to prepare you for the exam but to ensure that you gain hands-on experience with real-world examples and case studies, enabling you to apply your learning in a practical context.

→ Covers complete CEHv13 blueprint
→ Summarized content
→ Case Study based approach
→ Ready to practice labs on VM
→ Pass guarantee
→ Exam tips
→ Mind maps
→ Practice questions

In this course, you will learn the best ethical hacking practices and techniques to prepare for the CEHv13 certification using the latest tools and techniques currently available in the cybersecurity industry. Furthermore, this authoritative guide will remain a valuable resource long after you've passed the exam. Whether you're just starting out or advancing your career, the knowledge you gain here will be essential throughout your professional journey in ethical hacking.

Security Certification Tracks

	University Courses	Marketing/ Management	Information Security		Application Security
Chief Information Security Officer (CISO)					
Expert	MSS		CAT618 CAT616 CAT611 CAT614 CAT612		CAST613
Specialist	BCA BIS	PMITS	PM PM PM PM PM PM		
Advanced	ADCA ADIS	PM CIMP CRM	CEH		PM PM PM PM
Intermediate	DCA DIS		CND		
Fundamental		FPM	FNS FIS FCF		FSP
		Certified Secure Computer User (CSCU)			

How does CEH Certification Help?

A Certified Ethical Hacker is a skilled professional who understands and knows how to look for weaknesses and vulnerabilities in target systems and uses the same knowledge and tools as a clever hacker, but lawfully and legitimately, to assess the security posture of a target system(s). The CEH credential certifies individuals in the specific network security discipline of Ethical Hacking from a vendor-neutral perspective.

The purpose of the CEH credential is to:

→ Establish and govern minimum standards for credentialing professional information security specialists in ethical hacking measures.

→ Inform the public that credentialed individuals meet or exceed the minimum standards.

→ Reinforce ethical hacking as a unique and self-regulating profession.

Prerequisites

CEH requires the candidate to have two years of work experience in the Information Security domain and should be able to provide proof of the same as validated through the application process unless the candidate attends official training.

About the CEHv13 Exam

The Certified Ethical Hacker (CEH) v13 exam by EC-Council is a comprehensive certification that validates a professional's ability to identify vulnerabilities, assess security threats, and defend against various cyberattacks using ethical hacking techniques. CEH v13 has been updated to incorporate cutting-edge technologies such as artificial intelligence (AI), cloud security, and Internet of Things (IoT) vulnerabilities, reflecting the evolving cybersecurity landscape.

Exam Questions	MCQs
Number of Questions	125
Time to Complete	240 minutes
Exam Fee	850 USD
Certification Validity	3 years
Passing Score	70%

With the help of this updated version of the book, you will learn about the most powerful and latest hacking techniques, categorized into four phases.

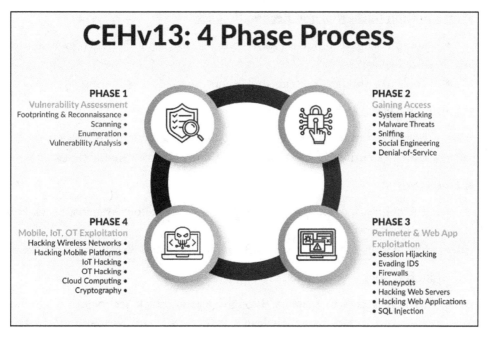

Figure 01: 4 Phases of CEHv13

Key Highlights of the CEHv13 Exam

- **AI-Powered Security Techniques**: CEHv13 introduces a strong emphasis on AI-driven tools for both defense and attack purposes. Candidates will gain knowledge of how to use AI to identify, exploit, and defend against cyber threats.
- **Cloud Security**: The certification updates coverage of cloud-specific vulnerabilities and ethical hacking tools tailored to cloud environments.
- **IoT Security**: With the growth of IoT devices, CEHv13 expands its focus on securing these devices and networks from potential attacks.
- **Modern Cybersecurity Threats**: The exam integrates modern cybersecurity threats, such as machine learning-based attacks, AI-driven malware, and vulnerabilities in AI systems.

Key Modules in CEHv13 Exam

CEHv13 retains the core structure of different modules that cover a wide range of cybersecurity and ethical hacking topics. Below are the key areas:

1. Introduction to Ethical Hacking

- Ethical hacking concepts, methodologies, and lifecycle.
- Overview of cybersecurity frameworks and standards.

2. Information Gathering and Reconnaissance

- Footprinting techniques, social engineering, and OSINT (Open Source Intelligence).
- Tools like Shodan, Maltego, and others are used for gathering intelligence.

3. Scanning Networks

- Network scanning techniques and tools, such as Nmap and Nessus.
- How to identify live hosts, open ports, and network vulnerabilities.

4. Enumeration

- Techniques for obtaining detailed information about systems, users, and network resources.
- Use of tools such as Netcat, SMB enumeration, and SNMP enumeration.

5. System Hacking

- Gaining access to systems through various attack techniques, including password cracking, privilege escalation, and exploiting system vulnerabilities.

6. Malware Threats

- AI-driven malware, including self-learning malware and its defense mechanisms.
- Malware analysis techniques and tools.

7. Sniffing and Social Engineering Attacks

- Using sniffing tools such as Wireshark and tcpdump to capture traffic.
- Mitigating social engineering attacks (phishing, pretexting, baiting).

8. Cloud Security

- Ethical hacking techniques for cloud platforms (AWS, Azure, Google Cloud).
- Addressing vulnerabilities related to cloud configurations, container security, and cloud service misconfigurations.

9. AI-Based Attack Techniques

- Use of machine learning models and AI-powered tools in both attacks and defenses.
- Detecting and mitigating AI-driven threats.

10. IoT Security

- Ethical hacking techniques for securing IoT devices and networks.

- Identifying vulnerabilities in IoT protocols (CoAP, MQTT) and defending against IoT-specific attacks.

11. Web Application Security

- Web application penetration testing (SQL injection, XSS, CSRF).
- Secure coding practices to mitigate common vulnerabilities.

12. Wireless Networks

- Hacking techniques specific to wireless networks (WEP, WPA, WPA2 cracking).
- Securing wireless communications and mitigating risks.

13. Cryptography

- Cryptographic algorithms and their vulnerabilities.
- Implementing strong cryptography practices to protect sensitive data.

14. AI in Vulnerability Detection

- AI-driven vulnerability scanners and their use in identifying system weaknesses.
- Integrating AI tools into security systems for proactive threat management.

Domain	Sub-Domain	No of Questions	Weightage
Information Security and Ethical Hacking Overview	Introduction to Ethical Hacking	8	6%
Reconnaissance Techniques	Footprinting and Reconnaissance	10	21%
	Scanning Networks	10	
	Enumeration	6	
Vulnerability Assessment	Vulnerability Analysis	9	17%
	System Hacking	6	
	Malware Threats	6	
Network and Perimeter Hacking	Sniffing	3	14%
	Social Engineering	5	
	Denial-of-Service	2	
	Session Hijacking	3	

Web Application Hacking	Hacking Web Servers	8	16%
	Hacking Web Applications	8	
	SQL Injections	4	
Wireless Network Hacking	Hacking Wireless Networks	8	6%
Mobile Platform, IoT, and OT Hacking	Hacking Mobile Platforms	4	8%
	IoT and OT Hacking	6	
Cloud Computing	Cloud Computing	7	6%
Cryptography	Cryptography	7	6%

Table 01: Domains

About this Book:

This comprehensive guide goes beyond just exam preparation. It offers a practical, hands-on approach with real-world examples and case studies, ensuring that you gain both theoretical knowledge and practical experience. From operating systems and network security to penetration testing and cyber threat intelligence, every domain essential to the CEHv13 exam is covered in-depth.

What sets this book apart is its focus on both foundational concepts and advanced hacking techniques. Each domain is explained clearly, equipping you with the knowledge and skills needed to tackle the exam and excel in real-world ethical hacking tasks.

How to Access CEHv13 Exam Resources

To access a detailed version of study guide of CEHv13 Exam including all topics, navigate to resources present at:

GitHub: https://github.com/IP-Specialist/CEHv13

Scan Me

To access a detailed step-by-step guide of each lab of CEHv13 Exam with the respective screenshots, navigate to resources present at:

GitHub: https://github.com/IP-Specialist/CEHv13---Hands-on-Labs

Scan Me

Other CEHv13 Products

- CEHv13 Study Guide
- CEHv13 Hands-on Labs
- CEHv13 Practice Questions
- CEHv13 Exam Cram Notes
- CEHv13 Glossary Booklet
- CEHv13 Study Cards
- CEHv13 Countermeasures
- Ethical Hacking AI Technologies

Ethical Hacking Essential Concepts

Ethical Hacking Essential Concepts serve as the backbone of the CEH certification and provide a comprehensive understanding of the ethical hacking landscape. At the core, these concepts revolve around the ethical hacker's role in identifying vulnerabilities before malicious attackers can exploit them. This includes a solid grasp of the types of hackers—white hat (ethical), black hat (malicious), and grey hat (a mix of both)—and their intentions and legal boundaries. Ethical hackers must understand the five critical phases of hacking:

- **Reconnaissance** – gathering preliminary data through passive and active techniques.
- **Scanning** – identifying live hosts, open ports, and potential vulnerabilities.
- **Gaining Access** – exploiting vulnerabilities to enter a system.
- **Maintaining Access** – ensuring long-term access using backdoors, Trojans, or rootkits.
- **Covering Tracks** – erasing digital footprints to avoid detection.

Additionally, these concepts cover the CIA triad (Confidentiality, Integrity, and Availability), which represents the guiding principles of information security. Learners are also introduced to threat modeling, risk assessment, types of malware (viruses, worms, Trojans), and key attack vectors such as phishing, social engineering, and DoS/DDoS attacks. Understanding network fundamentals, operating systems, and security controls is equally crucial.

By mastering these essential concepts, aspiring ethical hackers are equipped with the mindset and skills to think like an attacker, apply legal hacking techniques, and contribute effectively to strengthening an organization's cybersecurity posture.

Domain 01: Introduction to Ethical Hacking Essentials

Information Security Overview

System security consists of methods and processes for protecting information and information systems from unauthorized access, disclosure, usage, or modification. It ensures the confidentiality, integrity, and availability of information. If an organization lacks security policies and appropriate security rules, its confidential information and data will not be secure, putting it at great risk. Well-defined security policies and procedures help protect an organization's assets from unauthorized access and disclosures.

Millions of users interact with each other every minute in the modern world using latest technologies and platforms. These sixty seconds can be very vulnerable and costly to private and public organizations due to the presence of various types of old and modern threats present worldwide. The public internet is the most common and rapid option for spreading threats worldwide. Malicious codes and scripts, viruses, spam, and malware are constantly waiting to be accessed. This is why security risks to a network or a system can never be eliminated. Implementing a security policy that is effective and efficient, rather than consisting of unnecessary security implementations that can result in a waste of resources and create loopholes for threats, is a continual challenge.

It is necessary to understand key cybersecurity terminologies to better understand information security concepts. Here are some fundamental terms:

- **Hack Value:** It refers to the attractiveness, interest, or value of target to the hacker. The value describes the target's level of attractiveness to the hacker.

- **Zero-Day Attack:** It refers to threats and vulnerabilities that can be used to exploit the victim before the developer identifies or addresses them and releases a patch for them.

- **Vulnerability:** It refers to a weak point or loophole in any system or network that can be helpful and utilized by attackers to hack into the system. Any vulnerability can be an entry point from which they can reach their target.

- **Daisy Chaining:** It is a sequence of hacking or attacking attempts to gain access to a network or system, one after another, using the same information and the information obtained from the previous attempt.

- **Exploit:** It is a system security breach through vulnerabilities, zero-day attacks, or any other hacking technique.

- **Doxing:** It means publishing information, or a set of information, associated with an individual. This information is collected from publicly available databases, mostly social media and similar sources.

- **Payload:** It refers to the actual section of information or data in a frame as opposed to automatically generated metadata. In information security, a payload is a section or part of a malicious and exploited code that causes potentially harmful activities and actions such as exploiting, opening backdoors, and hijacking.

- **Bot:** It is software that controls the target remotely and executes predefined tasks. It is capable of running automated scripts over the internet. Bots are also known as internet bots or web robots. These Bots can be used for social purposes, for example, chatterbots and live chats. Furthermore, they can also be used for malicious purposes in the form of malware. Hackers use malware bots to gain complete authority over a computer.

Elements of Information Security

Confidentiality

The National Institute of Standards and Technology (NIST) defines confidentiality as "preserving authorized restrictions on information access and disclosure while including means for protecting personal privacy and proprietary information." It is essential to ensure that secret and sensitive data remains secure. Confidentiality ensures that only authorized personnel can access and manage the digital resources within our infrastructure. It also implies that unauthorized persons should not have any access to the data.

Data is categorized into two types: data in motion and data at rest. Data in motion, which travels across networks, should be encrypted before transmission. Additionally, sensitive data can be protected by using a separate network. Data at rest, stored on media like servers, hard drives, or the cloud, should also be encrypted to prevent unauthorized access in case of theft.

Integrity

The NIST defines integrity as "Guarding against improper information modification or destruction; this includes ensuring information non-repudiation and authenticity". Preventing unauthorized access to sensitive and personal data is essential to ensure its integrity and security. Data integrity ensures that only authorized parties can modify data. NIST SP 800-56B defines data integrity as a property whereby data has not been altered in an unauthorized manner since it was created, transmitted, or stored. This recommendation states that a cryptographic algorithm "provides data integrity," which means that the algorithm is used to detect unauthorized alterations.

Availability

Ensuring timely and reliable access to and using information applied to systems and data is termed as Availability. Suppose authorized personnel cannot access data due to general network failure or a Denial-of-Service (DoS) attack. In that case, it is considered a critical problem from the point of view of business, as it may result in loss of revenue or of records of some important results. The term "CIA" is used to remember these basic yet most important security concepts.

CIA	Risk	Control
Confidentiality	Loss of privacy, Unauthorized access to information and identity theft	Encryption, Authentication, Access Control
Integrity	Information is no longer reliable or accurate. Fraud	Maker/Checker, Quality Assurance, Audit Logs
Availability	Business disruption, Loss of customer confidence, Loss of revenue	Business continuity, Plans, and tests Backup storage, Sufficient capacity

Table 1-01: Cyber Risk and Protection with respect to CIA

Authenticity

Authentication is the process of identifying the credentials of authorized users or devices before granting privileges or access to a system or network and enforcing certain rules and policies. Similarly, authenticity ensures the appropriateness of certain information and whether it has been initiated by a valid user who claims to be the source of that information. Authenticity can be verified through the process of authentication.

Non-Repudiation

Non-repudiation is one of the Information Assurance (IA) pillars. It guarantees transmitting and receiving information between the sender and receiver via different techniques, such as digital signatures and encryption. Non-repudiation is the assurance of communication and its authenticity so that the sender is unable to deny the sent message. Similarly, the receiver cannot deny what they have received. Signatures, digital contracts, and email messages use non-repudiation techniques.

The Security, Functionality, and Usability Triangle

In a system, the level of security is a measure of the strength of a system's Security, Functionality, and Usability. These three components form the Security, Functionality, and Usability triangle. Consider a ball in this triangle—if it is sitting

in the center, all three components are stronger. On the other hand, if the ball is closer to Security, it means the system is consuming more resources for Security, and the system's Function and Usability require attention. A secure system must provide strong protection and offer the user complete services, features, and usability.

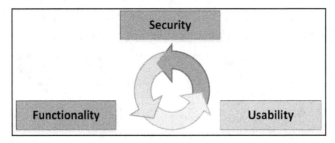

Figure 1-01: Security, Functionality, and Usability Triangle

Implementation of high-level security typically impacts the level of functionality and ease of usability. High-level security will quite often make the system nonuser-friendly and cause a decrease in performance. While deploying security in a system, security experts must ensure a reliable level of functionality and ease of usability. These three components of the triangle must always be balanced.

Threats and Attack Vectors

Motives, Methods, and Vulnerabilities

An attacker attacks the target system to penetrate information security with three attack vectors in mind: motive or objective, method, and vulnerability. These three components are the major blocks on which an attack depends.

- **Motive or Objective:** The reason an attacker focuses on a particular system

- **Method:** The technique or process used by an attacker to gain access to a target system

- **Vulnerability:** These help the attacker in fulfilling his intentions

An attacker's motive or objective for attacking a system may be a thing of value stored in that specific system. It may be ethical, or it may be non-ethical. However, there is always a goal for the hacker to achieve that leads to a threat to the system. Some typical motives behind attacks are information theft, manipulation of data, disruption, propagation of political or religious beliefs, attacks on the target's reputation, or revenge. The method of attack and vulnerability run side by side. To achieve their motives, hackers use various tools and techniques to exploit a system once a vulnerability has been detected.

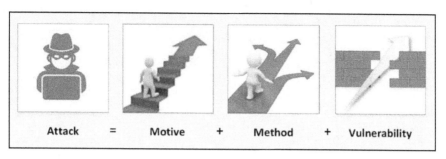

Figure 1-02: Attack Methodology

Top Information Security Attack Vectors

Cloud Computing Threats

Cloud computing has become a popular trend today. Its widespread implementation has exposed it to several security threats. Many of the threats resemble those encountered by traditionally hosted environments. Securing cloud computing is crucial for protecting important and confidential data.

The following are common threats in cloud security:

- A major threat to cloud security is a single data breach that results in a significant loss. It allows the hacker to have access to records; hence, a single breach may compromise all the information available on the cloud. It is an extremely serious situation, as the compromise of a single record can lead to multiple records being compromised.

- Data loss is one of the most common potential threats to cloud security. Data loss may be due to intended or accidental means. It may be large-scale or small-scale; though massive data loss is catastrophic and costly.

- Another major threat to cloud computing is hijacking an account or a service over the cloud. Applications running on a cloud with flaws, weak encryption, loopholes, and vulnerabilities allow the intruder to gain control, manipulate data, and alter the functionality of the service.

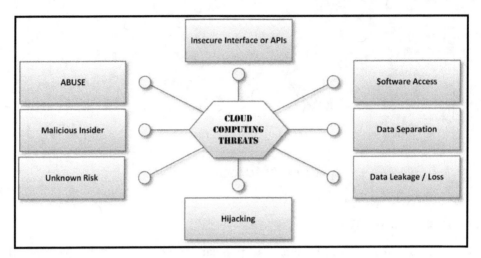

Figure 1-03: Cloud Computing Threats

Additionally, cloud computing faces several other threats, including:

- Insecure APIs

- Denial of Services

- Malicious Insiders

- Misconfigurations

- Poorly Secured Multi-Tenancy

Advanced Persistent Threats

An Advanced Persistent Threat (APT) is the process of stealing information through a continuous procedure. An advanced persistent threat usually focuses on private organizations or political motives. The APT process relies upon advanced and sophisticated techniques to exploit vulnerabilities within a system. The term "persistent" defines the process of an external command and controlling system that continuously monitors and fetches data from a target. The term "threat" indicates the involvement of an attacker with potentially harmful intentions.

Table 1-02 shows the characteristics of APT criteria are:

Characteristics	Description
Objectives	Motive or goal of threat
Timeliness	Time spent in probing & accessing the target
Resources	Level of knowledge & tools
Risk Tolerance	Tolerance to remain undetected
Skills & Methods	Tools & techniques used throughout the event
Actions	Precise action of threat

Table 1-02: APT Criteria Characteristics

Viruses and Worms

The term virus in network and information security describes malicious software. This malicious software is designed to spread by attaching itself to other files. Attaching itself This malicious software is designed to spread by attaching itself to other files, facilitating its transfer to different systems to trigger, infect, and initiate malicious activities on the resident system.

Worms are a type of malicious software that, unlike viruses, do not require a host program to replicate. They are self-replicating and can autonomously spread across systems, networks, or devices without user interaction. This self-propagating nature allows worms to infect systems rapidly, often exploiting vulnerabilities in network protocols or software. Since their emergence in the 1980s, worms have evolved in complexity and impact. Some modern variants are specifically designed to cause severe disruption, including launching Denial of Service (DoS) attacks, consuming bandwidth, and degrading network performance. These destructive worms can spread widely in a very short time, making them a significant threat in cybersecurity.

Mobile Threats

Emerging mobile phone technology, especially smartphones, has raised the focus of attacks on mobile devices. As smartphones became popularly used all over the world, attackers' focus shifted to stealing business and personal information through mobile devices. The most common threats to mobile devices are:

- Data Leakage
- Unsecure Wi-Fi

- Network Spoofing

- Phishing Attacks

- Spyware

- Broken Cryptography

- Improper Session Handling

Insider Threat

An insider can also misuse a system within a corporate network. Users are termed "Insider" and have different privileges and authorization power to access and grant the network resources.

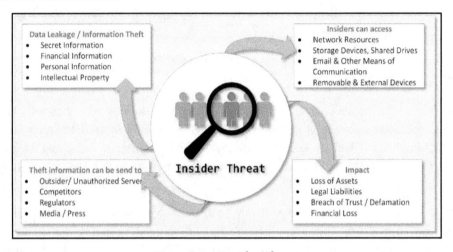

Figure 1-04: Insider Threat

Botnets

Botnets are the group of bots connected through the internet to perform a distributed task continuously. They are known as the workhorses of the internet. These botnets perform repetitive tasks (Robot) over the internet (Network). Botnets are mostly used in Internet Relay Chats. These types of botnets are legal and useful.

A bot may be used for positive intentions, but illegal bots are also intended for malicious activities. These malicious bots can gain access to a system by using malicious scripts and codes, either directly exploiting the vulnerability of the system or through a "Spider". A Spider program crawls over the internet and searches for security holes. Bots introduce the system to the hacker's web by contacting the master computer. It alerts the master computer when the system is under control. Attackers remotely control all bots from the master computer.

Information Warfare

Information warfare refers to the use of Information and Communication Technology (ICT) to gain a competitive advantage over an opponent. Information warfare is classified into two types:

Defensive Information Warfare

The term Defensive Information Warfare refers to all defensive actions taken to protect oneself from attacks executed to steal information and information-based processes. Defensive Information warfare areas are:

- Prevention
- Deterrence
- Indication and Warning
- Detection
- Emergency Preparedness
- Response

Offensive Information Warfare

Offensive warfare is an aggressive operation that proactively takes against a rival rather than waiting for the attackers to launch an attack. The fundamental concept of offensive warfare is accessing their territory to occupy it rather than lose it. In offensive warfare, the attacker identifies the opponent and their strategies, then decides to strike based on the available information. Offensive Information warfare prevents the information from being used by considering integrity, availability, and confidentiality.

Hacking Concepts

The term hacking in information security refers to exploiting vulnerabilities in a system and compromising the security to gain unauthorized command and control of the system. The purpose of hacking may include altering a system's resources or disrupting features and services to achieve other goals. Hacking can also be used to steal confidential information for any use, such as sending it to competitors or regulatory bodies or publicizing it.

Hacker

A Hacker is a person capable of stealing information such as business data, personal data, financial information, credit card information, username, and password from a system she or he has no authorized access to. An attacker gains access by taking unauthorized control over that system using different techniques and tools. They have great skills and abilities for developing and exploring software and hardware.

There can be several reasons for hacking, the most common: being fun, money, thrills, or a personal vendetta.

Hackers usually fall into one of the following categories, according to their activities:

White Hat Hackers

White hat hackers also known as penetration testers are people who apply their hacking expertise for defensive objectives. Nowadays, most companies employ security experts to protect their networks and information systems from cyberattacks using countermeasures. These experts are authorized by the system owner.

Black Hat Hackers

Black hat hackers also known as crackers are the ones who exploit their exceptional computer skills for malevolent or unlawful ends. This type of hacker frequently engages in illegal activity.

Gray Hat Hackers

People who work both offensively and defensively at different periods are known as gray hats. Gray hats can assist hackers in identifying different weaknesses in a system or network while also assisting businesses in enhancing their goods (hardware or software) by examining their limitations and enhancing their security.

Hacktivists

Hacktivism is a form of activism in which hackers infiltrate corporate or government computer networks as a form of protest. Hacktivists employ hacking to improve their reputations both online and offline and to raise notice of their social or political agendas. They specifically use hacking to deface or disable websites to further a political cause. Hacktivists have occasionally been known to access and make public sensitive material. Governmental organizations, financial institutions, global enterprises, and any other organization they believe poses a threat are common targets for hacktivists. Unauthorized access is illegal, regardless of the motivations of hacktivists.

Script Kiddies

Script kiddies are inexperienced hackers who use software, tools, and scripts created by professional hackers to compromise systems. Typically, they prioritize the number of attacks they launch over their quality. Their goal is to gain attention or demonstrate their technical skills, without a specific target or objective when launching the attack

Hacking Phases

The following are the five phases of hacking:

1. Reconnaissance
2. Scanning
3. Gaining Access
4. Maintaining Access
5. Clearing Tracks

Reconnaissance

Reconnaissance is an initial preparation phase in which the attacker gathers information about the target using various tools and techniques before launching the attack.. Gathering information about the target makes it easier for an attacker. It helps to identify the target range for large-scale attacks.

In passive reconnaissance, a hacker acquires information about the target without directly interacting with the target. An example of passive reconnaissance is searching social media to obtain the target's information.

Active reconnaissance is gaining information by directly interacting with the target. Examples of active reconnaissance include interacting with the target via calls, emails, help desk, or technical departments.

Scanning

Scanning is a pre-attack phase. In this phase, an attacker scans the network through information acquired during the initial phase of reconnaissance. Scanning tools include dialers, scanners such as port scanners, network mappers, and client tools such as ping and vulnerability scanners. During the scanning phase, attackers finally fetch the ports' information, including port status, Operating System information, device type, live machines, and other information depending on scanning.

Gaining Access

In this hacking phase, the hacker gains control over an Operating System (OS), application, or computer network. The control gained by the attacker defines the access level, whether the Operating System level, application level, or network level. Techniques include password cracking, denial of service, session hijacking, buffer overflow, or other techniques used for gaining unauthorized access. After accessing the system, the attacker escalates the privileges to a point to obtain complete control over services and processes and compromise the connected intermediate system.

Maintaining Access / Escalation of Privileges

The maintaining access phase is the point where an attacker tries to maintain access, ownership, and control over the compromised systems. The hacker usually strengthens the system to secure it from being accessed by security personnel or some other hacker. They use Backdoors, Rootkits, or Trojans to retain their ownership. In this phase, an attacker may either steal information by uploading it to the remote server, download any file on the resident system, or manipulate the data and configuration settings. The attacker uses this compromised system to launch attacks to compromise other systems.

Clearing Tracks

An attacker must hide his identity by clearing or covering tracks. Clearing tracks is an activity that is carried out to hide malicious activities. To achieve their goals without being detected, attackers must erase any traces or evidence that could reveal their identity and to do this, attackers usually overwrite the system, applications, and other related logs.

Ethical Hacking Concepts

Ethical hacking and penetration testing are common terms and have been popular in information security environments for a long time. Over the last decade, the increase in cybercrimes and hacking has created a great challenge for security experts, analysts, and regulations. The virtual war between hackers and security professionals has become very common.

Security experts' fundamental challenges include finding weaknesses and deficiencies in running upcoming systems, applications, or software and proactively addressing them. Investigating before an attack occurs is less costly than after facing or dealing with it. To ensure security, organizations appoint both internal teams and external experts for penetration testing, depending on the severity and scope of the threat.

Why Ethical Hacking is Necessary

The rising number of malicious activities and cybercrimes and the appearance of different forms of advanced attacks have created the need for ethical hacking. An ethical hacker penetrates the security of systems and networks in order to determine their security level and advises organizations to take precautions and remediation actions against aggressive attacks. These aggressive and advanced attacks include:

- Denial-of-Services Attacks
- Manipulation of Data

- Identity Theft
- Vandalism
- Credit Card Theft
- Piracy
- Theft of Services

The increase in these types of attacks, hacking cases, and cyber-attacks is mainly due to the increase in the use of online transactions and online services over the last decade. It has become much easier for hackers to steal financial information. Cybercrime law has only managed to slow down prank activities, whereas real attacks and cybercrimes have risen. Ethical hacking focuses on the requirement of a pentester, penetration tester in short, who searches for vulnerabilities and flaws in a system before it is compromised.

To succeed in defending against attackers, one must think and act like them. Hackers are highly skilled, with deep knowledge of hardware, software, and exploration techniques. As a result, ethical hacking has become essential. An ethical hacker can counter malicious hackers' attacks by anticipating their methods. Ethical hacking is also needed to uncover the vulnerabilities in systems and security controls to secure them before they are compromised.

Scope and Limitations of Ethical Hacking

Ethical Hacking is crucial component of risk assessment, auditing, and countering fraud. Ethical hacking is widely used as penetration testing to identify vulnerabilities and risks and highlight loopholes to take preventive action against attacks.

However, there are some limitations to ethical hacking. In some cases, ethical hacking is insufficient for resolving the issue. For example, an organization must first figure out what it is looking for before hiring an external pentester. This helps achieve goals and save time, as the testing team can then focus on troubleshooting the actual problem and resolving the issues. The ethical hacker also helps to understand an organization's security system better. It is up to the organization to take action recommended by the pentester and enforce security policies over the system and network.

Skills of an Ethical Hacker

An expert ethical hacker has a set of technical and non-technical skills, as outlined below:

Technical Skills

1. In-depth knowledge of almost all Operating Systems, including all popular, widely-used OSes such as Windows, Linux, Unix, and Macintosh.

2. Skilled at networking, basic and detailed concepts and technologies, and exploring hardware and software capabilities.
3. Strong command over security areas, information security-related issues, and technical domains.
4. Detailed knowledge of all older, advanced, and sophisticated attacks.

Non-Technical Skills

1. Must possess a strong commitment to ongoing education to stay abreast of the rapidly evolving cybersecurity landscape.
2. Exceptional analytical and critical thinking capabilities to effectively identify, assess, and mitigate complex security vulnerabilities.
3. Proficiency in articulating technical concepts to both technical and non-technical stakeholders is essential for conveying security assessments and recommendations.
4. A deep commitment to ethical principles and security policies is crucial, given the sensitive nature of their work and the trust placed in them to protect organizational assets.

Cybersecurity Laws and Regulations

Cybersecurity laws and regulations are essential frameworks established by governments and regulatory bodies to protect information systems, networks, and data from cyber threats. These laws aim to ensure organizations implement adequate security measures, protect individual privacy, and maintain the integrity of critical infrastructures. Below is an overview of key cybersecurity laws and regulations across various regions:

1. United States

The U.S. lacks a singular, comprehensive federal cybersecurity law; instead, it enforces a combination of sector-specific regulations:

- **Health Insurance Portability and Accountability Act (HIPAA):** Enacted in 1996, HIPAA mandates healthcare organizations to implement measures safeguarding the confidentiality and security of health information.

- **Gramm-Leach-Bliley Act (GLBA):** This act requires financial institutions to protect consumers' personal financial information, enforcing privacy and information security provisions.

- **Federal Information Security Management Act (FISMA):** FISMA obligates federal agencies to develop, document, and implement programs to secure their information systems.

- **Cybersecurity Information Sharing Act (CISA):** Enacted in 2015, CISA facilitates the sharing of cybersecurity threat information between the federal government and private sector entities.

- **California Consumer Privacy Act (CCPA):** Effective in 2020, the CCPA grants California residents rights regarding their personal data, imposing obligations on businesses to ensure data privacy and protection.

Despite these regulations, challenges persist due to overlapping mandates and inconsistent requirements across different sectors and states, complicating compliance efforts for organizations.

2. European Union

The EU has implemented comprehensive regulations to bolster cybersecurity and data protection:

- **General Data Protection Regulation (GDPR):** Effective in 2018, GDPR sets stringent requirements for data protection and privacy, applying to all organizations processing personal data of EU residents, regardless of the organization's location.

- **NIS 2 Directive:** An update to the original Network and Information Security Directive, NIS 2 aims to enhance cybersecurity across the EU by setting stricter security requirements for a broader range of sectors.

- **Cyber Resilience Act (CRA):** Proposed in 2022 and adopted in 2024, the CRA introduces common cybersecurity standards for products with digital elements, such as mandatory incident reporting and automatic security updates.

3. United Kingdom

In 2024, the UK government announced the Cyber Security and Resilience Bill (CS&R), aiming to strengthen the nation's cyber defenses. The proposed legislation seeks to update existing regulations, expand reporting requirements, and empower regulators to proactively address vulnerabilities, thereby enhancing the resilience of critical infrastructure and digital services.

4. Australia

Australia has introduced new cybersecurity laws requiring businesses to report ransomware payments to authorities. These measures aim to improve transparency, assist in understanding vulnerabilities, and facilitate the development of strategies to combat cyber threats. The legislation also enhances the powers of the Cyber Incident Review Board to conduct investigations and share insights with businesses to bolster security.

5. Global Trends

Globally, there is a trend toward implementing more stringent cybersecurity regulations. In 2024, significant new cybersecurity rules were enacted in major economies worldwide, transforming the global regulatory environment. These regulations aim to enhance security, protect individuals' information, and ensure organizations manage threats effectively.

ISO/IEC 27001:2013

The International Organization for Standardization (ISO) and International Electro-Technical Commission (IEC) are organizations that globally develop and maintain their standards. ISO/IEC 2700 1:20 13 standard ensures the requirement for implementation, maintenance, and improvement of an information security management system. This standard is a revised edition (second) of the first edition of ISO/ISE 27001:2005. ISO/IEC 27001:2013 covers the following key points of information security:

- Implementing and maintaining security requirements
- Information security management processes
- Assurance of cost-effective risk management
- Status of information security management activities
- Compliance with laws

Challenges and Ethical Considerations

Organizations encounter significant challenges in navigating the intricate landscape of cybersecurity regulations, particularly when operating across multiple jurisdictions with differing requirements. The absence of regulatory harmonization often results in heightened compliance costs and increased operational complexities. Furthermore, the rapid evolution of cyber threats necessitates the continuous revision of existing laws and the formulation of new regulations to address emerging risks effectively.

Adhering to legal and ethical standards is fundamental in ethical hacking. Practitioners must operate within clearly defined guidelines to ensure that their activities remain both lawful and responsible. Key ethical considerations include:

- **Permission:** Secure formal authorization before initiating any security assessments or penetration testing.

- **Confidentiality:** Handle sensitive data with the utmost responsibility and ensure that vulnerabilities are disclosed only to authorized parties.

- **Integrity:** Maintain transparency and accuracy in all reports, ensuring that findings are presented fairly and objectively.

In conclusion, cybersecurity laws and regulations play a pivotal role in safeguarding digital infrastructures and personal data. As cyber threats continue to evolve, regulatory frameworks must also adapt, necessitating that organizations remain well-informed and agile in maintaining compliance and strengthening security measures.

Consequences of Illegal Hacking

Engaging in illegal hacking, and unauthorized access to or manipulation of computer systems can lead to severe consequences, encompassing legal penalties, financial liabilities, and personal repercussions.

Legal Penalties

In the United States, the Computer Fraud and Abuse Act (CFAA) serves as the primary federal statute addressing unauthorized computer access. Violations under the CFAA can result in both felony and misdemeanor charges, depending on the nature and severity of the offense. For instance, unauthorized access to a protected computer with intent to defraud can lead to significant fines and imprisonment.

Specific offenses and their corresponding penalties under the CFAA include:

- **Trafficking in Passwords or Access Devices:** Knowingly distributing passwords or similar access tools, especially those issued for government or financial institution computers, is illegal. First-time offenders can face fines and up to one year in prison.

- **Trespassing in Government Computers:** Simply accessing a government computer without authorization is considered trespassing, punishable by up to one year of imprisonment for first-time offenders.

Beyond the CFAA, other federal laws impose penalties for specific hacking-related activities. For example, the Electronic Communications Privacy Act (ECPA) addresses unauthorized interception of electronic communications, with violations carrying penalties of up to five years in prison and fines up to $250,000.

Financial Liabilities

Victims of hacking incidents often pursue civil litigation against perpetrators to recover damages. Under statutes like the ECPA, individuals can seek actual

damages, punitive damages, and attorney's fees. For instance, in December 2024, a U.S. judge held NSO Group Technologies liable for violating U.S. hacking laws by infecting and surveilling individuals with spyware, leading to potential substantial financial penalties.

Case Studies

- **University Website Breach:** In March 2025, an individual claimed responsibility for hacking the New York University website, replacing its content with apparent test scores and a racial epithet. Such actions not only lead to criminal charges but also civil suits from affected institutions and individuals.

- **Sale of Hacking Tools:** In February 2025, the FBI seized 39 domains associated with selling hacking and fraud tools. Individuals involved in creating, distributing, or selling such tools face significant legal actions, including asset seizures and criminal charges.

Engaging in illegal hacking activities carries profound legal, financial, and personal risks. Understanding these consequences underscores the importance of ethical behavior in the digital realm and adherence to cybersecurity laws and regulations.

Domain 02: Operating Systems

Introduction

An Operating System (OS) is the core software that manages computer software and hardware resources, providing a user-friendly interface for interaction. It enables task execution, resource allocation, security enforcement, and file management, ensuring seamless functionality across various computing environments. Operating systems serve as the foundation for modern computing, supporting personal devices, enterprise systems, and cloud platforms.

This domain explores four major operating systems, Windows, UNIX, Linux, and macOS, each with distinct architectures and features. A crucial aspect of operating systems is file systems, which organize and manage stored data.

Windows Operating System

The Windows operating system, developed by Microsoft Corporation, is one of the most widely used OS platforms across corporations, government agencies, and individual users. Since its initial release in 1985, Windows has continuously evolved, incorporating advanced security measures, an intuitive Graphical User Interface (GUI), and extensive software compatibility to enhance user experience and system performance. Designed to support a wide range of devices, including desktops, laptops, servers, and cloud infrastructures, Windows has proven to be a versatile and scalable solution for both personal and enterprise computing needs.

It offers enterprise-grade features such as Active Directory, which facilitates centralized user and resource management, BitLocker which provides data encryption and security, and Windows Defender, a built-in security suite that protects against malware and cyber threats. Furthermore, Windows seamlessly integrates with cloud services, enabling organizations to leverage Microsoft Azure for scalable computing and OneDrive for cloud storage and synchronization.

The OS also supports virtualization technologies, such as Hyper-V, which enables users to run multiple operating systems in isolated environments, enhancing flexibility and security. With the advent of AI-powered enhancements, Windows now provides automated system optimizations, intelligent voice recognition, and predictive computing capabilities, improving productivity and overall user experience. By continuously advancing in security, cloud computing, and AI-driven automation, Windows remains a reliable, secure, and efficient operating system tailored to meet the dynamic needs of modern users.

The Windows OS family tree, as shown in Table 2-01, represents the evolution of Microsoft's operating systems, branching into different categories based on their purpose and architecture.

Windows OS Family Tree		
MS-Dos-based and 9x Windows OS Versions	NT Kernel-Based Windows OS Version	
	For PC	For Server
MS-DOS 1.0	Windows NT 3.1	Windows Server 2003
MS-DOS 2.0	Windows NT 3.51	Windows Server 2003 R2
MS-DOS 2.1X	Windows NT 3.5	Windows Server 2008, Windows Home Server
MS-DOS 3.0	Windows NT 4.0	Windows Server 2008 R2
MS-DOS 3.1X	Windows 2000	Windows Server 2012
Windows 95	Windows XP	Windows Server 2012 R2
Windows 98	Windows XP Professional X64 Edition	Windows Server 2016
Windows 98 SE	Vista	Windows Server 2019
Windows ME	Window7	Windows Server 2022
	Windows 8	
	Windows 8.1	
	Windows 10	
	Windows 11	

Table 2-01: Windows OS Family Tree

Windows Architecture

Windows architecture is a modular and layered structure designed to provide stability, security, and efficient resource management. It is divided into two primary modes of operation, User Mode and Kernel Mode, ensuring a separation between application execution and core system functions.

When a User Mode application needs to perform a privileged operation, such as reading a file or accessing the network, it sends a request via the Windows API. The request is handled by NTDLL.DLL, which passes it to the Kernel Mode components. The kernel processes the request, interacts with the required hardware or system resources, and returns the results to the user application.

This separation ensures that even if a User Mode application crashes or becomes compromised, it does not directly affect the system's core functions, enhancing security, stability, and reliability.

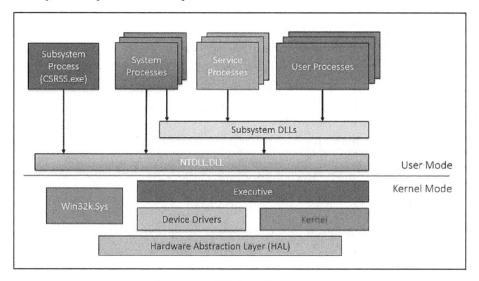

Figure 2-01: Windows Architecture

User Mode

User Mode is designed for running applications and system processes with limited access to system resources. Applications and processes in this mode interact with the system through the Windows Application Programming Interface (API) and rely on the kernel to perform privileged operations such as hardware access.

Key components of User Mode include:

User Processes

User processes are the applications that individuals start, such as internet browsers, text editing software, and media playback applications. These processes operate with limited permissions, granting them restricted access to essential system resources to avoid unauthorized changes. By operating within a regulated environment, user processes help maintain system stability and security. Even if a user application used by the user crashes, it does not affect the operating system directly, allowing other processes to continue running without interruption.

Service Processes

Service processes are background processes that perform essential system tasks without direct user interaction. These include services such as Windows Update Auto Update Service (wuauserv), Print Spooler (spoolsv.exe), and Task Scheduler (taskschd.exe), which ensure that the system remains updated, printing services

function properly, and scheduled tasks execute as expected. Many of these services are configured to start automatically when the system boots, continuing to operate in the background to provide uninterrupted system functionality.

System Processes

System processes are critical components of the Windows operating system and are responsible for managing system-wide functions such as session management, authentication, and initialization. These processes are vital for maintaining system integrity and security. Examples include winlogon.exe, which manages user logins and session maintenance, and Local Security Authority Subsystem Service (lsass.exe), which handles security policies and authentication procedures. These processes are essential role for enforcing system security and ensuring that user sessions and authentication mechanisms function properly.

Subsystem Processes (CSRSS.exe - Client/Server Runtime Subsystem)

The Client/Server Runtime Subsystem (CSRSS.exe) is a crucial User Mode process responsible for handling console windows, process creation, and thread management. Despite operating in User Mode, CSRSS.exe is integral to system stability. It manages essential functions such as text-mode applications and GUI-related console interactions. Terminating CSRSS.exe can cause severe system instability, often resulting in a critical failure that forces the system to crash.

Subsystem DLLs

Subsystem Dynamic Link Libraries (DLLs)provide additional functionality to user applications by acting as intermediaries between user processes and the underlying Windows system. These libraries contain predefined functions that applications can use without needing to implement them from scratch. Examples include Graphics Device Interface (GDI32.dll) for rendering graphics, USER32.dll for managing window interactions, and KERNEL32.dll for handling core system functions such as memory management and file operations. By modularizing system functionality, DLLs improve efficiency and allow multiple applications to share common resources.

NTDLL.DLL (Native API)

NT Layer Dynamic Link Library or NTDLL.DLL is a critical system library that serves as an interface between User Mode applications and Kernel Mode components. It contains a collection of low-level system functions that handle essential tasks such as process management, memory allocation, and exception handling. As a bridge between the Windows API and the kernel's native system calls, NTDLL.DLL enables user applications can request system services securely and efficiently. Its role is fundamental to both standard user applications and system-critical processes.

Kernel Mode

Kernel Mode provides unrestricted access to system memory and hardware. The kernel operates at the highest privilege level, ensuring process execution, resource allocation, and security enforcement.

Key components of Kernel Mode include:

Executive

The Executive manages core operating system functions like process management, memory allocation, security, file system operations, and I/O handling. Key subsystems include the Process Manager, which handles process creation and termination; the Memory Manager, which controls RAM allocation and virtual memory; and the I/O Manager, which processes input and output requests. The Security Reference Monitor enforces access control to protect system resources. Together, these components ensure the stability and security of the Windows operating system.

Win32k.sys (Graphical Subsystem)

Win32k.sys is a critical Kernel Mode component that manages Graphical User Interface (GUI) functions, including window rendering, mouse and keyboard input processing, and font management. Unlike standard User Mode applications that rely on APIs for graphical operations, Win32k.sys operates directly in Kernel Mode to enhance performance and responsiveness. This direct access to system resources allows for efficient rendering of user interfaces and processing of input events, ensuring a smooth and responsive user experience.

Device Drivers

Device drivers act as intermediaries between the operating system and hardware components, such as printers, network adapters, and graphics cards. These drivers run in Kernel Mode, granting them direct access to system memory and hardware resources. While this access is necessary for optimal hardware performance, it also introduces risks—faulty or malicious drivers can cause severe system instability, often leading to a Blue Screen of Death (BSOD). To mitigate these risks, Windows employs driver signing and verification mechanisms to ensure that only trusted drivers are loaded into the system.

Kernel

The kernel is the core component of the Windows operating system, managing CPU scheduling, thread execution, and low-level hardware interactions. It controls interrupt handling, synchronization between processes, and power management, ensuring efficient execution of system tasks. The kernel also enforces system

security by implementing privilege levels and access control mechanisms, preventing unauthorized processes from interfering with critical system functions. By maintaining a structured and secure execution environment, the kernel plays a crucial role in the stability and performance of the operating system.

Hardware Abstraction Layer (HAL)

The Hardware Abstraction Layer (HAL) functions as a bridge between the operating system kernel and physical hardware components. It abstracts hardware-specific details, enabling Windows to operate on various architectures, including Intel, AMD, and ARM, without necessitating modifications to the OS. By standardizing hardware communication, HAL enables seamless compatibility across various devices, ensuring that applications and system components can function correctly regardless of the underlying hardware configuration. This abstraction simplifies driver development and enhances the portability of the Windows operating system.

Windows Commands

Windows commands are instructions executed in Command Prompt (CMD) or PowerShell to perform system tasks, manage files, configure settings, and troubleshoot issues. These commands provide an efficient way to interact with the Windows operating system without using the graphical interface.

Command	Meaning
ipconfig	Shows the IP address of the system
netstat	Displays all active network connections and ports
nslookup	Displays information that you can use to diagnose Domain Name System (DNS) infrastructure
ping	Verifies connectivity to another TCP/IP computer
chdir	Shows the name of the current directory or changes the current folder
dir	Displays a directory's file list and subdirectories
echo	Turns the command-echoing feature on or off
format	Formats the disk
help	Provides online information about system commands
label	Creates, changes, or deletes the volume label of a hard disk
mkdir	Creates a directory or subdirectory
nbtstat	Displays protocol statistics and current TCP/IP connections
system info	Displays comprehensive configuration information about a computer and its operating system

Table 2-02: Windows Commands

UNIX Operating System

UNIX is a powerful, multi-user, and multitasking operating system developed in the late 1960s at AT&T's Bell Labs by Ken Thompson, Dennis Ritchie, and others. Designed for portability and efficiency, it operates on various devices, ranging from personal computers to mainframes. Its defining feature is its ability to support multiple users simultaneously, enabling resource sharing while ensuring security through strict user permissions. UNIX also supports multitasking, allowing multiple processes to run at the same time. It utilizes a modular design with small utilities that can be combined using pipes and shell scripting, and it features a hierarchical file system, treating everything as a file for easier management.

UNIX's Command-Line Interface (CLI) offers powerful tools for system administration, file manipulation, and process management, making it a preferred choice among developers and IT professionals. It is recognized for its stability, security, and robustness, which leads to its widespread use in enterprise environments, academia, and research institutions. Over time, UNIX has evolved into various variants, including BSD, macOS, AIX, HP-UX, and Solaris, while also inspiring the development of UNIX-like systems such as Linux.

UNIX Components

UNIX consists of three main components: Kernel, Shell, and Programs.

Kernel

The kernel is the core of the UNIX operating system, managing CPU scheduling, memory, processes, and file systems. It interacts with hardware and provides essential services through system calls, ensuring security and stability.

Shell

The Shell serves as an interface between users and the kernel, interpreting and executing commands. UNIX offers various shells like Bash, C Shell, Korn Shell, and Z Shell, which support scripting for automation and efficiency.

Programs

Programs include system utilities, applications, and background processes. UNIX provides tools like ls, grep, chmod, and more, as mentioned table 2-03 along with development utilities like gcc and make, making it a powerful and flexible Operating System.

UNIX Directory Structure

UNIX follows a hierarchical directory structure, where all files and directories are organized in an inverted tree format. At the top of this structure is the root directory (/), which serves as the starting point for all files and subdirectories.

Each directory can contain files and other directories, allowing for a well-organized and structured file system. Key system directories under root include:

- /home: User home directories
- /var: Variable data like logs and caches
- /usr: User applications and libraries
- /tmp: Store temporary files created by users and applications
- /bin: Essential binary executables
- /etc: System configuration files

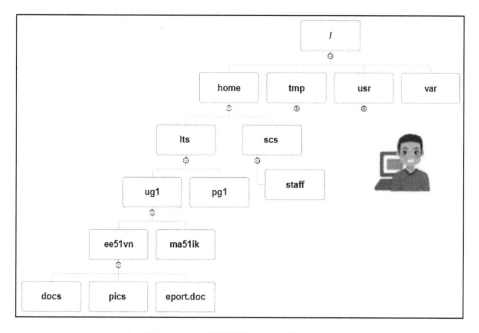

Figure 2-02: UNIX Directory Structure

UNIX Commands

UNIX commands are text-based instructions used to interact with the operating system for file management, process control, system monitoring, and networking. These commands are executed in a shell, such as Bash or Zsh.

Command	Syntax	Meaning
ls	ls options files(s)	List the contents of a directory
cd	cd path	Change directory
mkdir	mkdir dirname	Create a directory
rmdir	rmdir dirname	Remove directory
cp	cp file1 file2	Copy files or directories
rm	rm filename	Remove or delete specific files
mv	mv old.html new.html	Move or rename files
passwd	passwd	Change password
grep	grep string file	Search for a character string in a file
diff	diff file1 file2	Compare two files and report the differences
head	head filename	Show the first 10 lines of a file
ispell	ispell file	Check the spelling of the contents of a file
pr	pr file	Prepare text for printing with headers and page breaks
pwd	pwd	Display the current directory's full pathname
id	id username	Display your system ID numbers

Table 2-03: UNIX Commands

Linux Operating System

Linux is an open-source, UNIX-like operating system popular in enterprises, government, and personal use due to its security, flexibility, and performance. Developed by a global community, it features various distributions (distros), such as Ubuntu, Red Hat, and Debian, suited for desktop or server needs. Its stability and scalability make it ideal for servers, cloud computing, and cybersecurity applications.

Components of Linux Operating System

Linux comprises several key components that work together to manage system resources and provide user functionality, such as:

- **Hardware:** The physical components of a computer, including the CPU, RAM, HDD, and monitor, which interact with the operating system.

- **Kernel:** The core of the OS, responsible for managing system resources, memory, processes, and hardware interactions.

- **Shell:** A command-line interface that allows users to interact with the kernel by executing commands.

- **Applications/Utilities:** Programs and tools that extend the OS's functionality, including text editors, compilers, and system utilities.

- **System Libraries:** Collections of functions that enable applications to interact with the system without requiring direct access to the kernel.

- **Daemons:** Background services that handle tasks like printing, scheduling, and networking.

- **Graphical Server (X Server):** Manages graphical display and enables GUI-based applications to run.

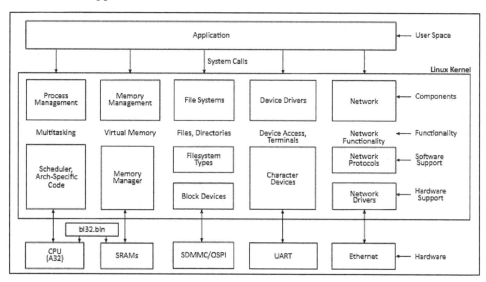

Figure 2-03: Linux System Architecture

Linux Features

Some key features of Linux are as follows:

- Linux Characteristics Portability

- Open Source

- Multiuser

- Multiprogramming

- Hierarchical File System

- Shell
- Security

macOS Operating System

macOS is a closed-source, UNIX-based operating system developed by Apple Inc. for Mac computers. It is known for its stability, security, and optimized performance, utilizing a Darwin-based kernel with features like preemptive multitasking and memory protection. Seamlessly integrating with Apple hardware, it offers functionalities such as Handoff, AirDrop, and iCloud synchronization. macOS features a user-friendly GUI, robust file management, and security options like Gatekeeper and FileVault encryption, making it popular in creative and professional fields.

Layers of macOS

macOS is built on a layered architecture, ensuring modularity, security, and efficiency. Each layer provides specific functionalities, from user interface components to low-level system operations. The architecture consists of five primary layers:

Cocoa Application Layer

The Cocoa Application Layer is responsible for the user interface and offers frameworks for macOS application development. It includes AppKit for GUI components, Foundation for utilities such as file management, SwiftUI for modern UI design, and Objective-C/Swift APIs for OS interaction. This layer allows developers to create visually rich and responsive applications.

Media Layer

The Media Layer manages audio, video, graphics, and animation, making macOS ideal for media-intensive applications. It includes Core Animation for smooth animations, Core Image for image processing, Core Video for video rendering, Core Audio for high-quality sound processing, and Metal for GPU-accelerated graphics. This ensures optimized performance for creative applications like video editing and game development.

Core Services Layer

The Core Services Layer provides essential system functionalities such as data management, networking, and security. It features Automatic Reference Counting (ARC) for memory management, Grand Central Dispatch (GCD) for multi-threading, Core Data for persistent storage, CloudKit for cloud integration, and the Security Framework for encryption and authentication. This layer is the backbone of macOS applications.

Core OS Layer

The Core OS Layer interacts with hardware and manages low-level system operations. It includes POSIX APIs for UNIX-based programming, networking APIs for TCP/IP and Wi-Fi, file system APIs for managing storage, energy management for power efficiency, and sandboxing for security. This layer ensures system stability and efficiency.

Kernel and Device Drivers Layer

The kernel and device drivers layer is the core of macOS, managing hardware resources, memory, and process scheduling. It includes the XNU kernel, which combines Mach and BSD for performance and security. It also offers file system support Apple File System (APFS), a networking stack (TCP/IP, VPNs), Inter-Process Communication (IPC) for process interaction, and device drivers for hardware interaction. This layer guarantees efficient hardware abstraction and system security.

macOS Layered Architecture

The macOS Layered Architecture describes the organized framework that arranges the different elements of macOS into separate layers, with each layer tasked with particular functions. This tiered structure enables the operating system to be modular, efficient, and straightforward to manage.

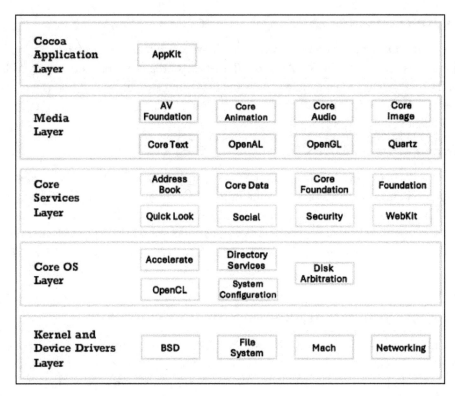

Figure 2-04: macOS Layered Architecture

Understanding File Systems

A file system refers to a method utilized by operating systems to save, arrange, manage, and access data on storage devices. It offers a systematic way to structure files and directories in a hierarchical format, facilitating effective navigation, access control, and data recovery.

File systems determine how information is stored and accessed, using directory structures, file paths, and access permissions. They usually adopt a tree-like configuration, which facilitates organized data management while enforcing authorization procedures to control user access.

Some notable file systems are:

- **File Allocation Table (FAT):** Utilized in older systems and removable drives

- **New Technology File System (NTFS):** A contemporary file system for Windows featuring advanced capabilities such as encryption and journaling

- **Hierarchical File System (HFS / HFS+):** Employed in earlier versions of macOS

- **Apple File System (APFS):** The default file system for macOS, tailored for SSDs

- **Ext2, Ext3, Ext4:** Frequently used across various Linux distributions

Types of File Systems

File systems are classified based on their design and purpose for storing, organizing, and retrieving data.

Shared Disk File Systems

A shared disk file system allows multiple servers to access the same external disk subsystem simultaneously. It is commonly used in high-availability clusters and enterprise storage environments, ensuring that data remains accessible even if a server fails. It is designed to manage concurrent access efficiently while preventing data corruption. Examples include the Global File System (GFS) and the Oracle Cluster File System (OCFS).

Disk File Systems

A disk file system is designed for storing and retrieving files on storage devices such as Hard Disk Drives (HDDs) and Solid-State Drives (SSDs). It provides essential features such as file organization, indexing, and access control. Disk file systems can also support journaling to track changes and prevent data loss in case of system crashes. Common examples are NTFS, FAT32, Ext4, and APFS.

Network File Systems

Network file systems enable users to access files stored on remote systems over a network as if they were stored locally. This file system is widely used in distributed computing environments to facilitate file sharing among multiple devices. It enhances collaboration by allowing seamless access to shared files across different operating systems. Examples include the Network File System (NFS), Server Message Block (SMB), and Andrew File System (AFS).

Database File Systems

Unlike traditional file systems that organize files hierarchically, database file systems store and manage files based on metadata attributes such as file type, author, or topic. This allows for faster searching and retrieval, making it suitable for applications that require structured data management. It is commonly used in database servers and enterprise content management systems. Examples include

Microsoft SQL Server FileStream and Oracle's Automatic Storage Management (ASM).

Flash File Systems

Flash file systems are designed to optimize the performance and longevity of flash memory devices such as USB drives, SSDs, and memory cards. These file systems use wear leveling and garbage collection techniques to prevent excessive wear on specific memory blocks, thereby extending the lifespan of the storage device. Examples include the Journaling Flash File System (JFFS), Yet Another Flash File System (YAFFS), and the Flash-Friendly File System (F2FS).

Tape File Systems

Tape file systems are used for storing and retrieving files on magnetic tape media, primarily for backup and archival purposes. They provide a self-describing format, which means the file system metadata is stored directly on the tape for easy retrieval. This file system is extremely reliable for long-term data preservation. One example is the Linear Tape File System (LTFS).

Special-Purpose File Systems

Special-purpose file systems are designed to handle specific system functions, such as inter-process communication, temporary file storage, or exposing system information. These file systems do not store traditional user data but are crucial for operating system functionality. Examples include Procfs (used for process management), Tmpfs (temporary file storage in RAM), and Sysfs (exposes system hardware details).

Windows File Systems

Windows file systems are structures utilized by the Windows operating system to store, organize, and manage files on storage devices. They define how data is written, accessed, and secured.

File Allocation Table (FAT)

The File Allocation Table (FAT) is one of the earliest file systems used in Windows operating systems, originally designed for Disk Operating System (DOS). It gained widespread adoption due to its simplicity, compatibility, and efficiency in managing files on storage devices such as floppy disks, hard drives, and USB flash drives. The FAT file system is named after its method of file organization, which relies on a table stored at the beginning of the volume to track file locations.

Structure and Functionality

The FAT file system organizes storage into clusters, the File Allocation Table tracks which clusters belong to which files and manages free and occupied space. When a file is created, deleted, or modified, the FAT structure updates accordingly. Its simplicity makes FAT easy to use and effective for small-scale storage devices

Versions of FAT

There are three primary versions of FAT, each differing in terms of entry size, storage capacity, and efficiency:

1. **FAT12:** FAT12 was the earliest version of the File Allocation Table (FAT) file system, primarily used for floppy disks and small storage devices. It supported volumes up to 32 MB in size and used 12-bit entries to manage clusters. Due to its limited storage capacity, FAT12 became obsolete as storage technology advanced, making it unsuitable for modern systems.

2. **FAT16:** FAT16 was introduced to accommodate larger hard drives and the early versions of Windows. It supported volumes up to 2 GB in size and used 16-bit entries, allowing for more efficient file organization compared to FAT12. Although newer file systems have mostly replaced FAT16, it is still utilized in embedded systems and legacy environments where simplicity and compatibility are prioritized.

3. **FAT32:** FAT32 is the most widely used version of the FAT file system, introduced with Windows 95 OSR2. It supports volumes up to 2 TB (although Windows limits it to 32 GB for compatibility purposes) and uses 32-bit entries, improving storage efficiency over its predecessors. However, FAT32 lacks the advanced security and journaling features of modern file systems like NTFS, making it less suitable for systems that require robust data protection and reliability.

System	Bytes Per Cluster within File Allocation Table	Cluster Limit
FAT12	1.5	Fewer than 4087 clusters
FAT16	2	Between 4,087 and 65,526 clusters, inclusive
FAT32	4	Between 65,526 and 268,435,456 clusters, inclusive

Table 2-04: Versions of FAT

FAT32

A significant benefit of FAT32 is its effective use of disk space. It achieves better space management by employing smaller cluster sizes, which minimizes wasted space on disk partitions, particularly when dealing with numerous small files. This efficiency makes FAT32 superior to FAT16, which utilized larger clusters and led to increased unused space.

Moreover, FAT32 offers a degree of redundancy by making copies of the File Allocation Table (FAT) rather than depending on a single version. This enhances data integrity and lowers the risk of corruption, resulting in greater reliability compared to previous FAT versions. Nonetheless, FAT32 is missing contemporary file system features like file permissions, encryption, and journaling that are found in NTFS, making it less appropriate for systems that demand heightened security and reliability. Regardless of its shortcomings, FAT32 continues to be widely adopted for USB drives, memory cards, and external storage solutions because of its compatibility across Windows, macOS, and Linux platforms.

Offset	Description	Size
000h	Executable code (boots computer)	446 bytes
1BEh	1st position entry	16 bytes
1CEh	2nd position entry	16 bytes
1DEh	3rd position entry	16 bytes
1EEh	4th position entry	16 bytes
1FEh	Boot record signature	2 bytes

Table 2-05: MBR Table of FAT32

New Technology File System (NTFS)

The New Technology File System (NTFS) is the default file system used by Windows operating systems, offering improved performance, security, and reliability over older file systems like FAT32. NTFS architecture is divided into different components that manage data storage, access control, journaling, and system recovery.

NTFS is the default file system for Windows NT and its successors, including Windows XP, Vista, 7, 8.1, 10, 11, and various Windows Server versions such as 2003, 2008, 2012, 2016, 2019, and 2022. Introduced with Windows NT 3.1, NTFS was created to replace the older FAT file systems by offering improved performance, security, and reliability, making it the preferred choice for modern Windows environments.

One key feature of NTFS is its support for metadata and advanced data structures, which enhance file retrieval speed and disk space management. Unlike FAT, NTFS uses a Master File Table (MFT) that improves file organization and access efficiency.

It also supports large file sizes and partitions, allowing storage devices to exceed 2 TB, a limitation found in FAT32.

Another significant advantage of NTFS is file system journaling, which records changes before they are finalized on the disk. This feature helps protect against data corruption and loss, ensuring system stability even during unexpected crashes or power failures. NTFS also includes Security Access Control Lists (ACLs), which enable administrators to define user permissions and control access rights for files and directories, significantly enhancing data security.

Additional enhancements of NTFS include file compression, encryption file system (EFS), disk quotas, symbolic links, and transactional NTFS (TxF). These features provide better storage efficiency, security, and system integrity, making NTFS ideal for enterprise environments, high-performance systems, and secure data management. With its robust architecture and advanced functionality, NTFS continues to be the standard file system for Windows-based operating systems.

NTFS Architecture

The NTFS boot process follows a structured approach, starting from hardware-level storage and transitioning to the operating system and user applications. The architecture can be divided into Kernel Mode and User Mode, as shown in Figure 2-05.

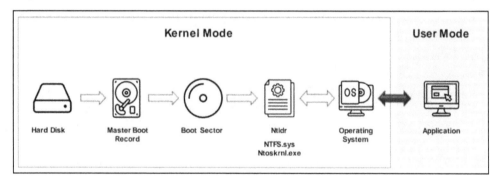

Figure 2-05: NTFS Architecture

Kernel Mode (System-Level Execution)

In Kernel Mode (System-Level Execution), the boot process begins with the hard disk, the primary storage medium that contains the NTFS file system. The first sector of the hard drive, called the Master Boot Record (MBR), identifies the active partition and loads the bootloader. The Boot Sector follows, containing NTFS-specific boot instructions that facilitate the loading of the Windows operating system. The Ntldr (NT Loader) plays a crucial role as the bootloader, loading essential system files required for startup. Once the boot process progresses, the

NTFS.sys file system driver initializes, enabling the OS to access NTFS partitions efficiently. The Ntoskrnl.exe, which is the Windows NT kernel, takes over system resource management and process execution. Finally, during Operating System Initialization, Windows completes its startup sequence by loading essential drivers and services, ensuring the system is ready for user interaction.

User Mode

Once the operating system has fully loaded, NTFS enables file and application access in User Mode, allowing users and applications to interact with stored data. Applications rely on the Win32 API for standard file operations such as reading, writing, and modifying files. For more advanced or low-level file system interactions, NTFS drivers handle direct communication with the file system, ensuring efficient data access and security enforcement. This separation between User Mode and Kernel Mode helps maintain system stability by preventing direct access to critical system resources, ensuring that applications operate within a controlled environment.

NTFS System Files

NTFS includes several system files that manage file storage, access control, and metadata handling. These system files are stored in the Master File Table (MFT) and are essential for the operation of NTFS.

Each NTFS volume contains several special system files, which are automatically created and managed by the file system. These files do not appear in the regular file explorer but are essential for maintaining the structure and integrity of the file system.

File Name	Description
$attrdef	Contains definitions of all system-and user-defined attributes of the volume
$badclus	Contains all the bad clusters
$bitmap	Contains a bitmap for the entire volume
$boot	Contains the volume's bootstrap
$logfile	Used for recovery purposes
$mft	Contains a record for every file
$mftmirr	Mirrors the MFT used for recovering files
$quota	Indicates a disk quota for each user
$upcase	Converts characters into uppercase Unicode
$volume	Contains the volume name and version number

Table 2-06: NTFS System Files

Encrypting File Systems (EFS)

The Encrypting File System (EFS) is a security feature introduced in NTFS version 3.0 that provides filesystem-level encryption to protect sensitive data. Unlike full-disk encryption, which secures an entire drive, EFS encrypts individual files and folders, allowing users to safeguard specific data while keeping the rest of the system accessible.

EFS encryption is designed to be transparent to authorized user. Once a file is encrypted, the encrypting user can access and modify it as if it were unencrypted. The system automatically decrypts the file when accessed and re-encrypts it upon closing, ensuring that encryption is always maintained without requiring manual intervention. This functionality enables seamless data protection without disrupting workflow.

When a file is encrypted using EFS, only the user who encrypted it (or an authorized recovery agent) can access it. Any unauthorized user attempting to open the file will be denied access, even if they have permission to view or modify other unencrypted files in the same directory. This level of security is particularly useful in shared environments where multiple users have access to a system.

Encryption and Decryption Process

To enable encryption, users must set the encryption attributes of the files and folders they want to secure. This is done through the file properties in Windows by selecting the "Encrypt contents to secure data" option. The encryption is managed

using a combination of the user's public and private keys, ensuring that only the rightful owner can decrypt the file.

When a user accesses an encrypted file, Windows automatically decrypts it using the corresponding private key. Once the user is finished, the file is automatically re-encrypted, maintaining its security without requiring additional actions from the user.

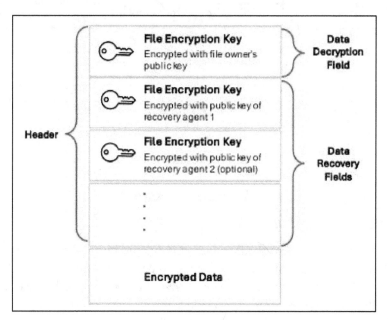

Figure 2-06: Operation of EFS

Components of EFS

The Encrypting File System (EFS) in Windows relies on multiple components working together to provide seamless file encryption and decryption. These components operate across User Mode and Kernel Mode, ensuring secure encryption, decryption, and key management.

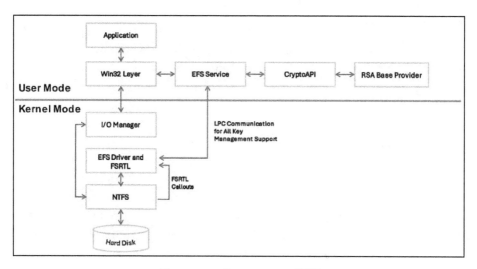

Figure 2-07: Components of EFS

User Mode Components

Application

The encryption process begins when a user or application attempts to access an encrypted file. Standard file operations such as opening, reading, and modifying are seamlessly handled by the system, allowing authorized users to work with encrypted files without needing to decrypt them manually.

Win32 Layer

The Win32 API facilitates user-mode file access by forwarding requests to the appropriate system services. When an application attempts to open an encrypted file, the Win32 Layer ensures that the request is correctly directed to the Encrypting File System (EFS). As an intermediary, it ensures that encryption and decryption requests comply with security protocols before passing them to the I/O Manager for processing.

EFS Service

The Encrypting File System (EFS) Service manages file encryption and decryption in User Mode. It works with CryptoAPI to securely handle encryption keys, ensuring that only authorized users can access encrypted files. By leveraging Local Procedure Call (LPC) to communicate with Kernel Mode components, the EFS Service maintains secure key management and access control while making encryption operations seamless for users.

CryptoAPI

The Cryptographic API (CryptoAPI) provides essential encryption functions for EFS, securely handling encryption keys throughout their lifecycle. It supports key generation, encryption, and decryption while safeguarding sensitive data from unauthorized access. CryptoAPI ensures that only authorized processes can utilize encryption keys to decrypting protected files.

RSA Base Provider

The RSA Base Provider is a cryptographic module within Windows that enables RSA-based encryption and secure key management. It generates and protects private keys associated with EFS-encrypted files, ensuring only authorized users can decrypt and access the secured data. Working alongside CryptoAPI, it strengthens the security of encrypted files, even if the system is compromised.

Kernel Mode Components

I/O Manager

The I/O Manager handles Input/Output (I/O) requests from applications in User Mode and directing them to the correct file system driver. It manages encryption and decryption, enforcing security policies to prevent unauthorized access to encrypted files.

EFS Driver and File System Runtime Library (FSRTL)

The EFS Driver is essential for managing encryption and decryption within the NTFS file system. It works with the File System Runtime Library (FSRTL), which manages encrypted files and enforces encryption policies. FSRTL callouts enable secure interactions between NTFS and the EFS driver, ensuring effective encryption while maintaining data integrity and security at the kernel level.

New Technology File System (NTFS)

NTFS serves as the foundation for EFS encryption, enabling the secure storage of encrypted files. Access to protected data is restricted to users possessing valid decryption keys. NTFS utilizes Access Control Lists (ACLs) to specify detailed permissions for file access, bolstering security. By integrating with EFS, NTFS guarantees that encrypted files remain safeguarded, even when accessed from various user accounts or network locations.

Hard Disk

The hard disk serves as the physical location for storing encrypted files. NTFS ensures that encryption is preserved at the file system level, preventing unauthorized access even if the storage device is compromised. Since encryption keys are not stored with files, attackers cannot decrypt or modify sensitive data

without authentication, ensuring strong protection against data breaches and unauthorized access.

Key Interactions

- **LPC Communication**: Used for secure communication between User Mode (EFS Service) and Kernel Mode (EFS Driver) for key management.

- **FSRTL Callouts**: Used to facilitate interaction between the EFS Driver and NTFS for encrypted file operations.

Sparse Files

Sparse files are a special type of file in the NTFS file system designed to efficiently store data while conserving disk space. Unlike regular files, which allocate physical disk space for their entire size, sparse files only allocate storage for portions of the file that contain actual data. Any empty or uninitialized sections remain unallocated, significantly reducing disk usage.

NTFS allocates disk clusters only to segments containing nonzero data. Any undefined or empty sections are represented as metadata rather than taking up actual disk space. This allows applications to create large files without consuming unnecessary storage, making sparse files particularly useful for database systems, disk images, and certain types of log files.

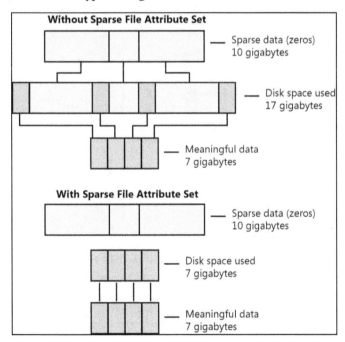

Figure 2-08: Sparse Files Attribute Set

By implementing sparse files, NTFS provides a space-efficient mechanism for managing large data sets while minimizing wasted disk space.

Linux File Systems

Linux file systems are structures used to store, organize, and manage data on Linux-based operating systems. They determine how files are named, stored, and accessed.

Linux File System Architecture

The Linux file system organizes and manages data in a hierarchical directory structure starting from the root (/). It treats everything as a file, including directories and devices, enforcing permissions and ownership for security. Linux supports multiple file systems like ext4, XFS, and Btrfs, many with journaling to prevent corruption. It allows dynamic mounting and unmounting and supports symbolic links, hard links, and case sensitivity, making it efficient for servers, cloud, and embedded systems.

The Linux file system architecture is structured into User Space and Kernel Space, with different components handling file operations efficiently. The architecture enables seamless interaction between user applications and the storage system while ensuring security, caching, and performance optimization.

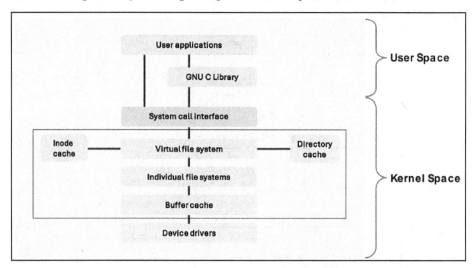

Figure 2-09: Linux File System Architecture

User Space

This layer consists of applications and libraries that interact with the file system using system calls.

User Applications

User applications are software programs that require file system access to function, such as text editors, web browsers, and command-line utilities. These applications do not directly interact with the Linux kernel; instead, they rely on system libraries and calls to request file operations. By abstracting file system interactions, Linux allows user applications to work across different distributions and file system types without direct kernel-level access.

GNU C Library (glibc)

The GNU C Library (glibc) acts as an intermediary between user applications and the Linux kernel. It provides standard APIs for system calls, translating high-level file operations, such as opening, reading, and writing files, into low-level instructions that the kernel can execute. Using glibc, developers can write programs that interact with the file system without handling kernel-specific complexities, ensuring compatibility across Linux environments.

System Call Interface (SCI)

The System Call Interface (SCI) serves as the boundary between User Space and Kernel Space, enabling user applications to communicate securely with the kernel. When an application requests a file operation, the SCI processes system calls like open(), read(), and write(), forwarding them to the appropriate kernel modules for execution. This mechanism ensures controlled access to system resources while maintaining system stability and security.

Kernel Space

This layer manages file system operations and communicates with hardware.

Virtual File System (VFS)

VFS is an abstraction layer that unifies access to different file systems like ext4, XFS, and NTFS. It enables seamless file operations and optimizes performance through inode and directory caching.

Inode Cache and Directory Cache

The inode cache stores frequently accessed file metadata, while the directory cache speeds up path lookups. Both reduce disk reads, enhancing file system performance.

Individual File Systems

File systems like ext4, XFS, and Btrfs manage storage uniquely. VFS forwards file operations to the appropriate driver, ensuring compatibility and security.

Buffer Cache

The buffer cache temporarily stores frequently used data, reducing disk I/O and improving read/write speeds, especially for intensive workloads.

Device Drivers

Device drivers enable communication between the OS and storage devices, translating file system operations into hardware-specific commands for efficient data transfer.

Filesystem Hierarchy Standard (FHS)

The Filesystem Hierarchy Standard (FHS) defines a consistent directory structure for Linux and Unix-like operating systems. It ensures that files and directories are systematically organized, making system administration and software compatibility more manageable. In FHS, all files and directories exist under the root directory (/), which serves as the starting point for the entire file system. Key directories like /bin (essential binaries), /etc (configuration files), /var (variable data), and /home (user directories) are structured under /, maintaining a logical and standardized layout.

Directory	Description
/bin	Essential command binaries. Ex: cat, ls, cp
/boot	Static files of the boot loader. Ex: Kernels, Initrd
/dev	Essential device files. Ex: /dev/null
/etc	Host-specific system configuration files
/home	Users' home directories, holding saved files, personal settings, etc.
/lib	Essential libraries for the binaries in /bin/ and /sbin/
/media	Mount points for removable media
/mnt	Temporarily mounted filesystems
/opt	Add-on application software packages
/root	Home directory for the root user
/proc	Virtual file system providing process and kernel information as files
/run	Information about running processes. Ex: running daemons, currently logged-In users
/sbin	Contains the binary files required for working
/srv	Site-specific data for services provided by the system
/tmp	Temporary files
/usr	Secondary hierarchy for read-only user data
/var	Variable data. Ex: logs, spool files, etc.
/sys	Contains information about connected devices

Table 2-07: Directories and their Description Specific to the FHS

Extended File System (EXT)

The Extended File System (EXT) The Extended File System (EXT), introduced in 1992, was the first file system designed specifically for Linux to overcome Minix's limitations. The Minix file system had a maximum partition size of 64 MB and imposed short file name restrictions, making it inadequate for growing storage needs. EXT solved this issue by allowing a maximum partition size of 2 GB and enabling file names to be up to 255 characters long, significantly enhancing file management capabilities.

However, despite these advancements, EXT possessed various limitations that resulted in its eventual replacement. A significant issue was the absence of distinct timestamps for access time, inode modification time, and data modification time, which complicated the process of monitoring file changes. This shortcoming

negatively impacted performance and system logging, making EXT less efficient for contemporary computing demands.

As a result of these limitations, the Second Extended File System (EXT2) was developed as a successor, offering additional improvements in stability, performance, and larger partition support. Although EXT was foundational for Linux file systems, it was rapidly replaced by more sophisticated file systems such as EXT2, EXT3, and EXT4.

Second Extended File System (EXT2)

The Second Extended File System (EXT2), introduced in 1993, improved upon the original EXT file system with better performance, larger storage capacity, and enhanced metadata tracking. It utilized more efficient algorithms for file allocation and directory indexing, which improved read and write speeds. EXT2 featured multiple timestamps to separately track access, inode modification, and data modification times, aiding in logging and auditing.

Additionally, EXT2 tracked the file system's status in the superblock, indicating whether it was in a clean or dirty state, which helped detect corruption and prompted checks during boot. However, its lack of journaling made it vulnerable to corruption during crashes or power failures, leading to potential data loss and requiring manual recovery. This limitation prompted the development of EXT3, which added journaling for better reliability. Despite this, EXT2 is still used for flash storage devices like USB drives due to its low write overhead, preserving the lifespan of flash memory.

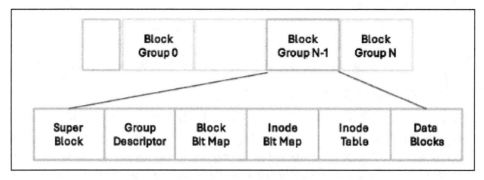

Figure 2-10: Physical Layout of the EXT2 File System

Third Extended File System (EXT3)

The Third Extended File System (EXT3) is an improved version of EXT2, introduced in 2001 to address EXT2's primary weakness—the lack of journaling. With journaling, EXT3 significantly improves data integrity and system reliability, reducing the chances of file system corruption due to unexpected shutdowns,

system crashes, or power failures. Instead of requiring a lengthy file system check (fsck) after a system crash, EXT3 can quickly recover lost data by replaying the journal, minimizing downtime.

EXT3 ensures stronger data integrity through journaling, which monitors changes before they are written to the disk. In the event of a system crash occurs, the journal helps restore the system to a consistent state, preventing file corruption.

Although journaling introduces some overhead, EXT3 often performs better than EXT2 because it reduces the need for full file system checks (fsck) after a crash. The file system supports three types of journaling modes:

1. **Journal mode:** Logs both metadata and actual file data, offering maximum reliability.

2. **Ordered mode (default):** Logs metadata and ensures file data is written before updating metadata.

3. **Writeback mode:** Logs metadata but does not guarantee order, improving performance but slightly reducing reliability.

One of EXT3's major advantages is that users can easily upgrade from EXT2 to EXT3 without reformatting or losing data. This is done using the following command:

```
# /sbin/tune2fs -j <partition-name>
```

EXT3 marked a significant advancement in Linux file system development, bringing journaling, reliability, and ease of transition from EXT2. However, as file storage demands grew, its limitations led to the creation of EXT4, which introduced further performance and scalability improvements.

EXT3 Features

Data Integrity

The EXT3 file system helps maintain data integrity even during an unclean system shutdown. It also allows users to choose the type and level of protection for their data. By default, EXT3 volumes are configured to maintain a high level of data consistency.

Speed

Although EXT3 may write some data multiple times, it generally offers higher throughput than EXT2. This is because EXT3's journaling features help optimize the movement of the hard drive's read/write head. Users can select from three journaling modes to improve speed, though each comes with trade-offs that may affect data integrity in the event of a system failure.

Easy Transition

Migrating from EXT2 to EXT3 is straightforward, allowing users to benefit from a robust journaling file system without needing to reformat.

Fourth Extended File System (EXT4)

The Fourth Extended File System (EXT4) is a journaling file system that emerged as the successor to the widely used EXT3, bringing significant advancements in performance, scalability, and reliability. Designed to address the limitations of its predecessors, EXT4 has become a cornerstone of Linux file management since its introduction in kernel version 2.6.19. One of the primary strengths of the EXT4 file system is its ability to manage vast storage capacities. It can support individual files up to 16 terabytes (TB) and an overall file system size of 1 exabyte (EB). This scalability is essential for modern applications that handle increasingly large datasets.

The performance improvements of EXT4 can be attributed to several key features. One significant enhancement is the introduction of extents, which replace the traditional block mapping scheme. Extents improve the management of large files by treating contiguous blocks of data as a single unit, enhancing efficiency. This approach reduces overhead, minimizes fragmentation, and leads to faster access times.

Delayed allocation further optimizes write operations by postponing the allocation of disk blocks, enabling the file system to make more informed decisions about data placement and reduce fragmentation. This is complemented by multi-block allocation, which enables the simultaneous allocation of multiple blocks, improving write performance.

Beyond performance, EXT4 also focuses on reliability. Journal check summing adds an extra layer of data integrity to the journal, ensuring more robust recovery in case of system crashes. Faster file system checking (fsck speed) minimizes downtime during repairs.

For specific needs, persistent preallocation allows users to reserve disk space for files in advance, ensuring availability and preventing fragmentation. For applications that require accurate time tracking, EXT4 offers enhanced timestamps with nanosecond resolution. Additionally, EXT4 is backward compatible with EXT3 and EXT2, enabling seamless mounting of older file systems and making it easier for users to transition smoothly.

macOS File System

The macOS file system has evolved, incorporating different technologies to enhance storage management, performance, and reliability.

Hierarchical File System (HFS)

One of the earliest file systems used in macOS was the Hierarchical File System (HFS), developed by Apple to support the Mac operating system. HFS introduced a structured way to organize files and directories, improving data retrieval efficiency compared to older file systems.

HFS Plus

As macOS advanced, Apple introduced HFS Plus (HFS+), an improved version of HFS, which became the primary file system for Macintosh computers. HFS+ was derived from the Berkeley Fast File System (FFS), originally developed at Bell Laboratories as part of the first UNIX File System (FS). This design allowed for larger file sizes, better disk space allocation, and improved performance, making it a more suitable option for modern computing needs.

UNIX File System (UFS)

Apart from HFS-based systems, macOS also supports the UNIX File System (UFS), commonly found in BSD UNIX derivatives such as FreeBSD, NetBSD, OpenBSD, NeXTStep, and Solaris. UFS provides a robust, journaled structure with strong multi-user support and file permissions, making it an alternative to HFS in some macOS environments. Although UFS was once available for macOS users, it was later phased out in favor of Apple-developed file systems like APFS, which provide superior performance, security, and optimization for modern SSD storage.

Domain 03: Computer Network Fundamental

Introduction

In today's digital world, computer networks form the backbone of communication, enabling seamless data exchange across various devices and systems. Understanding the fundamental concepts of computer networks is essential for anyone working in IT, as it lays the groundwork for designing, managing, and troubleshooting network infrastructures. From defining how data flows between devices to ensuring secure and efficient communication, network fundamentals cover crucial elements like protocols, network topologies, IP addressing, and security mechanisms.

However, even the most well-designed networks can experience issues, making troubleshooting a critical skill. Basic network troubleshooting techniques help identify and resolve connectivity problems, ensuring smooth operation. Whether it is diagnosing slow internet speeds, fixing IP conflicts, or resolving hardware failures, knowing the right troubleshooting steps can minimize downtime and enhance network performance.

Computer Network Fundamental Concepts

Computer Networks

Computer Networks

A computer network is a group of interconnected computing systems that facilitate electronic communication. It enables users to share information between resources such as computers, mobile phones, printers, scanners, and other devices. To ensure seamless communication between different computing systems, regardless of their internal architecture or technology, network models play a crucial role. These models establish a standardized framework for communication, ensuring interoperability across diverse systems. The two most widely recognized network models are the Open System Interconnection (OSI) Model and the TCP/IP Model, both of which define structured approaches for data transmission and networking protocols.

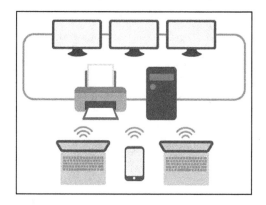

Figure 03-01: Computer Network

Open System Interconnection (OSI) Model

The Open System Interconnection (OSI) model serves as the standard reference framework for communication between two end users within a network. It is structured into seven layers, each with a specific role in facilitating data transmission. The top four layers primarily handle the communication process when a message is sent to or received from a user, ensuring proper data formatting, session management, and error handling. Meanwhile, the lower three layers handle the efficient transmission of messages by managing physical connections, data encoding, and ensuring reliable delivery across the network.

OSI MODEL			
	Data Unit	**Layer**	**Function**
Host Layers	Data	7. Application	Network process to application
		6. Presentation	Data representation, encryption, and decryption; convert data to machine-understandable format
		5. Session	Interhost communication, managing sessions between applications
	Segments	4. Transport	End-to-end connections, reliability, and flow control

Media Layers	Packet/Datagram	3. Network	Path determination and logical addressing
	Frame	2. Data Link	Physical addressing
	Bit	1. Physical	Media, signal, and binary transmission

Table 03-01: OSI Model

TCP/IP Model

Functions

The TCP/IP model is a foundational framework for the Internet Protocol (IP) suite, defining how communication occurs in an IP-based network. It establishes a structured approach for data transmission, enabling seamless communication between devices over the internet and other networks. By organizing networking functions into distinct layers, the TCP/IP model ensures efficient data routing, reliable delivery, and interoperability across diverse systems and technologies.

Layers

The TCP/IP model is structured into four layers, each with distinct functions and associated protocols that facilitate network communication.

- The Application layer handles high-level protocols, data representation, encoding, and dialog control. It enables services such as file transfer (TFTP, FTP), email (SMTP), remote login (Telnet, rlogin), network management (SNMP), and name resolution (DNS).
- The Transport layer establishes a logical connection between communication endpoints and ensures reliable data delivery from the source to the destination. It utilizes protocols such as the Transmission Control Protocol (TCP) for reliable, connection-oriented communication and the User Datagram Protocol (UDP) for faster, connectionless communication.
- The Internet layer is responsible for selecting the optimal path for data packets to travel across networks. It relies on protocols like the Internet Protocol (IP) for addressing and routing, the Internet Control Message Protocol (ICMP) for error reporting and diagnostics, and the Address Resolution Protocol (ARP) for mapping IP addresses to MAC addresses.
- The Network Access layer defines how data is physically transmitted across a network, ensuring communication between devices on a directly attached network. This layer includes protocols such as FDDI, Token Ring, CDP, VTP, and PPP, which govern data link and physical layer operations.

Protocols

Each layer in the TCP/IP model utilizes specific protocols that define communication rules and data exchange methods. These protocols ensure interoperability and efficient network operations:

- **Application Layer Protocols:** HTTP, FTP, SMTP, DNS, SNMP

- **Transport Layer Protocols:** TCP, UDP

- **Internet Layer Protocols:** IP, ICMP, ARP

- **Network Access Layer Protocols:** Ethernet, Wi-Fi, PPP, FDDI

Together, these layers and protocols form the backbone of IP-based networking, ensuring seamless communication across diverse computing environments.

Comparing OSI and TCP/ IP

The OSI and TCP/IP models serve as foundational frameworks for network communication, but they differ in their approach and design principles. The TCP/IP model is built around the practical implementation of protocols that have driven the development of the internet, making it a real-world, adaptable framework. In contrast, the OSI model is a conceptual reference model that provides a structured, protocol-independent standard for network communication. Another key difference lies in their level of specification—while the OSI model clearly defines services, interfaces, and protocols within its seven-layer structure, the TCP/IP model does not enforce a strict separation between these elements, making it more flexible but less structured compared to OSI.

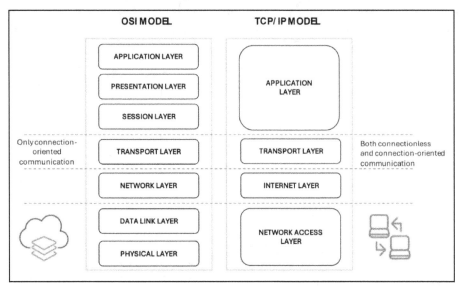

Figure 03-02: Comparing OSI and TCP/ IP

Types of Networks

A computer network is a group of interconnected computers that communicate over a shared communication medium to exchange data and share resources among network nodes. The primary purpose of a computer network is to enable resource sharing, such as files, applications, or hardware devices, among connected systems. The main types of computer networks include:

Local Area Network (LAN)

A Local Area Network (LAN) is typically owned and managed by private organizations to connect multiple computing devices within a limited area, such as an office, school, or building. It enables the seamless sharing of resources like files, printers, and internet connections among PCs or workstations within the same premises.

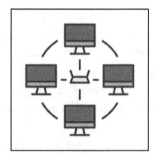

Figure 03-03: LAN

Wide Area Network (WAN)

A Wide Area Network (WAN) facilitates communication between multiple remote locations, which may be spread across different countries or even continents. It is commonly used by companies or organizations that require efficient data exchange across long distances. WANs ensure trustworthy, quick, and secure communication with minimal delays and low costs, making them a reliable solution for global networking needs.

Figure 03-04: WAN

Metropolitan Area Network (MAN)

A Metropolitan Area Network (MAN) is a large-scale network that spans an entire city. It can be owned and monitored by private organizations or provided as a service by public organizations such as telecommunications companies. MANs serve as an intermediary between LANs and WANs, offering high-speed connectivity across urban areas.

Figure 03-05: MAN

Personal Area Network (PAN)

A Personal Area Network (PAN) is a short-range network designed for individual use. It enables wireless communication between devices using radio and optical signals. PANs typically cover a small area, such as a person's workspace or home, and are often referred to as room-size networks.

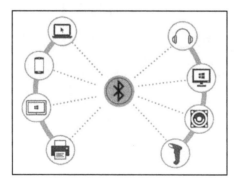

Figure 03-06: PAN

Campus Area Network (CAN)

A Campus Area Network (CAN) connects multiple local networks within a limited geographical area. This type of network is commonly used in university campuses, business parks, and industrial areas to provide seamless connectivity among buildings and departments.

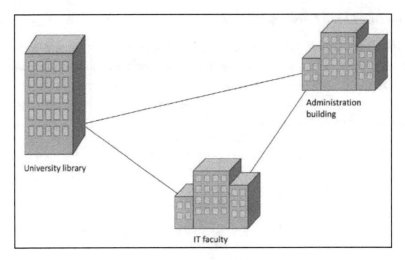

Figure 03-07: CAN

Global Area Network (GAN)

A Global Area Network (GAN) is an extensive network that interconnects multiple networks worldwide. It provides communication and data exchange across an unlimited geographical area. The internet is a well-known example of a GAN, facilitating global connectivity among users, organizations, and devices.

Figure 03-08: GAN

Wireless Networks (WLAN)

Wireless networks, also known as Wireless Local Area Networks (WLAN), rely on Radio Frequency (RF) signals to connect devices that are wireless-enabled. These networks operate based on the IEEE 802.11 standard and use radio waves for communication, allowing for seamless connectivity without the need for physical cables. One of the key advantages of wireless networks is their ease of installation, as they eliminate the need for cumbersome wiring. Additionally, users can access the network from anywhere within the coverage area of an access point, which

makes wireless LANs a popular choice for public spaces such as airports and schools, where they provide constant internet access.

However, there are some limitations associated with wireless networks. One major concern is Wi-Fi security, which may not always meet the expected standards, leaving the network vulnerable to potential threats. The network's bandwidth can also be negatively impacted by the number of users connected, leading to slower speeds and connectivity issues. Moreover, as wireless standards evolve, older equipment may need to be replaced to maintain compatibility with newer technologies. Additionally, certain electronic devices can interfere with the Wi-Fi signal, causing disruptions in service.

Figure 03-09: WLAN

Wireless Standards

Wireless standards define the protocols and specifications for wireless communication, ensuring interoperability between devices. Common standards include 802.11 (Wi-Fi) for wireless networking, Bluetooth for short-range connectivity, and 5G/4G LTE for mobile communication. These standards regulate aspects like frequency, speed, range, and security to optimize wireless data transmission.

Protocol	Frequency (GHz)	Bandwidth (MHz)	Stream Data Rate (Mbits/s)	Modulation	Range (Meters)	
					Indoor	Out door
802.11 (Wi-Fi)	2.4	22	1, 2	DSSS, FHSS	20	100
802.11a	5	20	6, 9, 12, 18, 24, 36, 48, 54	OFDM	35	120
	3.7				---	500 0

802.11ax	2.4 to 5	20, 40, 80, 160	2400	1024-QAM	30-50	100-300
802.11b	2.4	22	1, 2, 5.5, 11	DSSS	35	140
802.11be	2.4, 5, 6	20, 40, 80, 160, 320	3000	QAM	30-50	100-300
802.11d	An enhancement to 802.11a and 802.11b that enables global portability by allowing variation in frequencies, power levels, and bandwidth					
802.11e	Guides the prioritization of data, voice, and video transmissions, enabling QoS					
802.11g	2.4	20	6,9,12,18,24,36,48,54	OFDM		
802.11i	A standard for Wireless Local Area Networks (WLANs) that provides improved encryption for networks that use 802.11a, 802.11b, and 802.11g standards					
802.11n	5	20	7.2, 14.4, 21.7, 28.9, 43.3, 57.8, 65, 72.2	MIMO-OFDM	70	150
	2.4	40	15, 30, 45, 60, 90, 120, 135, 150		70	150
802.11ac	5	20	7.2, 14.4, 21.7, 28.9, 43.3, 57.8, 65, 72.2, 86.7, 96.3	MIMO-OFDM	35	
		40	15, 30, 45, 60, 90, 120, 135, 150, 180, 200		35	
		80	32.5, 65, 97.5, 130, 195, 260,		35	

			292.5, 325, 390, 433.3			
		160	65, 130, 195, 260, 390, 520, 585, 650, 780, 866.7		35	
802.11ad	60	2160	6.75 Gbit/s	OFDM, single carrier, low-power single carrier	60	100

Table 03-02: Wireless Standards

Wireless Technologies

Wireless technologies enable communication without physical cables, using electromagnetic waves such as radio, infrared, and microwave signals. They include Wi-Fi, Bluetooth, cellular networks (4G, 5G), and satellite communications. These technologies support mobile connectivity, IoT devices, and remote data transmission, enhancing flexibility and accessibility in various applications.

WIMAX

WIMAX, or Worldwide Interoperability for Microwave Access, is a wireless communication standard that is based on the IEEE 802.16 family of wireless networking protocols. Essentially, WIMAX serves as a wireless version of Ethernet, offering broadband access to both mobile and stationary devices. It provides an alternative to traditional wired technologies such as Cable Modems, DSL, and T1/E1 connections. One of the key advantages of WIMAX is its ability to cover long distances, spanning several miles while maintaining high data rates. This technology is capable of supporting high-speed data, voice, video calls, and internet connectivity, making it a versatile solution for a wide range of users.

Microwave Transmission

Microwave transmission is another form of wireless communication that relies on high-frequency radio waves to transmit data. It is particularly common in point-to-point communication due to its short wavelength, which allows for communication through narrow beams between small-sized antennas. The technology is advantageous because of its large information-carrying capacity, resulting from its wide bandwidth. However, one significant limitation of microwave transmission is

that it requires a direct line of sight between the transmitting and receiving points, meaning that obstacles in the path can disrupt the communication.

Optical Wireless Communication

Optical Wireless Communication (OWC) is a form of unguided transmission that utilizes optical carriers to transmit data. Unlike traditional wireless communication, OWC operates using visible light, Infrared (IR), and Ultraviolet (UV) wavelengths for data transmission. One of the key technologies within OWC is Visible Light Communication (VLC), which operates in the visible spectrum ranging from 390 to 750 nanometers. VLC systems use Light-Emitting Diodes (LEDs) that pulse at extremely high speeds to transmit data efficiently.

Another category of OWC is point-to-point Free-Space Optical (FSO) communication, which primarily transmits at IR frequencies between 750 and 1600 nanometers. These systems rely on laser transmitters and are capable of achieving high data rates, reaching up to 10 Gbit/s per wavelength. Additionally, Ultraviolet Communication (UVC) functions within the solar-blind UV spectrum, specifically within the 200–280 nanometer range. This enables communication in scenarios where other wireless technologies may face interference or limitations.

2G Mobile Network

2G, or the second generation of mobile cellular networks, operates under the Global System for Mobile Communications (GSM) standard. It introduced digitally encrypted signals for mobile data transmission, enhancing security and efficiency compared to its predecessor. An advanced version, known as 2.5G, emerged with the integration of General Packet Radio Service (GPRS), which extended GSM capabilities and supported transmission rates of 114 Kbit/s for downloads and 20 Kbit/s for uploads. Subsequently, Enhanced Data Rates for GSM Evolution (EDGE), also referred to as 2.75G, replaced GPRS, significantly increasing data rates to 384 Kbit/s for downloads and 60 Kbit/s for uploads.

3G Mobile Network

The third generation of wireless technology, commonly known as 3G, was introduced as the Universal Mobile Telecommunications Service (UMTS) network. The initial version of 3G, called High-Speed Packet Access (HSPA), combined two key protocols: High-Speed Downlink Packet Access (HSDPA) and High-Speed Uplink Packet Access (HSUPA). This enabled improved data transmission rates, offering speeds of 7.2 Mbit/s for downloads and 2 Mbit/s for uploads. In 2008, an upgraded version known as Evolved High-Speed Packet Access (HSPA+), or 3.5G, was introduced. This further enhanced network performance, delivering download speeds of up to 337 Mbit/s and upload speeds of 34 Mbit/s.

4G Mobile Network

4G, also known as Long-Term Evolution (LTE), is the fourth generation of wireless technology designed to meet the advanced communication requirements set by the International Telecommunication Union (ITU) and International Mobile Telecommunications-Advanced (IMT-Advanced) standards. This technology significantly improves data transmission rates, offering speeds of up to 100 Mbit/s for high-mobility communication, such as in moving vehicles, and up to 1 Gbit/s for low-mobility scenarios, like stationary or pedestrian users.

Terrestrial Trunked Radio (TETRA)

TETRA, or Terrestrial Trunked Radio, is a European standard developed to define a professional mobile radio communication infrastructure. It serves as a standard for both Private Mobile Radio (PMR) and Public Access Mobile Radio (PAMR), primarily catering to emergency and critical service sectors, including police forces, military, ambulance services, and public transport networks. One of the key advantages of TETRA is its use of low-frequency signals, which enable coverage over large geographic areas with fewer transmitters, thereby reducing infrastructure costs while maintaining reliable communication.

Bluetooth Technology

Bluetooth is a short-range wireless communication technology designed for device-to-device data transmission, primarily used in mobile devices. It enables seamless data transfer between cell phones, computers, and other networking devices without requiring physical connections. Bluetooth signals can cover distances of up to 10 meters, making it ideal for personal and peripheral device communication.

Operating within the frequency range of 2.4 GHz to 2.485 GHz, Bluetooth transfers data at speeds of less than 1 Mbps. It falls under the IEEE 802.15 standard and utilizes a radio technology known as Frequency-Hopping Spread Spectrum (FHSS) to ensure secure and efficient data transmission between Bluetooth-enabled devices.

Network Topologies

Network topology refers to the structural arrangement of a network, defining how devices are connected and how data flows within the system. It is categorized into two main types:

- **Physical Topology**: Represents the actual layout of nodes, workstations, and cables in the network

- **Logical Topology**: Describes how data moves between different components within the network

Types of Physical Network Topologies

1. **Bus Topology**: In this setup, all network devices are connected to a central cable, known as a bus, using interface connectors. Data travels along this main cable, and each device receives the transmitted signal.

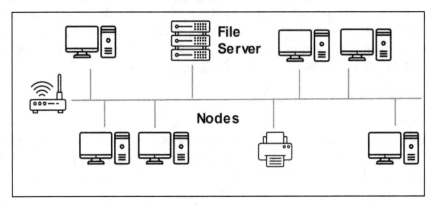

Figure 03-10: Linear Bus

2. **Ring Topology**: Devices in the network are connected in a closed-loop configuration. Data travels in one direction from node to node, with each node processing and forwarding the data until it reaches its destination.

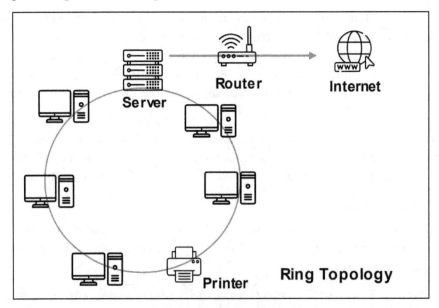

Figure 03-11: Ring Topology

3. **Tree Topology**: A hybrid model that combines elements of bus and star topologies. Groups of star-configured networks are linked together using a linear bus backbone cable, enabling hierarchical data flow.

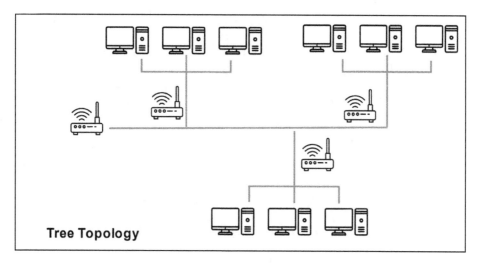

Figure 03-12: Tree Topology

4. **Star Topology**: All devices are connected to a central hub or switch, which functions as a router for managing communication. The hub relays messages between connected devices, ensuring efficient data transmission.

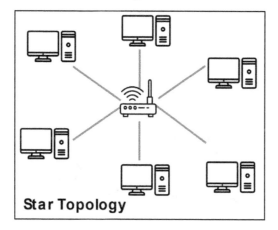

Figure 03-13: Star Topology

5. **Mesh Topology**: In this highly interconnected structure, each device is linked to every other device in the network through dedicated point-to-point connections, ensuring redundancy and fault tolerance.

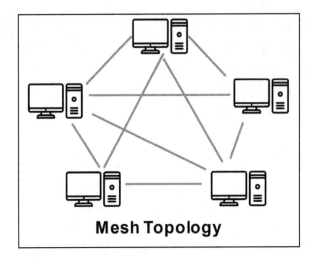

Figure 03-14: Mesh Topology

6. **Hybrid Topology**: A combination of two or more different topologies, allowing for flexible network design. Common examples include Star-Bus and Star-Ring configurations, which optimize performance and scalability.

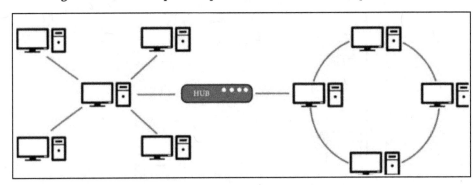

Figure 03-15: Hybrid Topology

Network Hardware Components

1. **Network Interface Card (NIC)**: A hardware component that enables computers to connect to and communicate within a network by facilitating data transmission and reception.

2. **Repeater**: A device used to amplify and regenerate weak or degraded network signals, extending the transmission range and maintaining signal quality.

3. **Hub**: A central connection point for multiple devices within a Local Area Network (LAN). It broadcasts incoming data packets to all connected devices, making network traffic visible to all segments.

4. **Switch**: Similar to a hub, but with enhanced efficiency. A switch directs data packets only to the intended recipient device within the LAN, reducing network congestion and improving performance.

5. **Router**: A networking device that receives data packets from one network and forwards them to another based on the best available path, enabling communication between different networks.

6. **Bridge**: A device that connects and manages traffic between two separate network segments, ensuring efficient data flow while maintaining network integrity.

7. **Gateway**: A networking component that facilitates communication between different network environments and protocols, allowing interoperability between diverse systems.

Types of LAN Technology

1. **Ethernet**: Ethernet is a widely used LAN technology that operates at the physical layer, balancing speed, cost, and ease of installation. It defines the number of conductors required for network connections, sets performance standards, and establishes a framework for data transmission. A standard Ethernet network can achieve transmission speeds of up to 10 Megabits Per Second (10 Mbps). The IEEE 802.3 standard governs Ethernet networks, specifying configuration rules and the interaction of network components.

2. **Fast Ethernet**: An enhanced version of Ethernet, Fast Ethernet operates at a minimum data transmission rate of 100 Mbps and follows the IEEE 802.3u standard. It comes in three variants:

   o **100BASE-TX**: Designed for use with Category 5 Unshielded Twisted Pair (UTP) cables

   o **100BASE-FX**: Utilizes fiber-optic cables for high-speed data transfer

   o **100BASE-T4**: Employs additional two wires with a Category 3 UTP cable for increased efficiency

3. **Gigabit Ethernet**: Defined by the IEEE 802.3-2008 standard, Gigabit Ethernet enables data transmission at a speed of 1 Gigabit Per Second (Gbps). It is widely used in high-speed communication networks, including multimedia streaming and Voice over IP (VoIP) applications. This technology is also known as "Gigabit Ethernet over copper" or 1000Base-T, as it offers speeds ten times faster than the 100Base-T standard.

4. **10 Gigabit Ethernet**: Introduced under the IEEE 802.3ae-2002 standard, 10 Gigabit Ethernet significantly enhances network performance by delivering

transmission speeds of 10 Gbps, making it ten times faster than standard Gigabit Ethernet. Unlike traditional Ethernet systems that use copper cables, 10 Gigabit Ethernet relies primarily on optical fiber connections to achieve high-speed data transfer.

5. **Asynchronous Transfer Mode (ATM)**: ATM is a high-speed, cell-based communication standard designed for transmitting various types of data, including voice, video, and general network traffic. It operates on the data link layer and utilizes fixed-size cells for efficient data transfer. ATM networks typically use fiber optic or twisted-pair cables and are primarily deployed in private long-distance networks, particularly by Internet Service Providers (ISPs).

6. **Power over Ethernet (PoE)**: Defined by the IEEE 802.3af and 802.3at standards, PoE enables Ethernet cables to deliver both data and power to network-connected devices. This eliminates the need for separate power sources. PoE devices are categorized into two types:

   o **Power Sourcing Equipment (PSE)**: Devices that provide power, such as switches and injectors.

   o **Powered Devices (PDs)**: Devices that receive power, such as IP cameras, wireless access points, and VoIP phones. Some devices can function as both PSE and PD, depending on network requirements.

Specifications of LAN Technology

Name	IEEE Standard	Data Rate	Media Type	Maximum Distance
Ethernet	802.3	10 Mbps	10Base-T	100 meters
Fast Ethernet/100Base-T	802.3u	100 Mbps	100Base-TX	100 meters
			100Base-FX	2000 meters
Gigabit Ethernet/GigE	802.3z	1000 Mbps	1000Base-T	100 meters
			1000Base-SX	275/550 meters
			1000Base-LX	550/5000 meters
10 Gigabit Ethernet	IEEE 802.3ae	10 Gbps	10GBase-SR	300 m
			10GBase-LX4	300m MMF/10 km SMF

				10GBase-LR/ER	10 km/40 km
				10GBase-SW/LW/EW	300 m/10 km/40 km

Table 03-03: Specifications of LAN Technology

Common Fiber Technologies

Fiber Optic Cable

Fiber optic cables are an advanced type of network cable designed for high-speed data transmission. These cables are composed of multiple layers, including the core, cladding, buffer, and jacket. The core, made of glass or plastic, serves as the main pathway for transmitting light signals. It has a higher refractive index than the surrounding cladding, which is also made of glass or plastic but with a lower refractive index to help contain the light within the core through total internal reflection. The buffer layer protects against physical damage and moisture, while the outermost jacket encases and secures multiple fiber strands within a single cable.

Fiber optic cables offer several advantages over traditional copper cables. They are cost-effective, lightweight, and compact while delivering an extremely wide bandwidth for high-speed data transfer. These cables provide enhanced security, as they are resistant to electromagnetic interference and immune to electrostatic disturbances. Additionally, fiber optic cables are more durable, resistant to corrosion, and easy to maintain. They also eliminate cross-talk, ensuring clearer signal transmission over longer distances.

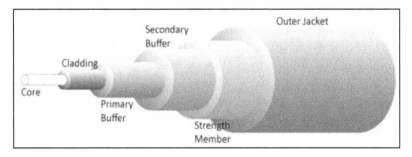

Figure 03-16: Fiber Optic Cable

Coaxial Cable

Coaxial cable is a type of copper cable designed to minimize signal interference through its unique construction. It consists of two conductors separated by a dielectric insulating material. The inner conductor, responsible for transmitting signals, is surrounded by an outer conductor that acts as a shield against external

electromagnetic interference. These conductors are arranged in a concentric cylindrical structure with a shared axis, ensuring efficient signal transmission.

There are two widely used types of coaxial cables: 50-ohm and 75-ohm variants. A 50-ohm cable is primarily used for digital signal transmission, while a 75-ohm cable is commonly employed for analog signals. Coaxial cables are known for their large bandwidth and low signal loss, making them suitable for various communication applications. They support a data rate of 10 Mbps, which can be increased by enlarging the diameter of the inner conductor.

One of the key advantages of coaxial cables is their cost-effectiveness, as both installation and production costs are relatively low. Additionally, they offer excellent channel capacity good bandwidth, and can be easily modified to suit different applications. These qualities make coaxial cables a reliable choice for transmitting signals in telecommunications, broadcasting, and networking systems.

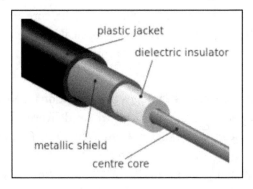

Figure 03-17: Coaxial Cable

CAT 3 and CAT 4

CAT 3: Category 3 (CAT 3) cable, also known as station wire, is a type of twisted pair cable primarily used for voice communication and 10BaseT Ethernet networks with data transmission speeds of up to 10 Mbps. It has a bandwidth capacity of 16 MHz, an attenuation level of 11.5 dB, and an impedance of 100 ohms. Though it was widely used in early networking applications, it has largely been replaced by higher-category cables that offer improved performance.

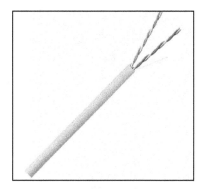

Figure 03-18: CAT 3

CAT 4: Category 4 (CAT 4) cable consists of four Unshielded Twisted Pair (UTP) copper wires and was designed for use in 10BaseT Ethernet networks. It provides a slightly higher bandwidth of 20 MHz compared to CAT 3, along with a lower attenuation of 7.5 dB, while maintaining an impedance of 100 ohms. Despite its improved characteristics, CAT 4 has become obsolete as newer standards like CAT 5 and beyond offer significantly better performance and reliability in modern networking environments.

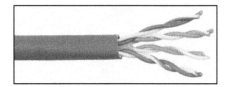

Figure 03-19: CAT 4

CAT 5

Category 5 (CAT 5) is an Unshielded Twisted Pair (UTP) cable commonly used in networking applications. It is terminated with RJ-45 connectors and has a maximum cable length of 100 meters. Supporting frequencies of up to 100 MHz, CAT 5 is suitable for various Ethernet standards, including 10BASE-T, 100BASE-TX, and 1000BASE-T. In addition to data networking, it can also carry telephonic and video signals, making it a versatile choice for communication infrastructure.

CAT 5 cables are typically connected using punch-down blocks and modular connectors, ensuring secure and reliable connections. With a bandwidth of 100 MHz, an attenuation level of 24.0 dB, and an impedance of 100 ohms, this cable is designed for efficient high-speed data transmission. It is widely applicable to different LAN topologies and is compatible with 4 and 16-Mbps UTP Token Ring systems. Despite the emergence of more advanced cable categories, CAT 5 remains a reliable solution for many networking environments.

Figure 03-20: CAT 5

CAT 5e and CAT 6

CAT 5e: Category 5e (CAT 5e), an enhanced version of Category 5, is designed for high-speed data transmission. It is widely used in Fast Ethernet (100 Mbps), Gigabit Ethernet (1000 Mbps), and Asynchronous Transfer Mode (ATM) networks operating at 155 Mbps. With a bandwidth of 350 MHz, an attenuation of 24.0 dB, and an impedance of 100 ohms, CAT 5e reduces crosstalk and improves signal quality compared to its predecessor. This makes it a reliable choice for networking applications requiring stable and efficient data transfer.

Figure 03-21: CAT 5e

CAT 6: Category 6 (CAT 6) is an advanced network cable that offers superior performance compared to CAT 5e. It supports Gigabit Ethernet (1000 Mbps) as well as 10 Gigabit Ethernet (10,000 Mbps), making it ideal for high-speed data transmission in modern networks. CAT 6 cables have a bandwidth of 250 MHz, an attenuation of 19.8 dB, and an impedance of 100 ohms. Their enhanced shielding and tighter twisted pair construction minimize interference, resulting in better signal integrity and reduced latency. As a result, CAT 6 is preferred for applications requiring faster and more reliable data communication.

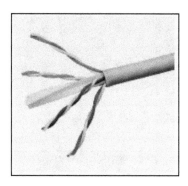

Figure 03-22: CAT 6

10/100/1000BaseT (UTP Ethernet)

The 10/100/1000Base-T Ethernet standards define network connection methods that utilize twisted pair cables for data transmission at speeds of 10 Mbps, 100 Mbps, and 1000 Mbps. In these standards, "BASE" signifies baseband transmission, while "T" refers to the use of twisted pair cabling.

- **10Base-T:** It operates at a transmission speed of 10 Mbps with a maximum cable length of 100 meters. It follows the IEEE 802.3i standard and is compatible with Category 3 and Category 5 cables. This standard uses four wires, specifically pins 1, 2, 3, and 6, for data transmission.
- **100Base-T**: This is also known as Fast Ethernet, supports a data transmission speed of 100 Mbps. It adheres to the IEEE 802.3u standard and is primarily designed for use with Category 5 cables. Like 10Base-T, it also utilizes four wires—pins 1, 2, 3, and 6—for communication.
- **1000Base-T:** 1000Base-T, or Gigabit Ethernet, enables data transmission at 1000 Mbps (1 Gbps) and follows the IEEE 802.3ab standard. It is best suited for Category 5e cables and requires all eight wires—pins 1, 2, 3, 4, 5, 6, 7, and 8—to facilitate high-speed communication efficiently. This makes it a preferred choice for modern high-performance networking environments.

TCP/IP Protocol Suite

The TCP/IP protocol suite is a set of communication protocols that enable data transmission over the internet and other networks. It is structured into four layers Application, Transport, Internet, and Network Access each responsible for specific networking functions. Key protocols include TCP (ensuring reliable communication), IP (handling addressing and routing), and UDP (supporting fast, connectionless communication). This suite forms the foundation of modern networking, ensuring seamless connectivity and data exchange.

Application Layer Protocol	Transport Layer Protocol	Internet Layer Protocol	Link Layer Protocol
DHCP	TCP	IP	FDDI
DNS	UDP	IPv6	Token ring
DNSSEC	SSL	IPsec	WEP
HTTP	TLS	ICMP	WPA
S-HTTP		ARP	WPA2
HTTPS		IGRP	TKIP
FTP		EIGRP	EAP
SFTP		OSPF	LEAP
TFTP		HSRP	PEAP
SMTP		VRRP	CDP
S/MIME		BGP	VTP
PGP			STP
Telnet			PPP
SSH			
SOAP			
SNMP			
NTP			
RPC			
SMB			
SIP			
RADIUS			
TACACS+			
RIP			

Table 03-04: TCP/IP Protocol Suite

Application Layer Protocols

Dynamic Host Configuration Protocol (DHCP)

Dynamic Host Configuration Protocol (DHCP) is a network protocol used by DHCP servers to automatically assign and distribute TCP/IP configuration settings to DHCP-enabled clients. This process occurs through a lease offer, where the server provides clients with essential network parameters such as IP addresses, subnet masks, default gateways, and DNS server information. By automating IP address allocation, DHCP simplifies network management and reduces the risk of configuration errors.

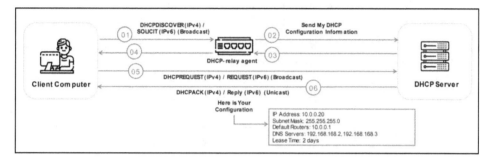

Figure 03-23: DHCP

Domain Name System (DNS)

The Domain Name System (DNS) is a distributed and hierarchical database that translates human-readable website URLs into corresponding IP addresses. This system enables users to access websites using domain names instead of numerical IP addresses, simplifying web navigation. By distributing the database across multiple servers worldwide, DNS ensures efficient and reliable domain resolution, making internet browsing seamless and scalable.

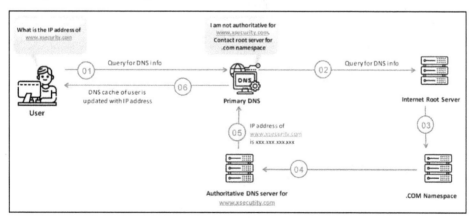

Figure 03-24: Domain Name System (DNS)

DNS Packet Format

A DNS packet consists of various fields that define the nature of the query and response. These fields help in the processing and resolution of domain name requests.

- **Query/Response (QR)**: Indicates the type of DNS message. A value of 0 represents a query, while 1 denotes a response
- **Opcode**: Defines the type of DNS query:
    - o   0 – Standard Query (QUERY)
    - o   1 – Inverse Query (IQUERY)
    - o   2 – Server Status Request (STATUS)
- **Authoritative Answer (AA)**: A value of 1 signifies that the responding server is authoritative for the domain
- **Truncation (TC)**: If set to 1, it indicates that the response was too large and had to be truncated
- **Recursion Desired (RD)**: A value of 1 request recursive resolution from the DNS server
- **Recursion Available (RA)**: A value of 1 means the server supports recursion
- **Reserved (Z)**: This field is reserved and must be set to 0
- **Response Code**: Indicates the status of the response:
    - o   0 – No Error
    - o   1 – Format Error (invalid request)
    - o   2 – Server Failure (DNS server issue)
    - o   3 – Non-existent Domain (domain not found)
    - o   4 – Query Type Not Implemented
    - o   5 – Query Refused (denied by the server)

These fields ensure efficient and structured communication between DNS clients and servers, enabling seamless domain resolution.

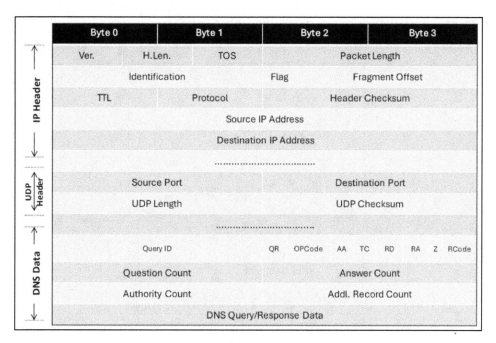

Figure 03-25: DNS Packet Format

DNS Hierarchy

The Domain Name System (DNS) hierarchy is a structured system that organizes domain names into different levels, ensuring efficient domain resolution. It consists of the following layers:

- **Root Level Domain**: This is the highest level in the DNS hierarchy. It responds to queries and maintains information about the global list of top-level domains, such as .com, .org, .uk, and .nz.
- **Top-Level Domains (TLDs)**: These domains fall under two main categories— organizational TLDs (such as .com, .edu, and .gov) and geographical TLDs (such as .uk and .jp).
- **Second-Level Domains**: This level represents the actual domain name chosen by the owner, allowing customization without restrictions. For instance, in example.com, "example" is the second-level domain.
- **Subdomains**: These are extensions of the main domain, dividing it into sections for better organization. For example, if an organization owns mydomain.com, it can create subdomains like about.mydomain.com and contact.mydomain.com.
- **Host**: A host is a device or server that holds DNS hierarchy domain names, enabling users to access websites and services through domain name resolution.

This hierarchical structure ensures a scalable and efficient way to manage domain names across the internet.

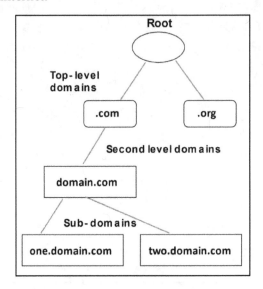

Figure 03-26: DNS Hierarchy

Domain Name System Security Extensions (DNSSEC)

DNSSEC is a suite of security extensions developed by the Internet Engineering Task Force (IETF) to enhance the security of the Domain Name System (DNS). It ensures that DNS responses are authentic and have not been altered in transit by digitally signing DNS records using public-key cryptography.

Guarantees Provided by DNSSEC:

- **Authenticity**: DNSSEC ensures that responses originate from a legitimate source. This is achieved through the use of cryptographic signatures, which confirm that the DNS data comes from an authorized entity.
- **Integrity**: By employing digital signatures, DNSSEC verifies that the DNS data has not been altered or tampered with during transit. This protects against various attacks, such as Man-In-The-Middle (MITM) or cache poisoning.
- **Verification of Non-Existence**: DNSSEC can cryptographically confirm when a domain name or record type does not exist. This feature prevents attackers from injecting false data by ensuring that the absence of a record is legitimate.

Limitations of DNSSEC:

While DNSSEC enhances security, it does not provide:

- **Confidentiality**: DNSSEC does not encrypt DNS queries or responses. As a result, while it verifies the authenticity and integrity of the data, the content of the communications remains visible to potential eavesdroppers.

- **Protection Against Denial-of-Service (DoS) Attacks**: DNSSEC does not include mechanisms to prevent or mitigate DoS attacks that target the DNS infrastructure. Attackers can still overwhelm DNS servers with high volumes of traffic, potentially disrupting service even when DNSSEC is in place.

DNSSEC plays a crucial role in strengthening internet security by ensuring the trustworthiness of DNS data, but it must be used alongside other security measures for comprehensive protection.

How DNSSEC Works

DNSSEC operates using asymmetric cryptography, which involves a pair of public and private keys to secure DNS data. It enhances DNS security by adding digital signatures to DNS records.

1. **Public and Private Key Pair**: DNSSEC relies on asymmetric encryption, where the private key signs the DNS data, and the public key is used to verify its authenticity.

2. **Digital Signatures for DNS Records**: Each piece of a domain's DNS information is digitally signed, ensuring its integrity.

3. **Verification by DNS Resolver**: When a user enters a domain name in a web browser, the DNS resolver checks the digital signature to confirm the authenticity of the DNS response.

4. **Validation Against Registry Records**: The resolver compares the digital signature with the one stored at the domain's registry. If they match, the response is accepted; otherwise, the resolver rejects the response, preventing access to potentially malicious data.

By implementing DNSSEC, organizations can protect users from DNS spoofing and ensure secure domain name resolution.

Managing DNSSEC for Domain Name

DNSSEC enhances the security of domain names by incorporating digital signatures into the Domain Name System (DNS) records. These digital signatures help prevent DNS spoofing and ensure data integrity.

1. **Adding Security with Digital Signatures**: DNSSEC strengthens domain security by appending cryptographic signatures to DNS records, ensuring authenticity and integrity.

2. **Delegation Signing (DS) Records**: DS records store the cryptographic signature details for a domain's DNS, allowing validation of the DNSSEC chain of trust.

3. **Supported Domain Extensions**: DNSSEC can be managed for domain names with extensions such as .com, .net, .biz, .us, .org, .eu, .co.uk, .me.uk, .org.uk, .co, .com.co, .net.co, and .nom.co.

4. **Multiple DS Records**: Depending on the domain extension, a domain may support one or more DS records simultaneously, ensuring enhanced DNSSEC protection.

By properly managing DS records, domain owners can reinforce the security of their domain names against DNS-based attacks.

What is a DS Record?

A Delegation Signing (DS) record is a type of DNS record that contains cryptographic details about a signed zone file. It plays a crucial role in the Domain Name System Security Extensions (DNSSEC) mechanism by establishing a chain of trust between a parent and a child DNS zone.

When enabling DNSSEC for a domain, the DS record is required to complete the setup. It ensures that DNS queries for the domain are authenticated and protected against spoofing or tampering.

How does DNSSEC Protect Internet Users?

DNSSEC is designed to protect users from forged or malicious DNS data, preventing attackers from redirecting them to fraudulent websites. It ensures that the DNS responses received are authentic and have not been altered during transmission.

Non-DNSSEC-Aware Lookups:

*   When a user requests a URL, the query is sent over the internet, and the browser accepts the first response it receives
*   A malicious attacker can intercept the request and send a fake response, directing the user to a fraudulent website
*   This can lead to security breaches, such as data theft or phishing attacks

DNSSEC-Aware Lookups:

*   The DNS query is validated against the digital signature stored in the domain's registry
*   If the response does not include a matching digital signature, the browser rejects it, ensuring that users are only directed to the intended website
*   This prevents attackers from misdirecting users to malicious or compromised websites

Operation of DNSSEC

DNSSEC ensures the authenticity and integrity of DNS records using cryptographic signatures.

- **Data Integrity & Authenticity:**
  - Each Resource Record Set (RRSET) is signed using a private key
  - A corresponding public key verifies the Resource Record Signature (RRSIG), ensuring data integrity
- **Proof of Non-Existence:**
  - DNSSEC uses Next Secure (NSEC) records to establish a chain of names in canonical order, proving the non-existence of a domain or record type
- **Delegated Zones (Child & Parent Validation):**
  - Child zones sign their RRSETs with a private key
  - The parent zone verifies the child's public key using the Delegation Signer (DS) record, which contains a hash of the child's DNSKEY

Hypertext Transfer Protocol (HTTP)

The Hypertext Transfer Protocol (HTTP) is a communication protocol used for transmitting web pages and other resources over the internet. It operates on a request-response model, where a client (browser) requests data from a web server, which then responds with the requested content. HTTP functions over TCP (port 80) and does not encrypt data, whereas Hypertext Transfer Protocol Secure (HTTPS) adds encryption via SSL/TLS for secure communication.

Key Features:

- Operates as the standard application protocol on top of TCP/IP
- Handles web browser requests and web server responses
- Transfers various data types, including audio, video, images, hypertext, and plain text
- Communication occurs through HTTP messages:
  - A client sends an HTTP request to the server
  - The server responds with an HTTP response

Weaknesses of HTTP:

- **Lack of Security:** Data is not encrypted, making it vulnerable
- **Man-In-The-Middle (MITM) Attacks:** Hackers can intercept and alter communication
- **No Encryption or Digital Certificates:** HTTP does not provide confidentiality or data integrity

115

Secure HTTP

Secure Hypertext Transfer Protocol (S-HTTP) is an extension of HTTP that provides encryption and security for individual messages between a client and a server. Unlike HTTPS, which secures the entire communication session using SSL/TLS, S-HTTP encrypts only specific messages, offering more flexible security options. However, it is less commonly used compared to HTTPS, which has become the standard for secure web communication.

Key Features:

- Ensures secure data transmission for individual messages
- Secure Sockets Layer (SSL) establishes a secure connection between two entities, protecting the entire communication
- Acts as an alternative to HTTPS (SSL/TLS)
- Commonly used when the server requires authentication from the user

Note: Not all Web browsers and servers support S-HTTP

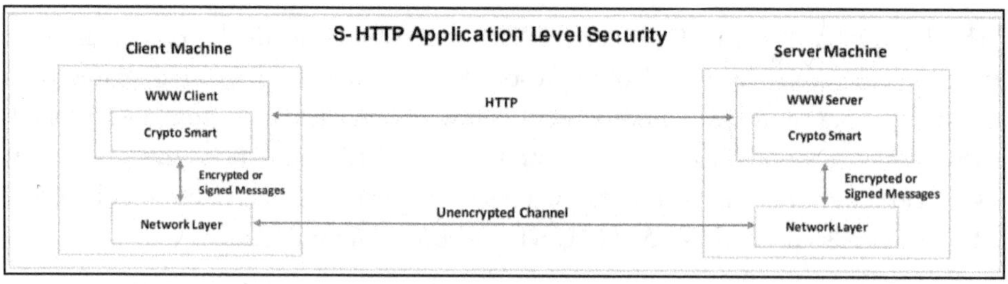

Figure 03-27: Secure HTTP

Hyper Text Transfer Protocol Secure (HTTPS)

HyperText Transfer Protocol Secure (HTTPS) is the secure version of HTTP, used for encrypted communication over the internet. It integrates SSL/TLS encryption to ensure data confidentiality, integrity, and authentication. HTTPS operates on TCP port 443, protecting sensitive information like login credentials and payment details. It is essential for secure browsing, online transactions, and safeguarding user privacy.

Key Features:

- Uses Transport Layer Security (TLS) or Secure Sockets Layer (SSL) to encrypt the connection
- Commonly used for secure online transactions such as banking and e-commerce
- Protects against Man-In-The-Middle attacks by transmitting data over an encrypted channel

Weaknesses of HTTP:

- **Potential vulnerability:** Can be exposed to Decrypting RSA with Obsolete and Weakened Encryption (DROWN) attacks if outdated SSL/TLS versions are used.

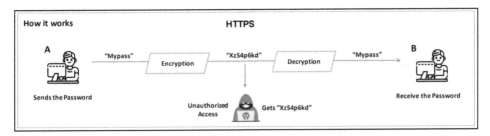

Figure 03-28: HTTPS

File Transfer Protocol (FTP)

File Transfer Protocol (FTP) is a standard network protocol used for transferring files between a client and a server over a network. It operates on a client-server model and uses TCP ports 20 and 21 for data transfer and control commands. FTP supports authentication via usernames and passwords but lacks encryption, making FTP Secure (FTPS) and SSH File Transfer Protocol (SFTP) preferred for secure file transfers.

Key Features:

- Follows a client-server architecture for file sharing
- Supports encryption mechanisms like SSL/TLS and SSH to enhance data security
- FTP servers authenticate users through a simple login mechanism to grant access

How does FTP Work?

FTP operates using two separate connections:

- **Control Connection**: Handles commands and responses between the client and server
- **Data Connection**: Manages the actual file transfer

Modes of Operation:

- **Active Mode:** The FTP client initiates the control connection, while the FTP server initiates the data connection to the client

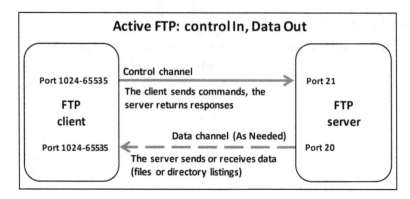

Figure 03-29: Active FTP

- **Passive Mode**: The FTP client initiates both the control and data connections to the server, which is useful when firewalls block incoming connections

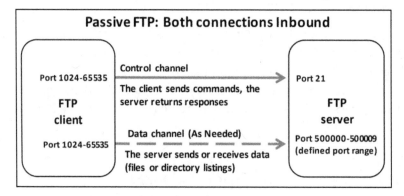

Figure 03-30: Passive FTP

Secure File Transfer Protocol (SFTP)

Secure File Transfer Protocol (SFTP) is a secure alternative to FTP and functions as an extension of the SSH2 protocol. It ensures secure file transfer and remote file access over an encrypted connection. SFTP operates on TCP port 22, providing data integrity and confidentiality.

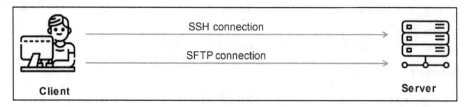

Figure 03-31: SFTP

Trivial File Transfer Protocol (TFTP)

Trivial File Transfer Protocol (TFTP) is a lockstep communication protocol that enables file transfers in both directions within a client-server application. It is commonly used for node booting on a local area network when operating system or firmware images are stored on a file server. TFTP only allows reading and writing files to or from a remote server without the ability to list, delete, or rename files or directories. It also lacks user authentication, making it primarily suitable for use within Local Area Networks (LAN). TFTP functions as an independent exchange but has significant weaknesses, including vulnerabilities to Denial-of-Service (DoS) attacks and directory traversal exploits.

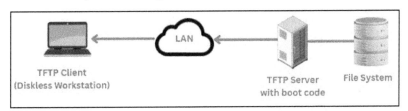

Figure 03-32: TFTP

Simple Mail Transfer Protocol (SMTP)

Simple Mail Transfer Protocol (SMTP) is an application layer protocol designed for the transmission of electronic mail (email). It operates as a text-based protocol that communicates with mail servers over TCP port 25. SMTP follows two models: the end-to-end model, which enables communication between different organizations, and the store-and-forward model, which is used within an organization.

SMTP offers features such as mail forwarding, mail gatewaying, mail relaying, address debugging, and mailing list expansion. It provides a simple and reliable method for sending emails, ensuring quick email delivery with low implementation and administration costs. It is also compatible with various platforms and flexible with existing applications.

However, SMTP has some drawbacks. Its security is weak, making it vulnerable to threats. It is limited to 7-bit ASCII characters, restricting the types of data that can be sent. Additionally, it lacks the advanced security protocols specified in X.400, and its simplicity limits its overall usefulness in complex email systems.

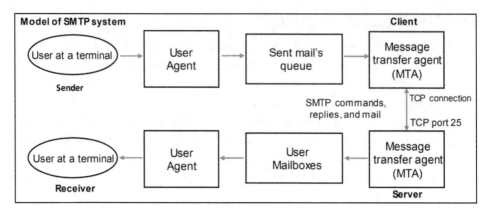

Figure 03-33: Model of SMTP System

S/MIME

Secure/Multipurpose Internet Mail Extensions (S/MIME) is an application layer protocol designed for sending digitally signed and encrypted email messages. It ensures email security by using RSA for digital signatures and DES for message encryption. To implement S/MIME-based security, administrators must enable it for mailboxes within their organizations. This enhances the confidentiality and integrity of email communication, protecting messages from unauthorized access and tampering.

How does it work?

S/MIME ensures the confidentiality, integrity, and authentication of email messages by utilizing asymmetric and symmetric cryptographic techniques. The process follows these key steps:

1. Signing the Message

When Alice wants to send a secure email to Bob, she first signs the message using her private key. This digital signature ensures that the message originates from her and has not been tampered with during transmission.

2. Encrypting the Message

To maintain confidentiality, Alice encrypts the message using a symmetric encryption algorithm (such as DES or AES). Since symmetric encryption is faster, it is used to encrypt the actual message content.

3. Encrypting the Secret Key

Alice then encrypts the symmetric key (used in the previous step) with Bob's public key using an asymmetric encryption algorithm like RSA. This ensures that only Bob, who possesses the corresponding private key, can decrypt and retrieve the symmetric key.

4. Sending the Encrypted Data

The encrypted message and the encrypted symmetric key are sent to Bob over a public network.

5. Decrypting the Secret Key

Upon receiving the message, Bob uses his private key to decrypt the symmetric key. This step is crucial because it enables Bob to decrypt the actual email content.

6. Decrypting the Message

Bob then uses the decrypted symmetric key to decrypt the email message, restoring it to its original readable format.

7. Signature Verification

Finally, Bob verifies Alice's digital signature using her public key. If the signature is valid, he can confirm that Alice indeed sent the email and was not altered in transit.

This process ensures message confidentiality, authentication, and integrity, making S/MIME a widely used standard for securing email communications.

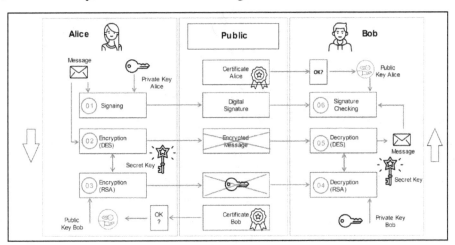

Figure 03-34: How S/MIME Works?

Pretty Good Privacy (PGP)

Pretty Good Privacy (PGP) is an application layer protocol that ensures cryptographic privacy and authentication for network communication. It secures email communication by encrypting and decrypting messages while also using digital signatures for authentication. Additionally, PGP encrypts stored files to protect sensitive data from unauthorized access.

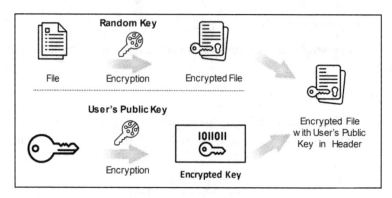

Figure 03-35: File Encryption

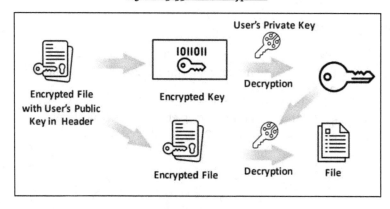

Figure 03-36: File Decryption

Difference between PGP and S/MIME

Pretty Good Privacy (PGP) and Secure/Multipurpose Internet Mail Extensions (S/MIME) are encryption protocols for securing email communication. PGP uses a web of trust for key management and is more flexible, working with various email clients. S/MIME, backed by Certificate Authorities (CAs), is integrated into major email providers like Outlook and supports built-in digital signatures. While PGP is user-managed, S/MIME relies on centralized trust through CAs.

Mandatory Features	S/MIME v3	OpenPGP
Message Format	Binary, Based on CMS	Application/Pkcs 7-mime
Certificate Format	Binary, Based on X.509v3	Binary, Based on the previous PGP
Symmetric Encryption Algorithm	Triple DES (DES, EDE3, and CBC)	Triple DES (DES, EDE3, and Eccentric CFB)

Signature Algorithm	Diffie-Hellman (X9.42) with DSS or RSA	ElGamal with DSS
Hash Algorithm	SHA-1	SHA-1
MIME Encapsulation of Signed Data	Choice of Multipart/signed or CMS Format	Multipart/signed ASCII armor
MIME Encapsulation of Encrypted Data	Application/ Pkcs 7-mime	Multipart/Encrypted

Table 03-05: PGP vs. S/MIME

Telnet

Telecommunications Network (Telnet) is a TCP/IP protocol used within a LAN that enables users or administrators to access and manage remote computers over a network. It allows logging into remote systems, executing programs, and controlling web servers, facilitating communication with other network servers. Telnet remains fast and efficient even under high network and system loads. However, it lacks security, as all data is transmitted in clear text, making it susceptible to Denial-of-Service attacks, packet sniffing, and eavesdropping threats.

```
Administrator: Command Prompt - telnet                                    —    □    ×
Welcome to Microsoft Telnet Client

Escape Character is 'CTRL+]'

Microsoft Telnet> help

Commands may be abbreviated. Supported commands are:

c      - close             close current connection
d      - display           display operating parameters
o      - open hostname [port]   connect to hostname (default port 23).
q      - quit              exit telnet
set    - set               set options (type 'set ?' for a list)
sen    - send              send strings to server
st     - status            print status information
u      - unset             unset options (type 'unset ?' for a list)
?/h    - help              print help information
Microsoft Telnet>
```

Figure 03-37: Telnet

SSH

SSH, or Secure Shell, is a network management protocol primarily used in UNIX and Linux environments for secure remote login. It establishes an encrypted tunnel

for securely exchanging information between network management software and devices. Administrators authenticate using a combination of a username, password, and port number.

SSH supports multiple authentication mechanisms:

1. **Simple Authentication**: Users authenticate using a password.

2. **Key-based Authentication**: Users generate a public and private key pair using ssh-keygen -t rsa or ssh-keygen -t dsa. The private key is used for authentication, while the public key is stored in ~/.ssh/authorized_keys.

3. **Host-based Authentication**: If enabled, users on a trusted host can log into a target machine using the same username. This requires setting the setuid bit on /usr/lib/ssh/ssh-keysign for 32-bit systems or /usr/lib64/ssh/ssh-keysign for 64-bit systems.

Simple Object Access Protocol (SOAP)

Simple Object Access Protocol (SOAP) is an XML-based messaging protocol designed for data transmission between computers. It facilitates data transport for web services while being platform- and language-independent, making it usable across different technologies.

SOAP is characterized by extensibility, neutrality, and independence. It functions similarly to Remote Procedure Calls (RPC) and is utilized in technologies like DCOM and CORBA.

Despite its advantages, SOAP has some weaknesses. It is stateless and heavily reliant on HTTP. It is slower compared to CORBA, RMI, or IIOP due to the verbose XML format and the need for envelope parsing. Additionally, SOAP depends on WSDL and lacks a standardized mechanism for dynamic service discovery.

Simple Network Management Protocol (SNMP)

Simple Network Management Protocol (SNMP) is an application layer protocol used for managing TCP/IP-based networks following a client-server architecture. It enables the collection and management of information about devices operating on these networks.

Devices that support SNMP include routers, hubs, modems, printers, bridges, switches, servers, and workstations.

However, SNMP configurations, particularly on Cisco IOS, are vulnerable to security risks such as Distributed Denial-of-Service (DDoS) attacks and SNMP Remote Code Execution.

Network Time Protocol (NTP)

Network Time Protocol (NTP) synchronizes the clock times of computers within a network. The NTP client initiates a time request exchange with the NTP server to maintain accurate timekeeping.

Key features include using Coordinated Universal Time (UTC) as a reference and its high scalability.

However, NTP is vulnerable to security threats such as Denial-of-Service (DoS) and DDoS amplification attacks. Intruders can intercept packets exchanged between an authentic client and server or replay previously transmitted packets to disrupt synchronization.

Remote Procedure Call (RPC)

Remote Procedure Call (RPC) is a protocol that enables inter-process communication between a client and a server, allowing them to interact without needing to understand the underlying network details. It facilitates seamless execution of procedures across different systems.

In Unix-based systems, RPC services include the Network Information Service (NIS), Network File System (NFS), and the Common Desktop Environment (CDE).

However, RPC has been associated with several security vulnerabilities on Windows and Linux platforms, including:

- Microsoft Windows RPC Security Feature Bypass Vulnerability
- Microsoft RPC DCOM Interface Overflow
- RPC Runtime Remote Code Execution Vulnerability (CVE-2024-20678)
- Multiple Linux Vendor rpc.statd Remote Format String Vulnerability
- Port 111 rpcbind Vulnerability
- Linux Kernel RPC Message Type Memory Corruption Vulnerability

These vulnerabilities can be exploited to execute remote code, gain unauthorized access, or cause service disruptions.

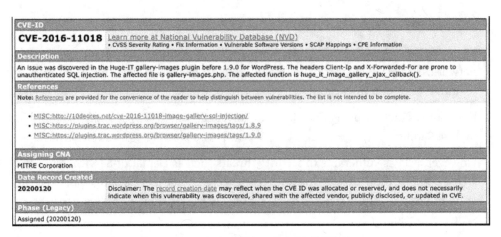

CVE-ID	
CVE-2016-11018	Learn more at National Vulnerability Database (NVD) • CVSS Severity Rating • Fix Information • Vulnerable Software Versions • SCAP Mappings • CPE Information
Description	
An issue was discovered in the Huge-IT gallery-images plugin before 1.9.0 for WordPress. The headers Client-Ip and X-Forwarded-For are prone to unauthenticated SQL injection. The affected file is gallery-images.php. The affected function is huge_it_image_gallery_ajax_callback().	
References	
Note: References are provided for the convenience of the reader to help distinguish between vulnerabilities. The list is not intended to be complete.	
• MISC:http://10degres.net/cve-2016-11018-image-gallery-sql-injection/ • MISC:https://plugins.trac.wordpress.org/browser/gallery-images/tags/1.8.9 • MISC:https://plugins.trac.wordpress.org/browser/gallery-images/tags/1.9.0	
Assigning CNA	
MITRE Corporation	
Date Record Created	
20200120	Disclaimer: The record creation date may reflect when the CVE ID was allocated or reserved, and does not necessarily indicate when this vulnerability was discovered, shared with the affected vendor, publicly disclosed, or updated in CVE.
Phase (Legacy)	
Assigned (20200120)	

Figure 03-38: Remote Procedure Call (RPC)

Server Message Block (SMB) Protocol

The Server Message Block (SMB) protocol is an application layer network protocol that facilitates shared access to files, printers, serial ports, and other resources across networked devices. It provides an authenticated inter-process communication mechanism and is widely used in Microsoft Windows environments.

SMB operates using a client-server model, where the client sends specific requests, and the server responds by granting access to file systems and other shared resources. The protocol commonly works over NetBIOS over TCP/IP (NBT) at the transport layer, ensuring reliable communication between networked systems.

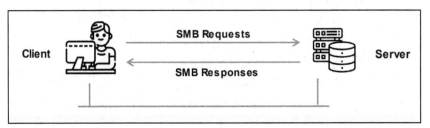

Figure 03-39: SMB Protocol

> **Note:** The enhanced version of SMB called Common Internet File System (CIFS) was developed by Microsoft for open use on the internet

Session Initiation Protocol (SIP)

The Session Initiation Protocol (SIP) is a communications protocol designed for signaling and managing real-time multimedia sessions, including voice, video, and instant messaging. It works alongside other protocols such as SDP, RTP, SRTP, and TLS to facilitate secure and efficient communication.

SIP is responsible for determining user attributes such as location, availability, and capability. It also manages session setup and control, ensuring seamless communication between users in a networked environment.

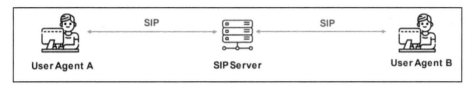

Figure 03-40: Session Initiation Protocol (SIP)

RADIUS

Remote Authentication Dial-In User Service (RADIUS) is an authentication protocol that centralizes Authentication, Authorization, and Accounting (AAA) for remote access servers, enabling secure communication with a central server.

Radius Authentication Steps:

- The authentication process begins when the client sends an Access-Request packet to the server
- The server then verifies the credentials against its database
- If the credentials are valid, it responds with an Access-Accept message, often accompanied by an Access-Challenge for additional authentication
- If the credentials do not match, the server sends an Access-Reject message, denying access

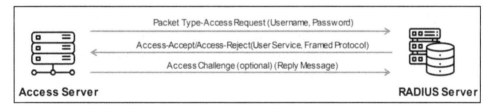

Figure 03-41: Radius Authentication Steps

A RADIUS Client is typically a Network Access Server (NAS) that interacts with the RADIUS server to authenticate and authorize users attempting to connect to the network.

RADIUS Accounting Process:

- Once authentication is successful, the client initiates the accounting process by sending an Accounting-Request message to the server containing details about the session
- The RADIUS server processes this request and responds with an accounting response message, confirming that the session has been successfully recorded and tracked in the system

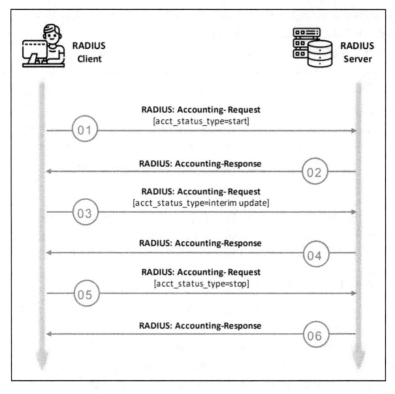

Figure 03-42: Radius Accounting Process

TACACS+

Terminal Access Controller Access-Control System Plus (TACACS+) is a network security protocol used for Authentication, Authorization, and Accounting (AAA) in network devices such as switches, routers, and firewalls. It operates through one or more centralized servers to manage user access.

TACACS+ encrypts the entire communication between the client and server, including the user's password, offering protection against sniffing attacks. It follows a client-server model, where the client (user or network device) sends a connection request, and the server authenticates the user by verifying their credentials.

Security Issues with TACACS+:

- Lack of integrity checking, making data susceptible to tampering
- Vulnerability to replay attacks, where an attacker intercepts and reuses authentication data
- Accounting information is sent in clear text, exposing session logs to potential interception
- Weak encryption, which may be exploitable if not properly configured

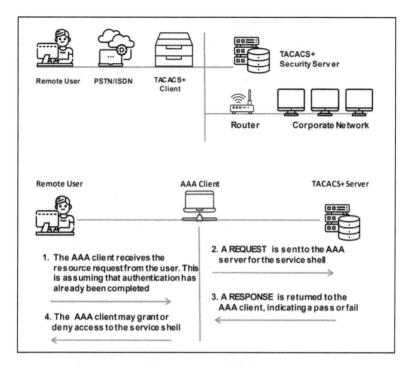

Figure 03-43: TACACS+

Routing Information Protocol (RIP)

Routing Information Protocol (RIP) is a distance vector routing protocol primarily designed for smaller networks. It uses Internet Protocol (IP) to exchange routing information between connected networks.

Characteristics of RIP:

- **Periodic Routing Updates**: Sends updates every 30 seconds
- **Broadcast Updates**: Transmits full routing tables to all RIP-enabled neighbors
- **Distance Vector Algorithm**: Uses the Bellman-Ford algorithm to determine the best path to a destination
- **Maximum Hop Count**: Limited to 15 hops, making it unsuitable for large networks

RIP Request/Response Process:

1. A router requests the full routing table from its neighbors.

2. RIP-enabled neighbors respond with their routing tables.

3. The startup router then sends a triggered update to all RIP-enabled interfaces.

Features of RIP:

- Supports IP and IPX routing

- Uses UDP port 520 for communication
- The administrative distance of RIP routes is 120, making it less preferred than other protocols like OSPF or EIGRP

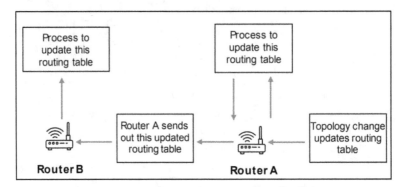

Figure 03-44: Routing Information Protocol (RIP)

Transport Layer Protocols

Transmission Control Protocol (TCP)

Transmission Control Protocol (TCP) is a connection-oriented protocol that operates across four layers of the networking model. It ensures reliable communication between devices by breaking messages into smaller segments, transmitting them to the destination, and reassembling them in the correct order. If any segment fails to reach its destination, TCP automatically detects the loss and resends the missing packets, ensuring data integrity and completeness. Several essential protocols rely on TCP for their operations, including File Transfer Protocol (FTP) for secure file exchanges, Hypertext Transfer Protocol (HTTP) for web communication, Telnet for remote access, and Simple Mail Transfer Protocol (SMTP) for email transmission.

TCP Header Format

Figure 03-45 represents the structure of a Transmission Control Protocol (TCP) header, which consists of multiple fields that help manage reliable communication between devices. Below is a detailed description of each field in paragraph form:

The TCP header plays a crucial role in ensuring reliable data transmission across networks. It consists of several fields, starting with the Source Port Number (16 bits) and the Destination Port Number (16 bits), which help identify the sending and receiving applications. The Sequence Number (32 bits) is used to keep track of the order of transmitted data packets, ensuring they are received in the correct sequence. Similarly, the Acknowledgment Number (32 bits) confirms the successful reception of data by indicating the next expected sequence number.

The Header Length (4 bits) specifies the size of the TCP header, while the Reserved (6 bits) field is kept for future use. Several control flags, including URG, ACK, PSH, RST, SYN, and FIN, help manage the connection by indicating various states, such as acknowledgment, synchronization, or termination of communication. The Window Size (16 bits) field determines how much data the receiver can accept at a given time, playing a critical role in flow control.

To ensure data integrity, the TCP Checksum (16 bits) is used to detect errors in the transmitted segment. The Urgent Pointer (16 bits) is relevant when the URG flag is set, indicating priority data that should be processed immediately. The Options field is used for additional functionalities such as selective acknowledgments and time stamping. Finally, the Data section contains the actual payload being transmitted if present.

Together, these fields enable TCP to provide a reliable, connection-oriented communication mechanism, ensuring that data is delivered accurately and in the correct order.

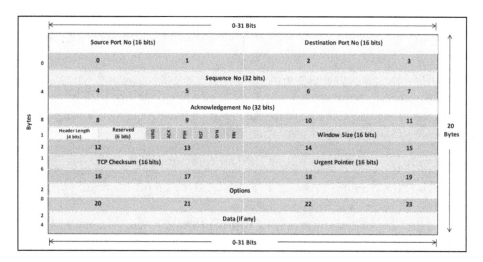

Figure 03-45: TCP Header

TCP Services

Transmission Control Protocol (TCP) supports different modes of communication based on how data flows between devices. These include Simplex, Half-Duplex, and Full-Duplex modes.

1. **Simplex Communication:** In this mode, data flows in only one direction, meaning one device acts as the sender while the other acts as the receiver. Each flow maintains its own window size, sequence numbers, and acknowledgment numbers, ensuring reliable data transmission.

2. **Half-Duplex Communication:** This mode allows data transmission in both directions between two nodes; however, at any given time, data can only flow in one direction. The sender and receiver must take turns to communicate, preventing simultaneous transmission.

3. **Full-Duplex Communication:** In this mode, data can flow in both directions simultaneously and independently. Each direction operates with its own window size, sequence numbers, and acknowledgment numbers, allowing continuous and efficient communication without waiting for the other side to finish transmitting.

These modes determine how TCP manages data exchange, optimizing network communication based on specific requirements.

User Datagram Protocol (UDP)

User Datagram Protocol (UDP) is a connectionless transport protocol that enables the exchange of datagrams without requiring acknowledgments or guaranteeing delivery. Unlike TCP, UDP does not implement mechanisms such as windowing or retransmissions, making it a lightweight and faster option for applications where speed is prioritized over reliability.

Since UDP does not provide built-in reliability, error-checking and retransmission must be handled at the application layer if needed. This makes it suitable for applications that can tolerate some data loss or have their own error-handling mechanisms.

Several widely used protocols rely on UDP for communication, including:

- **Trivial File Transfer Protocol (TFTP):** Used for simple file transfers, often in network booting and firmware updates
- **Simple Network Management Protocol (SNMP):** Enables monitoring and management of network devices
- **Dynamic Host Configuration Protocol (DHCP):** Assigns IP addresses dynamically to devices in a network

UDP is preferred for real-time applications, such as video streaming, online gaming, and VoIP, where low latency is more critical than guaranteed delivery.

UDP Segment Format

The UDP segment format consists of a simple 8-byte header followed by the data payload. Based on the provided figure:

1. **Source Port (16 bits):** Identifies the sender's port.
2. **Destination Port (16 bits):** Identifies the receiver's port.

3. **Length (16 bits)**: Specifies the total length of the UDP segment (header + data) in bytes.
4. **Checksum (16 bits)**: Optional field for error detection (covers header, data, and a pseudo-header).
5. **Data**: Variable-length payload (size determined by application).

The header fields are each 16 bits wide, as shown in the Figure 03-64. The Length field ensures the receiver knows where the segment ends, while the Checksum adds basic integrity verification. The Data field carries the actual application layer message.

# of Bits	16	16	16	16	16
	Source Port	Destination Port	Length	Checksum	Data

Figure 03-46: UDP Segment Format

UDP Operation

User Datagram Protocol (UDP) operates as a connectionless protocol, meaning it does not establish or maintain a dedicated connection between sender and receiver. Unlike TCP, UDP does not use windowing, acknowledgments, or retransmissions, making it a lightweight option for fast, low-latency communication. Instead, error detection and recovery, if required, are handled by the application layer protocols.

The Source Port field in UDP is optional and is only used when a response is expected from the receiving host. If no response is needed, this field can be left empty.

A key characteristic of UDP is that it does not rely on request-response mechanisms. For example, when a router receives a routing update, it is not because the sending router explicitly requested information. Instead, routing protocols such as Routing Information Protocol (RIP) use UDP to broadcast updates to other routers without expecting acknowledgments.

However, not all routing protocols use UDP.

- Border Gateway Protocol (BGP) uses TCP for reliable transmission
- Interior Gateway Routing Protocol (IGRP) sends data directly over IP, bypassing both UDP and TCP
- Enhanced Interior Gateway Routing Protocol (EIGRP) and Open Shortest Path First (OSPF) also send updates directly over IP. Still, they include their reliability mechanisms instead of using UDP or TCP.

UDP is ideal for applications where speed is more critical than guaranteed delivery, such as DNS lookups, VoIP, video streaming, and real-time gaming.

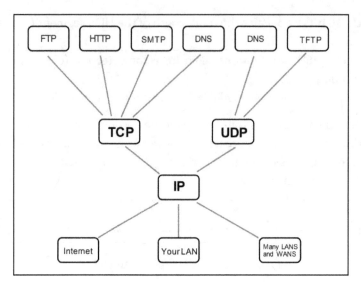

Figure 03-47: UDP Operation

Secure Socket Layer (SSL)

Secure Socket Layer (SSL) is an application layer protocol originally developed by Netscape to secure communication over the internet. It ensures confidentiality, integrity, and authentication between two communicating applications, such as a client (browser) and a server.

Key Features of SSL:

1. **Authentication & Encryption**

   o SSL provides a secure authentication mechanism between two communicating parties

   o It uses RSA asymmetric encryption (public and private key cryptography) to secure data transmission

2. **Transport Layer Dependency**

   o SSL requires a reliable transport protocol, such as TCP, for data transmission and reception

   o It does not work with UDP, as SSL relies on connection-oriented communication

3. **Data Security**

   o The encryption mechanism ensures that data transferred over SSL connections is protected from eavesdropping and tampering

- o It also verifies the identity of both the client and server through digital certificates issued by Certificate Authorities (CAs)

Transport Layer Security (TLS)

Transport Layer Security (TLS) is a protocol designed to establish a secure connection between a client and a server, ensuring the privacy and integrity of transmitted information. It employs a symmetric key for bulk encryption, an asymmetric key for authentication and key exchange, and message authentication codes to maintain message integrity. The RSA algorithm, with key strengths of 1024 and 2048 bits, is commonly used in TLS for encryption. By implementing TLS, security risks such as message tampering, forgery, and interception can be significantly reduced.

Internet Layer Protocols

Internet Protocol (IP)

Internet Protocol (IP) is a fundamental network layer protocol within the TCP/IP protocol suite. It serves as the backbone of internet communication, enabling the transmission of data packets, known as datagrams, across network boundaries. IP is responsible for addressing and routing these packets, ensuring they reach the correct destination. The protocol operates in a connectionless manner, meaning each packet is treated independently and may take different paths to reach the target system. To support this functionality, IP includes various header fields, such as the version field, which indicates the IP version in use, and the header length field, which defines the structure of the packet. The two widely used versions of IP are IPv4 and IPv6, with IPv4 being the more prevalent but gradually being replaced by IPv6 due to the need for a larger address space.

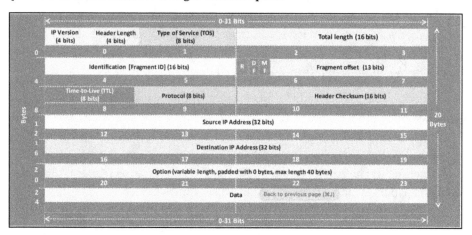

Figure 03-48: Internet Protocol

IP Header: Protocol Field

The IP header contains a protocol field that plays a crucial role in identifying the type of transport layer protocol used in the packet. This field specifies whether the encapsulated segment belongs to the Transmission Control Protocol (TCP) or the User Datagram Protocol (UDP). By analyzing this field, the receiving device determines how to process the packet and which transport layer protocol should handle the data. This distinction is essential for ensuring proper communication between networked systems, as TCP provides reliable, connection-oriented communication, while UDP offers a faster, connectionless transmission method.

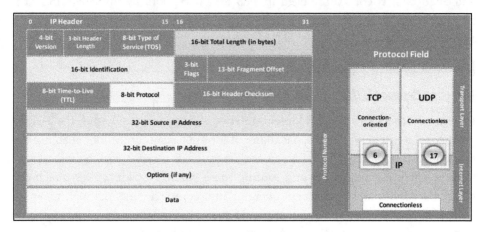

Figure 03-49: IP Header: Protocol Field

What is Internet Protocol v6 (IPv6)?

Internet Protocol version 6 (IPv6), also known as Next Generation Protocol (IPng), is designed to support the growing needs of the modern internet by providing a foundation for enhanced network functionalities. One of the most significant advancements of IPv6 over its predecessor, IPv4, is its vastly expanded address space, which allows for a greater number of unique IP addresses to accommodate the increasing number of internet-connected devices.

IPv6 is responsible for both addressing and controlling data to route packets across networks efficiently. Unlike IPv4, IPv6 has security features built into its core architecture, improving authentication, privacy, and overall network security. Additionally, IPv6 introduces several features that support the evolution of IT infrastructure, including an expandable and diverse address space, improved routing capabilities, and scalability for new users and services.

Other key features of IPv6 include auto-configuration (plug-and-play functionality), enhanced mobility support, end-to-end security, and extension headers that enable future protocol enhancements. It also supports the Source

Demand Routing Protocol and ensures Quality of Service (QoS), making it well-suited for modern networking demands. With these advancements, IPv6 serves as a critical enabler for the continued growth and development of internet technologies.

IPv6 Header

The IPv6 header is a fundamental component of the IPv6 packet structure, designed to improve efficiency and scalability compared to IPv4. Unlike IPv4, which has a variable-length header with multiple fields, the IPv6 header has a fixed length of 40 bytes, simplifying packet processing and enhancing performance. The streamlined header structure eliminates several fields from IPv4, such as the header checksum and options field, reducing overhead and making routing more efficient.

Key fields in the IPv6 header include the Version field (which indicates the IP version), the Traffic Class field (used for prioritizing packets and QoS), and the Flow Label (which helps in identifying and handling specific traffic flows). The Payload Length field specifies the size of the data being transmitted. In contrast, the Next Header field allows for the inclusion of extension headers, enabling additional functionalities such as security and mobility without affecting the core packet structure. The Hop Limit field, similar to the Time-to-Live (TTL) in IPv4, ensures that packets do not circulate indefinitely by decrementing at each hop until it reaches zero.

By incorporating these design improvements, the IPv6 header enhances routing efficiency, supports advanced networking capabilities, and provides a solid foundation for the next generation of internet applications.

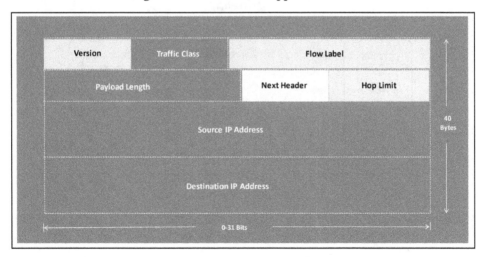

Figure 03-50: IPv6 Header

IPv4 and IPv6 Transition Mechanisms

There are three primary transition mechanisms for deploying IPv6 on existing IPv4 networks, and they can be used in combination based on requirements.

1. **Dual Stack**: Allows devices to run both IPv4 and IPv6 simultaneously, enabling seamless communication with both network types.

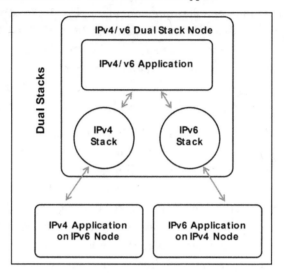

Figure 03-51: Dual Stack

2. **Tunneling**: Encapsulates IPv6 packets within IPv4 packets, enabling them to travel across IPv4-only networks. Examples include 6to4, Teredo, and ISATAP.

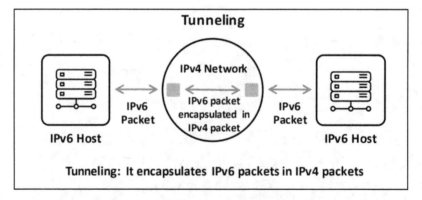

Figure 03-52: Tunneling

3. **Translation**: Converts IPv6 packets into IPv4 and vice versa, ensuring compatibility between the two protocols. NAT64 and NAT-PT are commonly used translation techniques.

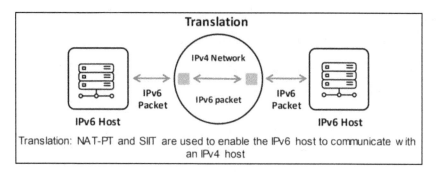

Figure 03-53: Translation

These mechanisms enable a smooth transition to IPv6 while maintaining interoperability with IPv4 networks.

IPv4 vs. IPv6

IPv4 and IPv6 are internet protocol versions used for device communication. IPv4 uses a 32-bit address system, supporting about 4.3 billion addresses, while IPv6 uses a 128-bit address, providing virtually unlimited addresses. IPv6 also offers improved security, efficiency, and scalability compared to IPv4.

IPv4	IPv6
Length of addresses is 32 bits (4 bytes)	The length of addresses is 128 bits (16 bytes)
Header consists of a checksum	The header does not consist of a checksum
Header consists of options	Extension headers support optional data
IPsec header support is optional	IPsec header support is required
Address can be organized physically or through DHCP	Stateless auto-organized link-local address can be obtained
ARP uses broadcast ARP requests to solve IP to MAC/Hardware address	Multicast neighbor solicitation communication solves both IP and MAC addresses
Broadcast addresses are used to send traffic to all nodes on a subnet	IPv6 uses an all-nodes multicast address with a link-local scope

Figure 03-54: IPv4 vs. IPv6

Internet Protocol Security (IPsec)

Internet Protocol Security (IPsec) is a suite of protocols designed by the IETF to provide secure communication at the IP layer. It ensures cryptographic security for both IPv4 and IPv6, offering features like peer authentication, data integrity, encryption for confidentiality, and protection against replay attacks. IPsec is

commonly used for securing Virtual Private Networks (VPNs) and enabling remote user access to private networks through dial-up connections.

Internet Control Message Protocol (ICMP)

The Internet Control Message Protocol (ICMP) is a crucial component of the TCP/IP protocol stack that helps address the lack of error notification in IP. Since IP itself is an unreliable method for data delivery and does not inform the sender of transmission failures, ICMP is used to send error messages and operational information about network conditions. However, ICMP does not resolve IP's unreliability; if reliability is required, it must be ensured by upper-layer protocols like TCP or specific application-level mechanisms.

Error Reporting and Correction

When datagram delivery errors occur, ICMP reports the following errors back to the source of the datagram:

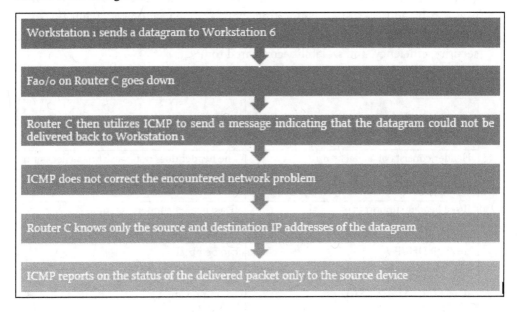

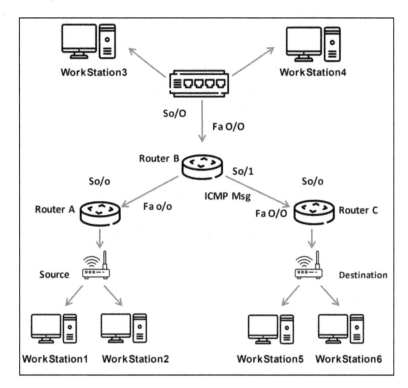

Figure 03-55: Error Reporting and Correction

ICMP Message Delivery

ICMP messages are transmitted by encapsulating them within IP datagrams. Since they rely on the same delivery mechanism as IP, they are also prone to the same delivery failures. This creates a potential issue where error messages could trigger additional error reports, leading to increased network congestion. To prevent such a recursive loop, ICMP-generated errors do not generate further ICMP messages. However, this also means that certain datagram delivery failures may remain unreported to the sender, leaving some transmission issues undetected.

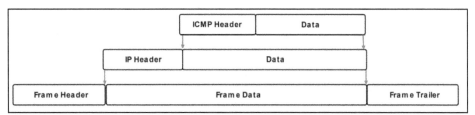

Figure 03-56: ICMP Message Delivery

Format of an ICMP Message

The Internet Control Message Protocol (ICMP) message format consists of various message types and codes that facilitate error reporting and network diagnostics.

Each ICMP message has a standardized structure, including a Type, Code, and Checksum field, followed by additional parameters and data.

ICMP message types define the nature of the message, such as Echo Request (Type 8) and Echo Reply (Type 0) for ping operations or Destination Unreachable (Type 3) for indicating network issues. The Code Field further classifies these messages by specifying the reason for an error, such as Host Unreachable (Code 1) or Port Unreachable (Code 3) under Destination Unreachable messages.

ICMP messages are encapsulated within IP packets, making them susceptible to the same delivery challenges as regular IP packets. To avoid excessive network congestion, ICMP-generated errors do not trigger further ICMP error messages. This structured approach ensures efficient communication and troubleshooting within IP networks.

Type(8 bit)	Code(8 bit)	CheckSum(16 bit)
Extended Header(32 bit)		
Data/Payload(Variable Length)		

Figure 03-57: Format of an ICMP Message

Table 03-06 lists common ICMP message types and their corresponding names:

ICMP Message Types

Type	Name
0	Echo Reply
1	Unassigned
2	Unassigned
3	Destination Unreachable
4	Source Quench
5	Redirect
6	Alternate Host Address
7	Unassigned
8	Echo

9	Router Advertisement
10	Router Solicitation
11	Time Exceeded
12	Parameter Problem
13	Timestamp
14	Timestamp Reply
15	Information Request
16	Information Reply
17	Address Mask Request
18	Address Mask Reply
19	Reserved (for Security)
20-29	Reserved (for Robustness Experiment)
30	Traceroute
31	Datagram Conversion Error
32	Mobile Host Redirect
33	IPv6 Where-Are-You
34	IPv6 I-Am-Here
35	Mobile Registration Request
36	Mobile Registration Reply
37	Domain Name Request
38	Domain Name Reply
39	SKIP
40	Photuris
41-255	Reserved

Table 03-06: ICMP Message Types

ICMP Destination Unreachable Codes (Type 3)

Code	Description

0	Net Unreachable
1	Host Unreachable
2	Protocol Unreachable
3	Port Unreachable
4	Fragmentation Needed and Don't Fragment was Set
5	Source Route Failed
6	Destination Network Unknown
7	Destination Host Unknown
8	Source Host Isolated
9	Communication with Destination Network is Administratively Prohibited
10	Communication with the Destination Host is Administratively Prohibited
11	Destination Network Unreachable for Type of Service
12	Destination Host Unreachable for Type of Service
13	Communication Administratively Prohibited
14	Host Precedence Violation
15	Precedence Cutoff in Effect

Table 03-07: ICMP Codes

Address Resolution Protocol (ARP)

The Address Resolution Protocol (ARP) is a stateless protocol designed to resolve IP addresses into their corresponding machine (MAC) addresses. When a device needs to communicate with another device on a local network, it sends an ARP request as a broadcast message to all devices on the network, asking for the MAC address associated with a specific IP address. The device that owns the IP address responds with an ARP reply, which is sent as a unicast message directly to the requester. To optimize network performance and reduce repeated requests, the IP-MAC address pair is temporarily stored in the ARP cache of the system, switch, or router through which the ARP reply is transmitted.

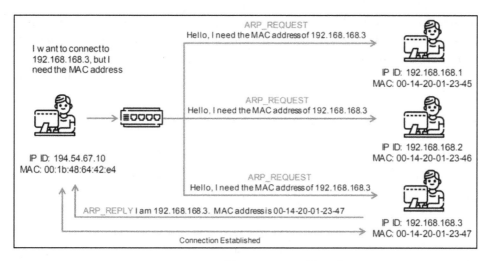

Figure 03-58: Address R Protocol (ARP)

ARP Packet Format

The ARP Packet Format consists of several fields that define how an Address Resolution Protocol (ARP) message is structured. Each field in the packet plays a crucial role in ensuring the proper resolution of IP addresses to MAC addresses.

The packet starts with the Hardware Type, which specifies the type of network being used. For example, a value of 1 indicates Ethernet, while other values correspond to different network types like Experimental Ethernet, Amateur Radio AX.25, or IEEE 802 Networks.

Next, the Protocol Type field defines the type of protocol for which the ARP request or response is being made. Common values include 0x0800 for IPv4 and 0x86DD for IPv6.

The Hardware Length and Protocol Length fields specify the length (in bytes) of the hardware address (MAC address) and the protocol address (IP address), respectively. For Ethernet, the hardware length is 6 bytes, and for IPv4, the protocol length is 4 bytes.

The Operation Code indicates whether the packet is an ARP Request (1) or an ARP Reply (2).

The packet then contains Sender Information, which includes the sender's hardware address (MAC address) and protocol address (IP address). The MAC address is divided into two parts: the first 4 bytes and the last 2 bytes.

Similarly, the Target Information contains the target's hardware address and protocol address. In the case of an ARP request, the target's MAC address is set to null because the sender is requesting this information.

By structuring the ARP packet in this way, devices on a network can efficiently determine the MAC address associated with a given IP address, ensuring smooth communication within the network.

Byte 0	Byte 1	Byte 2	Byte 3
Hardware Type		Protocol Type	
Hardware Length	Protocol Length	Operation (1 for Request, 2 for Reply)	
Sender's Hardware Address (First 4 Bytes of Ethernet Address)			
Sender's Hardware Address (Last 2 Bytes of Ethernet Address)		Sender's Protocol Address (First 2 Bytes of IP Address)	
Sender's Protocol Address (Last 2 Bytes of IP Address)		Target's Hardware Address (2 Bytes of Ethernet Address, Null in ARP Request)	
Target's Hardware Address (Last 4 Bytes of Ethernet Address, Null in ARP Request)			
Sender's Protocol Address (4-byte IP Address)			

Figure 03-59(a): ARP Packet Format

Hardware Type:
- 1 = Ethernet
- 2 = Experimental Ethernet
- 3 = Amateur Radio AX.25
- 4 = Proteon ProNET Token Ring
- 5 = Chaos
- 6 = IEEE 802 Networks, etc.

Protocol Type:
- IPv4 = 0x0800
- IPv6 = 0x86DD

Hardware Length:
- 6 for Ethernet

Protocol Length:
- 4 for IPv4

Operation Code:
- 1 For Request
- 2 For Reply

Figure 03-60(b): ARP Packet Format

ARP Packet Encapsulation

Figure 03-60 and Figure 03-61 illustrate ARP Packet Encapsulation, showcasing the structure of both an ARP Request and an ARP Reply.

1. ARP Request (With Null Destination MAC Address)

- The ARP request is used when a device wants to discover the MAC address of another device using its IP address

- **Key Fields in the ARP Request:**

    o **Hardware Type (0x0001):** Indicates Ethernet

    o **Protocol Type (0x0800):** Specifies IPv4

    o **Hardware Length (0x06):** MAC address length is 6 bytes

    o **Protocol Length (0x04):** IP address length is 4 bytes

    o **Operation Code (0x0001):** Represents an ARP request

    o **Sender MAC Address (0x645A04531E65):** The MAC address of the requesting device

    o **Sender IP Address (0xC0A80019):** The IP address of the sender (192.168.0.25)

    o **Target MAC Address (0x000000000000 - NULL):** The device does not know the MAC address of the target

    o **Target IP Address (0xC0A8001B):** The IP address whose MAC address is being requested

- **Encapsulation Details:**

    o **Preamble and SFD (8 bytes):** Synchronization bits

    o **Destination MAC (0x000000000000 - NULL) (6 bytes):** Since the sender does not know the MAC, it is set to all zeros

    o **Source MAC (6 bytes):** Sender's MAC address

    o **Type (0x0806) (2 bytes):** Indicates ARP

    o **Data (28 bytes):** Contains the ARP request

    o **CRC (2 bytes):** Error-checking field

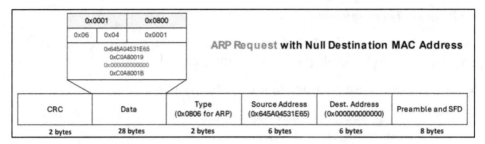

Figure 03-61: ARP Request (With Null Destination MAC Address)

2. ARP Reply (With Destination MAC Address)

- The ARP reply is sent by the device that owns the target IP address, providing its MAC address.

- **Key Fields in the ARP Reply:**

  o **Operation Code (0x0002):** Represents an ARP reply

  o **Sender MAC Address (0x0454530E2CAB):** The MAC address of the responding device

  o **Sender IP Address (0xC0A8001B):** The IP address of the responding device (192.168.0.27)

  o **Target MAC Address (0x645A04531E65):** The MAC address of the original requester

  o **Target IP Address (0xC0A80019):** The IP address of the original requester

- **Encapsulation Details:**

  o **Preamble and SFD (8 bytes):** Synchronization bits

  o **Destination MAC (0x645A04531E65) (6 bytes):** The MAC address of the requester

  o **Source MAC (6 bytes):** The MAC address of the responder

  o **Type (0x0806) (2 bytes):** Indicates ARP

  o **Data (28 bytes):** Contains the ARP reply

  o **CRC (4 bytes):** Error-checking field

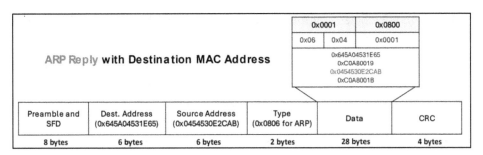

Figure 03-62: ARP Reply (With Destination MAC Address)

This breakdown explains how an ARP request is broadcast to the network, and upon receiving a reply, the requesting device updates its ARP cache with the resolved MAC address for future communication.

Interior Gateway Routing Protocol (IGRP)

IGRP is a distance vector routing protocol developed for transmitting routing data within an internetwork. Unlike IP RIP and IPX RIP, which were designed for multi-vendor environments, IGRP was specifically developed to enhance routing within Cisco networks.

By default, IGRP calculates the distance metric using Bandwidth and Delay of the line. Additionally, it can incorporate optional parameters such as Reliability, Load, and Maximum Transmission Unit (MTU) to refine path selection.

IGRP follows standard distance vector properties, including periodic routing updates every 90 seconds. It transmits a full routing table in each update and uses broadcast updates to communicate with neighboring routers. The protocol determines the best path using the Bellman-Ford Distance Vector algorithm, ensuring efficient routing within a network.

IGRP supports only IP routing and operates using IP protocol number 9. It has an administrative distance of 100, ensuring a moderate level of trust in the routing hierarchy. By default, IGRP supports up to 100 hops, but this limit can be extended to 255 hops for larger networks.

Enhanced Interior Gateway Routing Protocol (EIGRP)

EIGRP is a hybrid routing protocol that combines characteristics of both Distance-Vector and Link-State protocols. It enables routers to share routing information with other routers within the same network system while maintaining efficiency and scalability.

EIGRP utilizes the Diffusing Update Algorithm (DUAL) to determine the best path among all feasible routes, ensuring a loop-free routing environment. It maintains neighbor relationships with adjacent routers within the same Autonomous System

(AS) to facilitate efficient routing. Depending on the packet type, EIGRP traffic is sent as unicast or multicast on the address 224.0.0.10.

To ensure reliable packet delivery, EIGRP employs the Reliable Transport Protocol (RTP). Unlike traditional distance vector protocols, it does not send periodic, full-table updates. Instead, EIGRP transmits updates only when a change occurs and includes only the affected routes. It is a classless protocol, meaning it supports Variable Length Subnet Masks (VLSMs) for more flexible subnetting.

EIGRP supports routing for IP, IPX, and AppleTalk. It assigns an Administrative Distance (AD) of 90 for routes within the local Autonomous System and 170 for external routes received from outside the AS. By default, EIGRP calculates the distance metric based on Bandwidth and Delay of the line, with optional parameters like Reliability, Load, and MTU. The protocol allows a maximum of 100 hops, which can be extended to 255 hops for larger network implementations.

Open Shortest Path First (OSPF)

OSPF is an Interior Gateway Protocol (IGP) designed to distribute IP routing information within a single Autonomous System (AS) in an IP network. As a link-state routing protocol, it enables routers to exchange topology information with their immediate neighbors, ensuring an accurate and efficient view of the network.

The OSPF process maintains three key tables:

- **Neighbor Table:** Contains a list of all directly connected routers
- **Topology Table:** Stores all possible routes to known networks within the OSPF area
- **Routing Table:** Determines and stores the best route for each known network

OSPF supports only IP routing and uses cost as its metric, where lower cost values indicate better paths. It has an Administrative Distance (AD) of 110 and does not have a hop-count limit, making it highly scalable for large networks.

Hot Standby Router Protocol (HSRP)

HSRP is a fault-tolerant routing protocol designed to provide gateway redundancy by allowing multiple routers to function as a single virtual router. This ensures seamless failover in case the primary router fails, maintaining network availability.

Developed by Cisco, HSRP works by sharing a virtual IP and MAC address between two or more routers. The active router is responsible for forwarding traffic, while the standby router remains on standby to take over if needed.

To check the HSRP status, the "show standby" command is used. It is specifically designed for multi-access or broadcast LAN environments and automatically updates itself when the MAC address is modified.

However, HSRP can be vulnerable to Denial-of-Service (DoS) attacks, posing a security risk if not properly secured.

Virtual Router Redundancy Protocol (VRRP)

VRRP is a networking protocol that enables the automatic assignment of available IP routers to participating hosts, ensuring redundancy and high availability. Unlike traditional static routing, VRRP allows multiple routers to share a virtual IP address, so if the primary router fails, another router takes over automatically without disrupting network connectivity.

VRRP provides status information about the router but does not exchange or process routing table data. If the router handling traffic for the virtual router fails, another physical router is automatically elected to take its place, ensuring seamless failover.

However, VRRP can be vulnerable to DoS attacks, making it crucial to implement security measures to protect network infrastructure.

Border Gateway Protocol (BGP)

BGP is a routing protocol that manages packet transmission across the internet by exchanging routing information between Autonomous Systems (AS). Unlike traditional routing protocols, BGP makes routing decisions based on paths, reachability, hop counts, and administrator-defined policies, allowing for customized traffic control.

Each BGP router maintains a routing table to determine the best path for forwarding packets to the next hop. BGP version 4 (BGP4) is the current standard, widely used by Internet Service Providers (ISPs) to manage inter-domain routing and ensure efficient data transmission between networks.

Link Layer Protocols

Fiber Distributed Data Interface (FDDI)

FDDI is an optical standard designed for high-speed data transfer over fiber optic lines in a Local Area Network (LAN), covering distances of up to 200 km. It operates at a data transfer rate of 100 Mbps and supports voice and multimedia communication through its extended version, FDDI-2.

The network is structured with two fiber optic rings:

- The primary ring handles the main network traffic
- The secondary ring serves as a backup, taking over if the primary ring fails, ensuring network redundancy and reliability

Token Ring

Token Ring is a Local Area Network (LAN) technology that connects multiple computers using a transmission link arranged in either a ring topology or a star topology.

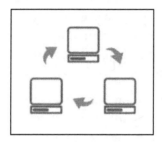

Figure 03-63: Ring or Star Topology

Data transmission follows a unidirectional flow, ensuring an orderly and collision-free communication process within the network.

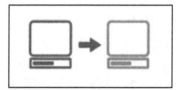

Figure 03-64: Unidirectional Flow

Cisco Discovery Protocol (CDP)

Cisco Discovery Protocol (CDP) is a Layer 2 (Data Link Layer) proprietary protocol developed by Cisco to facilitate the sharing of information between directly connected network devices. It is both media and network independent, making it compatible with various physical media and network layer protocols. CDP functions by using the destination MAC address 01.00.0c.cc.cc.cc to exchange data between neighboring Cisco devices.

This protocol operates between directly connected network entities and plays a role in On-Demand Routing (ODR) by discovering network topology and device information. CDP helps in obtaining details about neighboring devices, including device types, router interfaces they are connected to, interfaces used for connections, and model numbers of the devices.

Security Concerns

CDP can be vulnerable to Denial-of-Service (DoS) attacks, making it essential to secure its usage in critical network environments.

VLAN Trunking Protocol (VTP)

VLAN Trunking Protocol (VTP) is a Cisco-developed messaging protocol designed to facilitate the exchange of Virtual Local Area Network (VLAN) information across trunk links. Operating at the Data Link Layer of the OSI model, VTP helps manage VLAN configurations efficiently within a network.

By using VTP, a network manager can distribute VLAN configurations to all switches in the same VTP domain, ensuring consistency and reducing manual configuration effort. The VLAN configuration is stored in a VLAN database, allowing seamless plug-and-play integration when new VLANs are added to the network.

Security Concerns

Despite its advantages, VTP has several security vulnerabilities. It is susceptible to Denial-of-Service (DoS) attacks, which can disrupt network operations. Additionally, integer wrapping in VTP revision and buffer overflow vulnerabilities in VLAN name handling pose risks that could compromise the stability and security of the network.

Spanning Tree Protocol (STP)

Spanning Tree Protocol (STP) is a Layer 2 network protocol that operates on bridges and switches to prevent loop formation in a network. It ensures that redundant paths do not create broadcast storms or data loops by selectively disabling certain links.

STP is commonly used in entertainment and communication systems to manage streaming media servers, ensuring efficient and loop-free data transmission. By dynamically adjusting network topology, it maintains network stability and prevents congestion.

Security Concerns

STP is vulnerable to several security threats, including:

- Man-In-The-Middle attacks, where an attacker intercepts network traffic
- File and path name attacks, exploiting file structure vulnerabilities
- DNS spoofing, misleading devices by providing false DNS responses
- Denial-of-Service (DoS) attacks overwhelming network resources
- Session hijacking, allowing attackers to take control of active sessions
- Authentication mechanism attacks, where security loopholes are exploited to gain unauthorized access

Proper security measures, such as BPDU filtering, root guard, and loop guard, can help mitigate these vulnerabilities and enhance network resilience.

Point-to-Point Protocol (PPP)

Point-to-Point Protocol (PPP) is a data link layer protocol used for direct communication between two network nodes. It facilitates data transfer without any intermediate networking devices, making it ideal for dedicated and high-speed connections.

PPP is widely utilized for modem connections, DSL, ISDN, and VPNs, offering features such as encryption, authentication, and compression for secure and efficient data transmission. It supports multiple physical networks, including phone lines, cellular networks, fiber optics, and serial cables.

Authentication Mechanisms

PPP employs two primary authentication protocols:

- **Password Authentication Protocol (PAP):** Uses a simple username-password mechanism for authentication.
- **Challenge Handshake Authentication Protocol (CHAP):** Provides more security by periodically verifying the identity of the connecting device.

Issues & Limitations

Despite its advantages, PPP has some limitations:

- Lack of flow control, which can cause sender overload by transmitting multiple frames without regulation.

- Error detection without notification, as PPP discards corrupted frames using Cyclic Redundancy Check (CRC) without alerting the sender.

- No built-in addressing mechanism, making it unsuitable for multipoint network configurations.

To enhance performance, PPP is often combined with PPP over Ethernet (PPPoE) or PPP over ATM (PPPoA) in broadband and DSL connections.

IP Addressing and Port Numbers

Internet Assigned Numbers Authority (IANA)

The Internet Assigned Numbers Authority (IANA) is responsible for the global coordination of DNS Root, IP addressing, and other internet protocol resources. It plays a crucial role in maintaining the structure and stability of the internet.

IANA manages port number assignments, categorizing them into different ranges:

- **Well-known ports (0–1023):** Reserved for system (or root) processes and applications executed by privileged users.

- **Registered ports (1024–49151):** Assigned to specific services or applications, allowing ordinary users and applications to use them.

While the registration of these ports is primarily for organizational convenience, IANA ensures that conflicts are minimized, helping maintain an orderly and standardized approach to internet communication.

IP Addressing

An IP Address is a unique numerical identifier assigned to a node or network connection, enabling communication across a network. It follows a structured format to ensure proper identification and routing of data.

IP addresses are 32-bit binary numbers, typically represented in a dotted-decimal notation. They consist of four octets, each ranging from 0 to 255, and are separated by periods.

Examples of IP Addresses:

- 192.168.0.1
- 23.255.0.23
- 192.165.7.7

Figure 03-65: IP Addressing

Classful IP Addressing

Classful IP addressing was the first addressing scheme used on the internet, dividing IP addresses into five major classes: A, B, C, D, and E. This scheme helps in structuring and managing network communication by distinguishing between network and host portions within an IP address.

An IP address is composed of two parts:

- **Network Part:** Identifies the network to which a device belongs
- **Host Part:** Identifies a specific device (host) within that network

Key Rules:

- All hosts on the same network share the same network prefix but must have a unique host number.
- Hosts on different networks can have the same host number but must have different network prefixes.

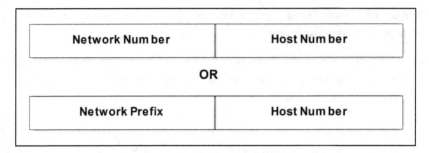

Figure 03-66: Two-Level Internet Address Structure

Address Classes

IP addresses are divided into five major classes: A, B, C, D, and E. Each class has a different structure for network and host identification.

Class A:

- **Network Prefix:** 8 bits
- **Binary Start:** 0
- **Decimal Range:** 1 – 126
- **Structure:** The first 8 bits represent the network, remaining 24 bits define hosts
- **Usage:** Suitable for large networks with many hosts

Class B:

- **Network Prefix:** 16 bits
- **Binary Start:** 10
- **Decimal Range:** 128 – 191
- **Structure:** The first 16 bits represent the network, remaining 16 bits define hosts
- **Usage:** Designed for medium-sized networks

Class C:

- **Network Prefix:** 24 bits
- **Binary Start:** 110
- **Decimal Range:** 192 – 223
- **Structure:** The first 24 bits represent the network, remaining 8 bits define hosts
- **Usage:** Best for small networks

Class D:

- **Binary Start:** 1110
- **Decimal Range:** 224 – 239
- **Usage:** Reserved for multicasting (sending data to multiple devices at once)

Class E:

- **Binary Start:** 1111
- **Decimal Range:** 240 – 255
- **Usage:** Reserved for experimental and future use

Table 03-08 summarizes the number of networks and hosts supported by different address classes.

Class	Leading Bits	Size of Network Number Bit Field	Size of Host Number Bit Field	Number of Networks	Addresses Per Network
Class A	0	7	24	126	16,277,214
Class B	10	14	16	116,384	65,534
Class C	110	21	8	2,097,152	254
Class D (Multi cast)	1110	20	8	1,048,576	254
Class E (Reserved)	1111	20	8	1,048,576	254

Table 03-08: IP Address Classes and Their Characteristics

Table 03-09 outlines the classifications, characteristics, and primary uses of IP address classes.

IP Address Class	Fraction of Total IP Address Space	Number of Network ID Bits	Number of Host ID Bits	Intended Use
Class A	1/2	8	24	Used for Unicast addressing for very large organizations
Class B	1/4	16	16	Used for Unicast addressing for medium or large organizations
Class C	1/8	24	8	Used for Unicast addressing small organizations
Class D	1/16	N/A	N/A	Used for IP multicasting

Class E	1/16	N/A	N/A	Reserved

Table 03-09: IP Address Classes and class characteristics and uses

Subnet Masking

A subnet mask is used to divide an IP address into network and host portions, enabling efficient utilization of IP address space. It plays a crucial role in segmenting networks by allowing Class A, B, and C networks to be divided into smaller, more manageable subnets. This division enhances network performance and security by reducing congestion and limiting the broadcast domain.

Additionally, Variable Length Subnet Masking (VLSM) allows multiple subnet masks within the same network, providing flexibility in IP address allocation. VLSM enables network administrators to assign different subnet sizes based on specific requirements, ensuring optimal use of available IP addresses. By implementing subnet masking and VLSM, organizations can effectively manage and scale their network infrastructure while minimizing IP address wastage.

IP Address Class	Total # bits for Network ID/Host ID	Default Subnet Mask			
		First Octet	Second Octet	Third Octet	Fourth Octet
Class A	8/24	11111111	00000000	00000000	00000000
Class B	16/16	11111111	11111111	00000000	00000000
Class C	24/8	11111111	11111111	11111111	00000000

Table 03-10: Subnet Masking

Subnetting

Subnetting is the process of dividing a Class A, B, or C network into multiple smaller, logical subnets. This segmentation helps in better network management, improved security, and efficient utilization of IP addresses. Instead of treating an entire network as a single entity, subnetting allows organizations to create isolated sections within the network, reducing congestion and optimizing routing.

To achieve subnetting, some bits from the host ID portion of an IP address are borrowed and used to extend the natural subnet mask. This reallocation of bits increases the number of subnetworks while reducing the number of available hosts per subnet. By implementing subnetting, businesses can efficiently distribute IP addresses, enhance network security, and control traffic flow more effectively.

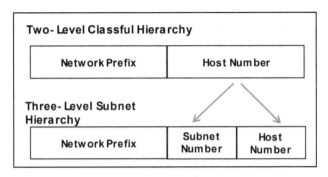

Figure 03-66: Subnet Address Hierarchy

Consider the Class C Address

IP Address: 192.168.1.12 11000000.10101000.00000001.00001010

Subnet mask: 255.255.255.0 11111111.11111111.11111111.00000000

Subnetting: 255.255.255.224 11111111.11111111.11111111.11100000

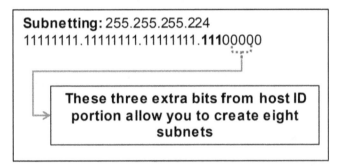

Figure 03-67: Subnetting

Supernetting

As Class A and B IP addresses have become scarce due to their high demand, and Class C addresses provide only 256 hosts per network—out of which only 254 are usable—supernetting was introduced as a solution. Supernetting is a technique that combines multiple Class C networks into a larger network, or supernetwork, allowing for more efficient IP address allocation and routing.

Supernetting applies specifically to Class C addresses and is commonly referred to as Classless Inter-Domain Routing (CIDR). CIDR was developed to prevent the rapid exhaustion of IP addresses by allowing flexible subnetting and supernetting instead of rigid class-based allocations. Unlike traditional subnetting, where a subnet mask is used to divide a network, a supernet mask works oppositely by aggregating multiple networks into a single, larger address space. This approach reduces the number of routing table entries, optimizes IP address usage, and enhances the scalability of modern networks.

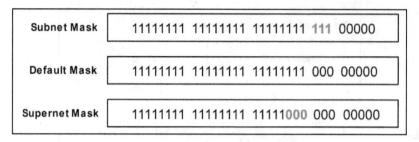

Figure 03-68: Supernetting

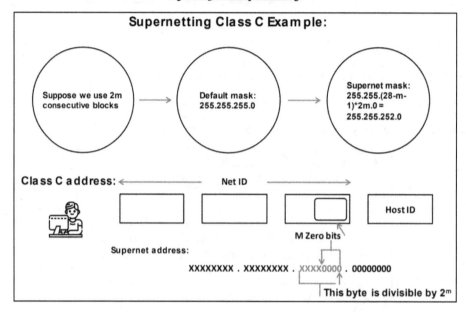

Figure 03-69: Example of Class C Supernetting

IPv6 Addressing

IPv6 addressing follows the standard defined in RFC 4291 and was introduced to overcome the limitations of IPv4, particularly the exhaustion of available IP addresses. It provides a significantly larger address space and supports multilevel subnetting, allowing for more efficient allocation and management of addresses within networks.

Unlike IPv4, which primarily supports unicast and broadcast, IPv6 supports unicast, anycast, and multicast addressing, eliminating the need for broadcast communication and improving network efficiency. Additionally, IPv6 addresses are structured hierarchically, enabling better organization and routing of network traffic. This hierarchical structure allows for improved scalability, simplified network management, and enhanced security features.

Allocation	Format prefix	Start of address range (hex)	Mask length (bits)	Fraction of address space
Reserved	0000 0000	0:: 8/	8	1/256
Reserved for Network Service Allocation Point (NSAP)	0000 001	200:: /7	7	1/128
Reserved for IPX	0000 010	400:: /7	7	1/128
Aggregatable global unicast addresses	001	2000:: /3	3	1/8
Link-local unicast	1111 1110 10	FE80:: /10	10	1/1024
Site-local unicast	1111 1110 11	FEC0:: /10	10	1/1024
Multicast	1111 1111	FF00:: /8	8	1/256

Table 03-11: IPv6: Format Prefix Allocation

Difference between IPv4 and IPv6

Internet Protocol (IP) is the primary protocol used for communication across networks. Internet Protocol version 4 (IPv4) has been the standard for decades, but due to its limited address space, Internet Protocol version 6 (IPv6) was introduced to accommodate the growing number of internet-connected devices. IPv6 offers a larger address space, improved security, and better performance compared to IPv4. The Table 03-12 highlights the key differences between IPv4 and IPv6:

	Internet Protocol version 4 (IPv4)	Internet Protocol version 6 (IPv6)
Year Deployed	1981	1999
Size	32-bit addresses	128-bit source and destination addresses
Format	Dotted-decimal notation (separated by periods)	Hexadecimal notation (separated by colons)
Example	192.168.0.77	3ffe:1900:4545:AB00: 0123:4567:8901:ABCD
Prefix Notation	192.168.0.7/74	3FFE:F200:0234::/77
Total Number of Addresses	2^{32} = ~4,294,967,296	2^{128} = ~340,282,366, 920,938,463,463,374, 607,431,768,211,456
Configuration	Manually perform static or dynamic configuration	Auto-configuration of addresses is available
Security	IPSec is optional	Inbuilt support for IPSec

Table 03-12: Ipv4 vs. IPv6

Port Numbers

Both Transmission Control Protocol (TCP) and User Datagram Protocol (UDP) use port numbers to facilitate communication between different applications running on a network. These port numbers help ensure that multiple conversations can occur simultaneously without interference.

Each network conversation is assigned a unique port number, enabling devices to distinguish between different types of communication. Well-known applications use predefined port numbers, while conversations that do not involve well-known applications are assigned randomly selected port numbers from a designated range.

Port numbers are categorized into different ranges based on their usage:

- **Well-Known Ports (0-1023):** Reserved for commonly used services such as HTTP (80), HTTPS (443), and FTP (21)
- **Registered Ports (1024-49151):** Assigned to vendor-specific applications but not as widely recognized as well-known ports
- **Dynamic or Private Ports (49152-65535):** Used for temporary assignments and dynamically allocated for specific sessions

Both TCP and UDP have some reserved port numbers, although not all applications may utilize them. End systems use port numbers to correctly identify and direct network traffic to the appropriate application, ensuring smooth and organized communication across networks.

Network Terminology

Routing

Routing is the process of determining the most efficient path for data packets to travel across a network. This task is typically handled by a router, which uses routing tables to store and manage information about various network destinations. The router relies on these tables to make forwarding decisions, ensuring that data reaches its intended destination efficiently.

Types of Routing

- **Static Routing**

In static routing, the routing table is manually configured and maintained by a network administrator. Since there is no automatic route discovery, any changes in the network require manual updates to the routing table. This method is suitable for smaller, stable networks where minimal changes occur.

- **Dynamic Routing**

Dynamic routing, in contrast, uses routing protocols to automatically create, maintain, and update routing tables. These protocols enable routers to communicate with each other, share route information, and adjust routes dynamically based on network conditions.

Common dynamic routing protocols include:

- **Routing Information Protocol (RIP)**: A distance-vector protocol that determines routes based on hop count
- **Enhanced Interior Gateway Routing Protocol (EIGRP)**: A Cisco proprietary protocol that improves efficiency by using bandwidth and delay as routing metrics
- **Open Shortest Path First (OSPF)**: A link-state protocol that determines the shortest and most efficient path using a cost-based metric.

Dynamic routing is ideal for large and complex networks where network topology frequently changes, ensuring efficient and adaptive data transmission.

Network Address Translation (NAT)

Network Address Translation (NAT) is a network protocol used in IPv4 networks to enable multiple devices within a private network to access the internet using a single public IPv4 address. NAT acts as a bridge between private and public networks, modifying the source or destination IP addresses of data packets as they pass through a router. Despite these modifications, port numbers for protocols such as TCP and UDP remain unchanged, ensuring seamless communication.

Benefits of NAT

- **Conserves IPv4 addresses**: Reduces the need for multiple public IP addresses by allowing multiple devices to share a single public IP

- **Enhances security**: Hides internal private IP addresses, making it difficult for external entities to access internal devices directly

- **Simplifies routing**: Reduces the complexity of network routing by allowing internal devices to use private IP addresses

- **Supports a wide range of services**: Works with various applications and network services without major configuration changes

- **Consumes fewer resources**: Reduces the demand for additional IP addresses, making network management more efficient

NAT plays a crucial role in extending the life of IPv4 while ensuring secure and efficient communication between private and public networks.

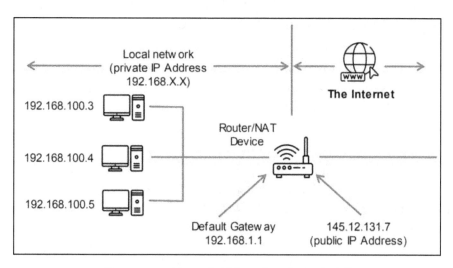

Figure 03-70: Network Address Translation (NAT)

Port Address Translation (PAT)

Port Address Translation (PAT) is a network technique that allows multiple devices within a Local Area Network (LAN) to share a single public IP address by assigning unique port numbers to each session. This method ensures that multiple devices can communicate with external networks while using the same public IP.

PAT is often referred to as port overloading, port-level multiplexed NAT, or single address NAT because it maps multiple internal private IP addresses to a single public IP by distinguishing sessions based on port numbers. This approach optimizes IPv4 address utilization and enhances network security by preventing direct exposure of internal devices to external networks.

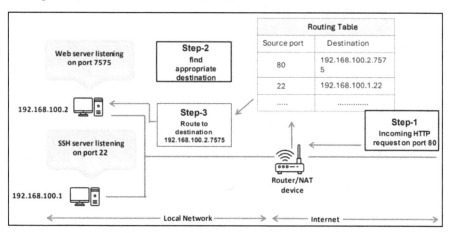

Figure 03-71: Port Address Translation (PAT)

Virtual Local Area Network (VLAN)

A Virtual Local Area Network (VLAN) is a logical grouping of devices that communicate as if they were on the same physical network, even if they are located in different geographical locations. Unlike traditional networks, VLANs are configured through software rather than hardware, making them more flexible and scalable.

One of the key advantages of VLANs is cost efficiency. Instead of investing in expensive routers, VLANs use switches to segment networks, reducing infrastructure costs while maintaining network segmentation and security. By logically dividing a network, VLANs enhance performance, security, and management without requiring physical reconfiguration.

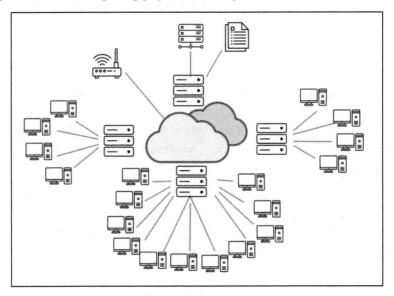

Figure 03-72: VLAN

Advantages, Disadvantages, and Security Implications of VLANs

VLANs offer several advantages that enhance network efficiency and security. By reducing the number of devices required for a specific network topology, VLANs help simplify network management and reduce complexity. They improve performance by segmenting network traffic, which minimizes congestion and enhances overall data transfer speeds. VLANs also provide security benefits by isolating devices, ensuring that communication occurs only within designated groups. This separation not only prevents unauthorized access but also enables the formation of virtual workgroups that operate independently while sharing the same physical infrastructure. Additionally, VLANs simplify administration by allowing

network changes to be managed through software rather than physical hardware adjustments.

Despite these benefits, VLANs have some disadvantages. Their functionality heavily relies on switches to operate correctly, which means improper configurations can lead to security vulnerabilities. Packet leaks between VLANs may occur due to misconfigurations, potentially exposing sensitive data. VLANs are also susceptible to injected packet attacks, where malicious packets are introduced into the network to compromise security.

To mitigate these risks, security measures should be implemented when using VLANs. Keeping hosts separated by VLANs ensures controlled communication, limiting unauthorized interactions. VLANs enhance security by delivering frames specifically to intended devices, reducing the risk of data exposure. Inter-VLAN routing should be carefully controlled using IP access lists to prevent unauthorized access between different VLANs. Additionally, deploying VTP domains, VTP pruning, and password protections strengthens network security by preventing unauthorized modifications and improving overall VLAN management.

Shared Media Network

A shared media network is a type of network where all nodes share a single communication channel and bandwidth. In this setup, every transmitted message is received by all nodes within the network, making data distribution straightforward but also presenting certain challenges.

Advantages of Shared Media Networks

One of the key benefits of shared media networks is their cost-effectiveness. Since fewer hardware components and communication channels are needed, the overall cost remains low. The absence of switches eliminates switching delays, leading to faster communication and a shorter response time. Additionally, broadcasting and multicasting are inherently simple, as all nodes receive transmitted messages without the need for complex routing mechanisms. The design of shared media networks is also relatively simple, making them easier to set up and maintain.

Disadvantages of Shared Media Networks

Despite their simplicity, shared media networks have several limitations. The available channel bandwidth is fixed, meaning that as more devices connect, the performance can degrade due to congestion. Since all nodes share the same channel, a router or gateway is required to connect different segments of the network. The distance span is also limited, as shared media networks do not scale efficiently over large areas. Traffic problems and network collisions can occur frequently, reducing overall network efficiency. Additionally, security concerns arise because every

message is broadcasted to all nodes, making it easier for unauthorized users to intercept and access sensitive information.

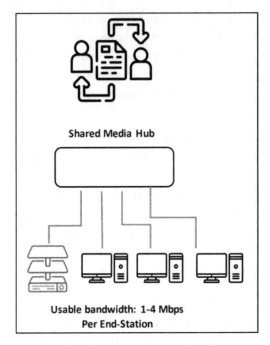

Figure 03-73: Shared Media Networks

Switched Media Network

A switched media network is a type of network where communication occurs through dedicated point-to-point connections established using network switches. Unlike shared media networks, switched networks ensure that data is transmitted directly between the sender and the receiver without being broadcast to all nodes. This setup enhances efficiency and reduces network congestion.

Advantages of Switched Media Networks

One of the major benefits of a switched media network is its high bandwidth, which allows multiple pairs of devices to communicate simultaneously without interference. Since each communication occurs over a dedicated path, collisions are eliminated, improving overall network performance.

Disadvantages of Switched Media Networks

Despite their advantages, switched media networks can be expensive due to the cost of switches and additional infrastructure. The design is complex, requiring careful configuration and management. Response time may be longer compared to shared media networks, as switches introduce some processing delays. Security concerns

also exist—if unauthorized ports on access switches are enabled, rogue devices can exploit vulnerabilities to gain network access, posing a significant security risk.

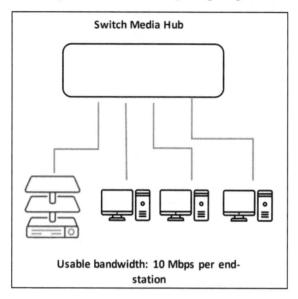

Figure 03-74: Switched Media Network

Basic Network Troubleshooting Techniques

Unreachable Networks

For successful network communication, certain fundamental conditions must be met. Both sending and receiving devices must have their TCP/IP protocol stacks correctly configured. This includes the proper assignment of an IP address and subnet mask. Additionally, if data packets need to travel beyond the local network, a default gateway must be configured. Routers play a crucial role in this process, as they must also have their TCP/IP settings properly configured on their interfaces and use an appropriate routing protocol to ensure seamless data transfer.

When these conditions are not met, network communication becomes impossible. Several issues can arise, such as a sending device addressing a datagram to a non-existent IP address, the destination device being disconnected from its network, or a router's connecting interface being down. Additionally, if a router lacks the necessary routing information to locate the destination network, data transmission will fail. In such cases, an Internet Control Message Protocol (ICMP) destination unreachable message is generated. This occurs when either the host or port is unreachable or when the network itself is deemed inaccessible.

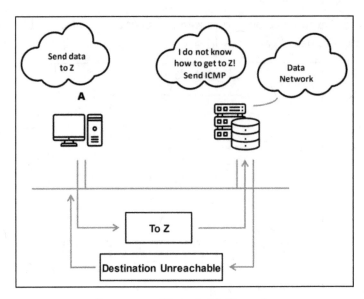

Figure 03-75: Unreachable Networks

Destination Unreachable Message

When a datagram cannot be forwarded to its destination, the Internet Control Message Protocol (ICMP) sends a destination unreachable message back to the sender. This notification indicates that the datagram could not be properly delivered. Such messages may also be triggered when packet fragmentation is required for forwarding a packet. Fragmentation typically becomes necessary when a datagram transitions from a token-ring network to an Ethernet network, as these networks have different Maximum Transmission Unit (MTU) sizes.

However, if a datagram has been configured to disallow fragmentation, the packet cannot be forwarded, leading to the generation of a destination unreachable message. Additionally, these messages may also be sent when IP-related services, such as FTP or web services, are unavailable, preventing successful communication.

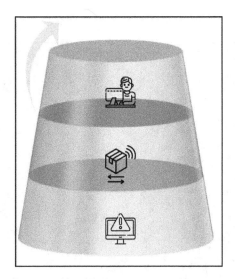

Figure 03-76: Destination Unreachable Message

ICMP Echo (Request) and Echo Reply

1. ICMP Echo Request and Echo Reply

- The Internet Control Message Protocol (ICMP) Echo Request and Echo Reply messages are used for network connectivity testing
- The ping command is typically used to send an Echo Request (Type 8), and the receiving device responds with an Echo Reply (Type 0), confirming network reachability

2. Command Prompt Output (Ping Test)

- Figure 03-77 shows a Windows command prompt where the user attempts to ping 10.10.1.22
- The responses from 10.10.1.22 indicate that the host is reachable, with the response times being minimal (less than 1ms) and 0% packet loss
- The Time-to-Live (TTL) value of 128 suggests that the packet has not traversed many hops

```
Select Command Prompt                                    —   □   ×

Microsoft Windows [Version 10.0.22000.469]
(c) Microsoft Corporation. All rights reserved.

C:\Users\Admin>telnet
'telnet' is not recognized as an internal or external command,
operable program or batch file.

C:\Users\Admin>ping 10.10.1.22

Pinging 10.10.1.22 with 32 bytes of data:
Reply from 10.10.1.22: bytes=32 time=1ms TTL=128
Reply from 10.10.1.22: bytes=32 time<1ms TTL=128
Reply from 10.10.1.22: bytes=32 time<1ms TTL=128
Reply from 10.10.1.22: bytes=32 time<1ms TTL=128

Ping statistics for 10.10.1.22:
    Packets: Sent = 4, Received = 4, Lost = 0 (0% loss),
Approximate round trip times in milli-seconds:
    Minimum = 0ms, Maximum = 1ms, Average = 0ms
```

Figure 03-77: Windows Command Prompt

3. ICMP Packet Structure

Figure 03-78 shows an ICMP packet's structure, breaking it down into different layers:

a. Ethernet Header (Layer 2 - Data Link Layer)

- Contains the MAC addresses (destination and source) of the devices communicating
- The Frame Type field specifies the type of payload being carried

b. IP Header (Layer 3 - Network Layer)

- Contains the source and destination IP addresses
- Includes the IP Protocol Field, which is set to 1 for ICMP

c. ICMP Message (Layer 3 - Internet Control Message Protocol)

- Consists of:
  - **Type** - 8 for Echo Request, 0 for Echo Reply
  - **Code** - Usually 0 for standard echo messages
  - **Checksum** - For error checking
  - **ID** and **Sequence Number** - Used to match requests with replies
  - **Data** - Contains additional information, usually part of the original request

Ethernet Header (Layer 2)			IP Header (Layer 3)	ICMP Message (Layer 3)							Eher. Tr.
Ethernet Destination Address (MAC)	Ethernet Source Address (MAC)	Frame Type	Source IP Add. Dest. IP Add. Protocol Field	Type 0 or 8	Code 0	Checksum	ID	Seq. Num.	Data		FCS

IP Protocol Field = 1
The echo request message is typically initiated using the ping command

Figure 03-78: ICMP Packet's Structure

4. Key Takeaways

- Ping works using ICMP Echo Request and Reply messages to verify network connectivity
- ICMP Type 8 = Echo Request, and Type 0 = Echo Reply
- IP Protocol Field = 1, indicating the packet is ICMP
- Ping statistics show packet loss, response time, and round-trip time, helping diagnose network issues

Time Exceeded Message

Each IP packet, also known as a datagram, has a Time-to-Live (TTL) value assigned to it. This TTL value determines how long the packet can exist in the network before it is discarded. Every time a router processes the packet, it decreases the TTL value by one. If the packet's TTL reaches zero before reaching its destination, the router discards the packet to prevent it from looping indefinitely in the network. To inform the sender about this event, Internet Control Message Protocol (ICMP) generates a Time Exceeded message. This notification helps in troubleshooting network issues, as it indicates that the packet could not reach its destination due to excessive hops along the way.

ICMP Time Exceeded Type = 11		
Type (8 bits)	Code (8 bits)	Checksum (16 bits)
Parameters		
Data..........		

Figure 03-79: Time-to-Live Packet Structure

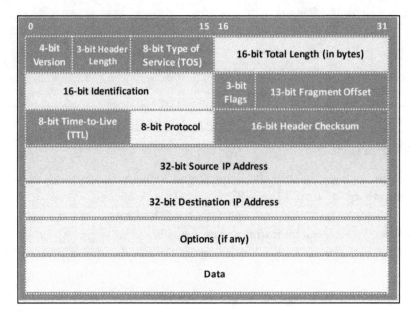

Figure 03-80: IP Header

IP Parameter Problem

When a network device processes an IP datagram, it examines the packet's header to ensure it is correctly formatted and contains valid information. If there is an issue with the header, such as a missing or incorrect field, the device may be unable to forward the packet. These errors are not related to the availability of the destination host or network but still prevent the datagram from being processed and delivered. In such cases, Internet Control Message Protocol (ICMP) generates a Type 12 Parameter Problem message. This message is sent back to the source, informing it of the issue so that corrective action can be taken.

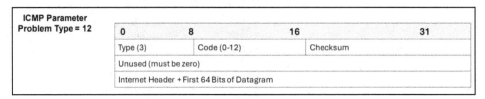

Figure 03-81: IP Parameter Problem

ICMP Control Messages

ICMP Control Messages serve a different purpose compared to error messages. Instead of being triggered by lost packets or transmission errors, these messages are used to provide important network-related information to hosts. They help optimize network communication by informing devices about specific conditions. For example, ICMP control messages can notify a host about network congestion,

allowing it to adjust its transmission rate accordingly. Additionally, they can indicate the presence of a better gateway to reach a remote network, helping in more efficient routing. These messages play a crucial role in maintaining and improving network performance.

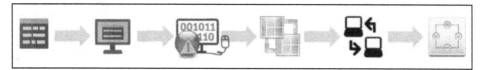

Figure 03-82: ICMP Control Messages

ICMP Redirects

Routers use ICMP Redirect messages (Type 5, Code 0-3) to inform hosts that a better route exists for a specific destination. This helps optimize routing decisions and reduce unnecessary traffic through inefficient paths. However, a router only sends an ICMP Redirect message under specific conditions:

- **Router Configuration:** The router must be explicitly configured to send redirect messages
- **Valid Routing Path:** The new route being suggested must not be another ICMP redirect or a default route; it should be a more specific and optimized path
- **No Source Routing:** The datagram must not be source-routed, meaning it should not have predetermined routing information from the sender
- **Same Interface Handling:** The packet must enter and leave the router through the same interface
- **Matching Subnets:** The source IP address of the incoming packet must belong to the same subnet/network as the next-hop IP address of the routed packet

If these conditions are met, the router sends an ICMP Redirect message to the sender, advising it to update its routing table and send future packets directly to the more efficient route.

Troubleshooting

Network troubleshooting is the process of identifying and diagnosing issues within a computer network to restore normal operations. It involves systematically analyzing different network components, including hardware, software, and configurations, to determine the root cause of connectivity problems.

Several common issues can affect network performance and reliability:

- **Physical Connection Issues:** Loose or faulty cables can disrupt network connectivity, making it essential to check and secure all physical connections.

- **Connectivity Issues:** Network failures or misconfigured ports and interfaces in both LAN and WAN environments may prevent proper communication with the host server.

- **Configuration Issues:** Incorrect settings in services such as DHCP and DNS, as well as routing misconfigurations, can lead to failed communication between devices.

- **Software Issues:** Incompatible software versions or mismatches in protocol implementations may cause disruptions in the transmission of IP data packets between the source and destination.

- **Traffic Overload:** When network traffic exceeds the capacity of network devices, it can lead to performance degradation and increased latency, affecting overall network behavior.

- **Network IP Issues:** Improper IP address assignments, incorrect subnet masks, or misconfigured routing settings can result in communication failures between the source and destination devices.

By systematically addressing these issues, network administrators can effectively troubleshoot and resolve network problems, ensuring smooth and reliable connectivity.

Steps for Network Troubleshooting

Effective network troubleshooting involves a systematic approach to diagnosing and resolving issues that impact network performance and connectivity. The following steps outline key areas that should be examined during the troubleshooting process:

1. **Troubleshooting IP Problems:** IP-related issues often arise due to incorrect configurations, subnet mismatches, or conflicting IP addresses. Ensuring that devices have the correct IP settings, subnet masks, and default gateways is crucial for seamless communication within the network.

2. **Troubleshooting Local Connectivity Issues:** Local network problems can stem from misconfigured network interfaces, incorrect VLAN assignments, or firewall restrictions. Checking the connection between devices within the same local network can help identify and resolve these issues.

3. **Troubleshooting Physical Connectivity Issues:** Faulty cables, damaged ports, or disconnected network devices can lead to connectivity failures. Verifying cable connections, testing network ports, and ensuring proper device functioning can help eliminate physical connectivity problems.

4. **Troubleshooting Routing Problems:** Misconfigured routing tables, missing routes, or incorrect default gateway settings can disrupt

communication between different networks. Analyzing routing tables, checking route propagation, and verifying the functionality of routing protocols help in resolving these issues.

5. **Troubleshooting Upper-Layer Faults:** Issues at the application or transport layers, such as problems with DNS resolution, firewall settings, or application misconfigurations, can impact network performance. Diagnosing these layers ensures that network services function properly.

6. **Troubleshooting Wireless Network Connection Issues:** Wireless networks can experience connectivity issues due to weak signal strength, interference, incorrect security settings, or device incompatibility. Adjusting wireless configurations, optimizing signal coverage, and updating firmware can help maintain a stable wireless network connection.

By following these structured troubleshooting steps, network administrators can efficiently identify and resolve network problems, ensuring reliable connectivity and optimal performance.

Troubleshooting IP Problems

Troubleshooting IP-related issues require a systematic approach to identify and resolve network connectivity problems. The process begins with using diagnostic tools to locate the devices that are experiencing issues along the communication path. Tools like ping, traceroute, and network analyzers help in pinpointing the source of the problem.

Next, it is essential to check the physical connections between the source and destination devices. Faulty or loose cable connections can often be the cause of network failures, especially in wired environments. Additionally, Local Area Network (LAN) connectivity faults can contribute to communication breakdowns, so verifying LAN settings and connections is crucial.

At each intermediate hop, the functionality of routers should be assessed to ensure they are operating correctly. If a router is malfunctioning or misconfigured, it may disrupt the flow of data packets across the network. Finally, all network devices should be checked for proper configuration settings, including IP addresses, subnet masks, gateways, and DNS configurations. Incorrect settings can lead to communication failures, preventing devices from connecting to the intended network.

By following these steps, network administrators can efficiently diagnose and resolve IP-related issues, ensuring stable and reliable network performance.

Troubleshooting Local Connectivity Issues

When troubleshooting local connectivity issues, the first step is to verify communication between the source and destination devices. If both devices are on the same subnet, use the ping command to test the connection directly. However, if they are on different subnets, the next step is to ping the gateway IP of the router to determine if communication is being routed correctly.

If the ping request fails, it is necessary to check whether the subnet mask and routing table are correctly configured. An incorrect subnet mask or missing route entry in the routing table can prevent proper data flow. If the routing configurations appear correct, verify whether the source device can ping intermediate hops or routers within the network. A failed ping response at this stage could indicate a configuration issue or an IP address conflict.

To resolve IP conflicts, disconnect the suspected device and attempt to ping the same IP address from another device on the network. If the new device successfully responds to the ping, it confirms that the previously disconnected device was using the same IP address as another device in the network. In such cases, the IP address needs to be reconfigured to ensure unique addressing within the network.

By following these steps, network administrators can efficiently diagnose and resolve local connectivity issues, ensuring smooth communication between devices.

Troubleshooting Physical Connectivity Issues

Troubleshooting physical connectivity issues involves verifying the integrity of hardware components such as cables, ports, and network devices. The first step is to verify cable connections, ensuring that the correct cables are in use and properly connected to the devices. Loose connections should be avoided, and if no loose connection is found, inspect the cables for wear and tear. If replacing the cable does not resolve the issue, the next step is to check the network port by testing it with a different cable or device to confirm whether the port is faulty.

Next, check for faulty ports by inspecting the ports where the network link is established. The indicator lights on the ports should be on, signaling proper functionality. If the lights are off, it could indicate a faulty port that needs further investigation or replacement.

Lastly, verify whether the issue is caused by traffic overload. Network devices have a specified capacity, and exceeding this limit can result in communication interruptions between the source and destination. Crosscheck the capacity of devices in the network and compare it with the amount of traffic flowing through them. If network congestion is detected, managing bandwidth allocation or upgrading network devices may be necessary to restore smooth communication.

By systematically checking these physical components, network administrators can identify and resolve connectivity issues, ensuring stable network performance.

Troubleshooting Routing Problems

When troubleshooting routing issues, the first step is to use the traceroute tool to identify the hop or router responsible for the problem. If the issue persists, systematically investigate each intermediate hop or router to pinpoint where the disruption has occurred. Once the problematic hop or router is detected, log in to the device using Telnet and attempt to ping both the source and destination.

If the ping is unsuccessful and the necessary routes are not defined, configure the appropriate routes between the source and destination with the correct subnet mask. After configuring the routes, verify the network path again.

Next, check for the possibility of a routing loop by executing another ping test. If a loop is detected, it must be resolved by tracing its origin and reconfiguring the routing settings to ensure proper path determination.

If the issue remains unresolved, review the routing protocol being used. Some network configurations may require a different protocol for optimal performance. If necessary, modify the routing protocol to align with the network's requirements, ensuring efficient and accurate data transmission.

By following these steps, network administrators can systematically identify and fix routing issues, restoring seamless communication across the network.

Troubleshooting Upper-layer Faults

various issues can arise in upper-layer network communication, impacting connectivity and service availability. One common problem is a firewall blocking incoming and outgoing traffic, preventing seamless communication. To resolve this, the affected host can be moved within the network to bypass the firewall restrictions and restore traffic flow.

Another frequent issue is when a server or a critical service goes down, disrupting operations. In such cases, the best solution is to replace the downed server with a temporary server to ensure continuity of services while diagnosing and fixing the primary server.

Additionally, authentication-related issues may prevent access to services between the host and the server. This can be caused by misconfigured authentication protocols or expired credentials. Deploying appropriate software tools to check and troubleshoot authentication-related errors can help resolve the problem effectively.

Lastly, software compatibility issues, such as version mismatches between networked devices, can disrupt communication. Upgrading all devices to

compatible software versions ensures smooth operation and prevents conflicts caused by outdated or mismatched software versions.

By following these troubleshooting steps, administrators can efficiently diagnose and resolve upper-layer faults, ensuring reliable network performance and service availability.

Troubleshooting Wireless Network Connection Issues

When facing issues with a wireless network connection, the first step is to check whether Wi-Fi is enabled on the device. This can be verified by navigating to Settings → Network & Internet → Wi-Fi and ensuring that the Wi-Fi toggle is switched on.

If the issue persists, the next step is to examine the SSID and access points. Incorrect or outdated SSID settings can prevent a device from obtaining an IP address. Modifying the SSID and reconfiguring access points can help allocate an IP address to the requesting device, restoring network connectivity.

For further troubleshooting, you can use the Windows Network Diagnostics tool. This built-in tool helps identify network-related issues by detecting errors and downloading and installing any available patches that may be required to resolve the problem.

If all else fails, a router reset may be necessary. Restoring the router to its factory settings and restarting it can help eliminate misconfigurations or firmware issues that might be causing connectivity problems.

By following these troubleshooting steps, you can efficiently diagnose and resolve most wireless network issues, ensuring a stable and reliable connection.

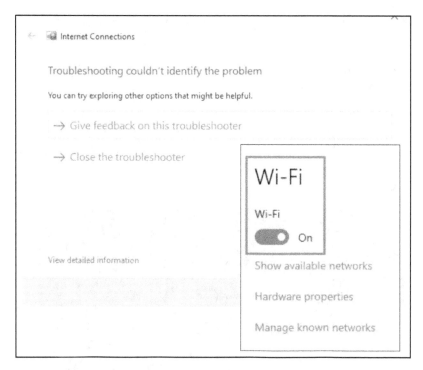

Figure 03-673: Troubleshooting Wireless Network Connection Issues

Network Troubleshooting Tools

Here are list of basic network troubleshooting utilities and tools

- Ping
- Tracert/ traceroute
- Ipconfig/ ifconfig
- NSlookup
- Netstat
- PuTTY/ Tera Term
- Subnet and IP Calculator
- Speedtest.net
- Pathping/ mtr
- Route

Ping

The ping utility is a network diagnostic tool that checks whether a specific IP address or website is accessible from a host system. It works by sending data packets to the specified destination and waiting for a response.

When a reply is received from the pinged IP address, it indicates that packets are successfully transferring between the system and the destination, confirming

connectivity. To use this utility, open the command prompt and execute the command:

- ping x.x.x.x (for an IP address)
- ping example.com (for a domain)

This command helps verify if a host is reachable from the computer. However, if the response shows "Request timed out," it indicates that the system cannot establish a connection with the host. This may be due to network issues, firewall restrictions, or the target server being unavailable.

```
Select Command Prompt                                    —    □    ×

Microsoft Windows [Version 10.0.22000.469]
(c) Microsoft Corporation. All rights reserved.

C:\Users\Admin>ping 8.8.8.8

Pinging 8.8.8.8 with 32 bytes of data:
Reply from 8.8.8.8: bytes=32 time=7ms TTL=114
Reply from 8.8.8.8: bytes=32 time=7ms TTL=114
Reply from 8.8.8.8: bytes=32 time=7ms TTL=114
Reply from 8.8.8.8: bytes=32 time=7ms TTL=114

Ping statistics for 8.8.8.8:
    Packets: Sent = 4, Received = 4, Lost = 0 (0% loss),
Approximate round trip times in milli-seconds:
    Minimum = 7ms, Maximum = 7ms, Average = 7ms
```

Figure 03-84(a): Ping

```
Command Prompt                                    —    □    ×

C:\Users\            >ping 8.8.8.8

Pinging 8.8.8.8 with 32 bytes of data:
Request timed out.
Request timed out.
Request timed out.
Request timed out.

Ping statistics for 8.8.8.8:
    Packets: Sent = 4, Received = 0, Lost = 4 (100% loss),
```

Figure 03-84(b): Ping

Traceroute and Tracert

The Traceroute utility is a network diagnostic tool used to trace the path of packets across a network and analyze the connection to a specific server. It helps identify where delays or failures occur in the transmission. Traceroute works by sending ICMP echo request messages to the designated destination.

If the destination is active and reachable, it responds with ICMP echo reply messages, confirming a successful connection. However, if there is no response, it

could indicate that the destination is inactive or that there is a connectivity issue between the source and destination.

In Windows, the tracert command is used to achieve the same functionality. By executing tracert <hostname> in the command prompt, the tool traces the route taken by packets to reach the target system. Each hop in the route appears as a numbered entry in the left column, displaying details such as the domain name and IP address of each intermediate network device. This information helps diagnose network latency issues and pinpoint the exact location of failures in the network.

```
Administrator: Command Prompt                                         —    □    ×

C:\Windows\system32>tracert facebook.com

Tracing route to facebook.com [157.240.229.35]
over a maximum of 30 hops:

  1    <1 ms    <1 ms    <1 ms  10.10.1.2
  2    <1 ms    <1 ms    <1 ms  172.18.0.1
  3    <1 ms    <1 ms    <1 ms  192.168.0.1
  4    <1 ms    <1 ms    <1 ms  103.186.82.26
  5    <1 ms    <1 ms    <1 ms  103.186.82.3
  6     1 ms     1 ms    <1 ms  dc5.pr01.iad2.tfbnw.net [206.126.236.191]
  7    <1 ms    <1 ms    <1 ms  po204.asw04.iad3.tfbnw.net [129.134.99.246]
  8    <1 ms    <1 ms    <1 ms  psw03.iad3.tfbnw.net [204.15.23.144]
  9     4 ms     3 ms     3 ms  157.240.39.139
 10    <1 ms     1 ms     2 ms  edge-star-mini-shv-02-iad3.facebook.com [157.240.229.35]

Trace complete.
```

Figure 03-85: Tracert to Facebook.com

Ipconfig and Ifconfig

Internet Protocol Configuration (ipconfig) is a command-line utility used in Windows that displays a system's current TCP/IP network configuration. It provides details such as the IP address, subnet mask, and default gateway for all network adapters.

To view the basic network configuration, simply open the command prompt and execute the ipconfig command. To obtain more detailed system configuration information, including DNS servers, MAC addresses, and DHCP settings, use the ipconfig /all command.

```
Command Prompt                                                    —    □    ×

C:\Users\Admin>ipconfig

Windows IP Configuration


Ethernet adapter Ethernet:

   Connection-specific DNS Suffix  . :
   Link-local IPv6 Address . . . . . : fe80::709f:40d1:26a1:f4ac%8
   IPv4 Address. . . . . . . . . . . : 10.10.1.11
   Subnet Mask . . . . . . . . . . . : 255.255.255.0
   Default Gateway . . . . . . . . . : 10.10.1.2

C:\Users\Admin>
```

Figure 03-86: Windows Computer Network Configuration Using ipconfig

For Linux-based systems, a similar utility called ifconfig is used. It provides network interface details and allows users to configure network parameters. While ifconfig is still available on some distributions, it has largely been replaced by the ip command in modern Linux environments.

```
● ● ●                          Parrot Terminal
File   Edit   View   Search   Terminal   Help
┌─[attacker@parrot]─[~]
└─➤ $ifconfig
eth0: flags=4163<UP,BROADCAST,RUNNING,MULTICAST>  mtu 1500
        inet 10.10.1.13  netmask 255.255.255.0  broadcast 10.10.1.255
        inet6 fe80::deb2:9b3b:5490:d89b  prefixlen 64  scopeid 0x20<link>
        ether 02:15:5d:21:aa:5c  txqueuelen 1000  (Ethernet)
        RX packets 4736  bytes 850055 (830.1 KiB)
        RX errors 0  dropped 0  overruns 0  frame 0
        TX packets 875  bytes 78438 (76.5 KiB)
        TX errors 0  dropped 0 overruns 0  carrier 0  collisions 0

lo: flags=73<UP,LOOPBACK,RUNNING>  mtu 65536
        inet 127.0.0.1  netmask 255.0.0.0
        inet6 ::1  prefixlen 128  scopeid 0x10<host>
        loop  txqueuelen 1000  (Local Loopback)
        RX packets 16  bytes 904 (904.0 B)
        RX errors 0  dropped 0  overruns 0  frame 0
        TX packets 16  bytes 904 (904.0 B)
        TX errors 0  dropped 0 overruns 0  carrier 0  collisions 0
```

Figure 03-87: Linux Computer Network Configuration Using ifconfig

NSlookup

The Name Server Lookup (NSlookup) utility retrieves the IP address associated with a domain name or vice versa. It helps diagnose DNS resolution issues, particularly when a user can access a resource using its IP address but not through its DNS name.

By executing the nslookup command in the command prompt, users can query DNS records and obtain the corresponding IP address of a given domain. Additionally, subcommands can be used to perform advanced queries or set specific options for DNS lookups. This tool is essential for troubleshooting network connectivity issues related to domain name resolution.

```
Command Prompt                                    —    □    ×

C:\Users\Admin>nslookup www.google.com
Server:  dns.google
Address:  8.8.8.8

Non-authoritative answer:
Name:     www.google.com
Addresses:  2607:f8b0:4004:c17::63
            2607:f8b0:4004:c17::93
            2607:f8b0:4004:c17::67
            2607:f8b0:4004:c17::68
            142.251.16.147
            142.251.16.103
            142.251.16.105
            142.251.16.99
            142.251.16.104
            142.251.16.106
C:\Users\Admin>
```

Figure 03-88: DNS Lookup Results of Google.com Using nslookup

Netstat

The Network Statistics (Netstat) utility is a command-line tool used to monitor incoming and outgoing TCP/IP traffic on a network. It helps identify active connections, network statistics, and the services associated with specific ports.

By executing the netstat command in the command prompt or terminal, users can view a list of active connections on the system. Additionally, using netstat -e provides detailed statistics of various network protocols, allowing administrators to diagnose potential network issues and monitor real-time network activity.

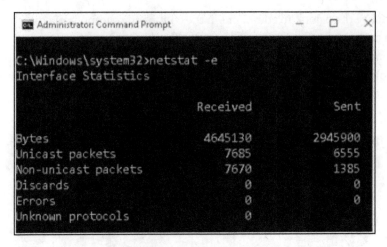

Figure 03-89: Network Interface Statistics via netstat

PuTTY and Tera Term

PuTTY is a widely used tool that functions as both a File Transfer Protocol (FTP) and Secure File Transfer Protocol (SFTP) client. It is commonly used for secure remote access and data transfer between systems. Additionally, PuTTY can generate hashes for passwords, enhancing security by encrypting login credentials.

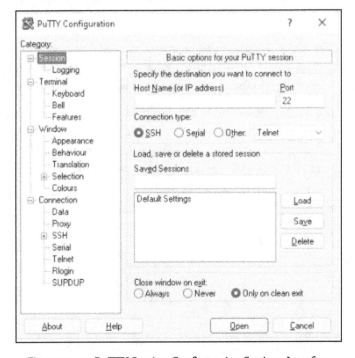

Figure 03-90: PuTTY Session Configuration Settings Interface

On the other hand, Tera Term is a terminal emulation tool primarily used to automate tasks in remote connections. It supports Telnet and SSH protocols, allowing users to access and manage remote systems with ease and security. Tera Term is particularly useful for scripting and automating repetitive network administration tasks.

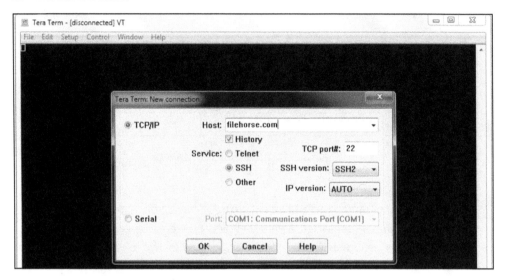

Figure 03-91: Tera Term Connection Setup Interface

Subnet and IP Calculators

A subnet defines the structure and classification of IPv4 and IPv6 networks. It helps divide IP address spaces into smaller, manageable subnetworks, optimizing network performance and security.

The IP subnet calculator is a useful tool for determining possible IP address ranges and classifying them into different IP classes. It calculates key details such as broadcast ranges, network addresses, and host ranges, allowing network administrators to allocate and manage IP addresses within a given network efficiently.

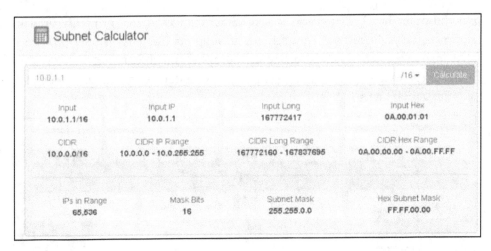

Figure 03-92: Subnet and IP Calculator

Speedtest.net

Speedtest.net is an online tool used to measure the available bandwidth of a host at the time of testing. It helps users assess their actual internet speed, which may differ from the values assigned by their Internet Service Provider (ISP). The platform evaluates both upload and download speeds, providing insights into the time required to transfer files over the network.

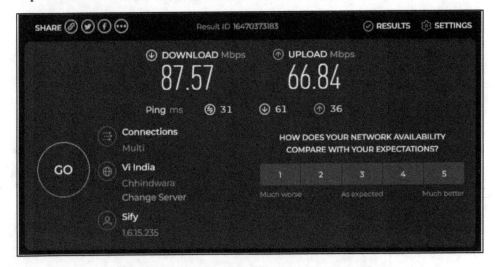

Figure 03-93: Internet Speed Test Using Speedtest.net

Pathping and mtr

Pathping is a network diagnostic tool that provides detailed insights into the route between a host and a destination. It combines the functionalities of ping and traceroute, offering a comprehensive view of network latency and packet loss. The

tool first traces the route to the destination and then runs a 25-second test, analyzing the packet loss rate at each router along the path. To display numeric IP addresses instead of DNS hostnames, use the pathping –n command.

```
Select Command Prompt - pathping 8.8.8.8                          —    □    ×

C:            >pathping 8.8.8.8

Tracing route to dns.google [8.8.8.8]
over a maximum of 30 hops:
  0  Windows11 [10.10.1.11]
  1  10.10.1.2
  2  172.18.0.1
  3  192.168.0.1
  4  103.186.82.26
  5  103.186.82.3
  6  gi0-1-1-15.rcr21.iad01.atlas.cogentco.com [38.104.207.233]
  7  be2956.ccr41.iad02.atlas.cogentco.com [154.54.30.193]
  8  be3083.ccr41.dca01.atlas.cogentco.com [154.54.30.53]
  9  be4943.ccr41.jfk02.atlas.cogentco.com [154.54.165.14]
 10  be3294.ccr31.jfk05.atlas.cogentco.com [154.54.47.218]
 11  tata.jfk05.atlas.cogentco.com [154.54.12.18]
 12  if-be-2-2.ecore1.n75-newyork.as6453.net [66.110.96.62]
 13  72.14.221.146
 14  142.251.225.85
 15  142.251.60.229
 16  dns.google [8.8.8.8]

Computing statistics for 400 seconds...
```

Figure 03-94: Network route trace via pathping

Route

The Route utility displays the current status of a host's routing table. It is particularly useful when a host has multiple IP addresses and is connected to multiple networks. The utility provides details about the network destination, netmask, and gateways under the Active Routes section.

To add, delete, or modify a route entry, use the following command format:

route [-p] command dest [mask subnet] gateway [-if interface]

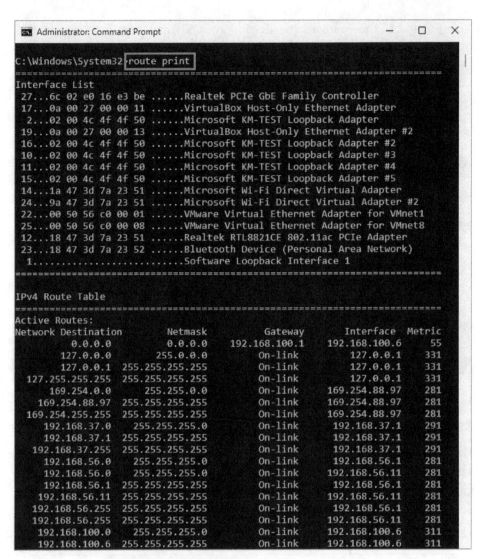

Figure 03-95: Routing Table Information Using Route Print

Domain 04: Virtualization

Introduction

Virtualization serves as a fundamental technology in contemporary computing, facilitating the generation of virtual representations of hardware, operating systems, storage, and networks on one physical machine. By decoupling physical resources, virtualization permits several Virtual Machines (VMs) to operate autonomously on the same hardware, with each functioning as an individual system complete with its own operating environment and applications.

This domain explores the core concepts, types, and benefits of virtualization, along with its role in optimizing resource utilization, improving scalability, and enhancing system flexibility. As organizations increasingly adopt virtualization to streamline operations, reduce costs, and support cloud computing, understanding its architecture, security considerations, and management practices becomes essential for IT professionals.

Introduction to Virtualization

Virtualization is the process of creating a virtual version of physical resources within a system, such as servers, operating systems, storage devices, or networks. The virtual version is referred to as a Virtual Machine (VM), and it operates independently of the physical resource. This approach allows multiple operating systems to run on a single physical machine, increasing efficiency and reducing costs. Additionally, virtualization offers greater flexibility and scalability for managing IT resources.

Difference Between Pre Virtualization and Post Virtualization

In a non-virtualized environment, a hardware platform, also known as the host machine, is designed to run a single Operating System (OS) directly on the physical hardware. This OS manages all the hardware resources, including the CPU, memory, Network Interface Card (NIC), and storage disk, while supporting various applications. The system follows a one-to-one relationship between the hardware and the OS, meaning that if different applications require separate operating systems (like Windows, macOS, or Linux) multiple physical servers are needed. This approach often leads to inefficient use of hardware resources, higher energy

consumption, and increased operational costs since each machine might not utilize its full hardware capacity.

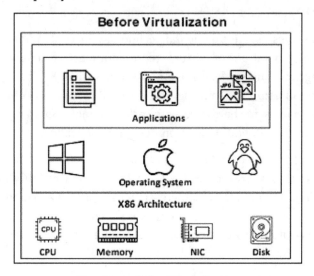

Figure 4-01: Before Virtualization

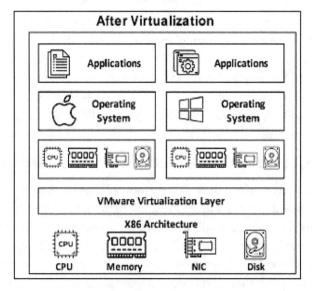

Figure 4-02: After Virtualization

With virtualization, the hardware platform is abstracted by a virtualization layer, often managed by a hypervisor (e.g., VMware, Hyper-V). This layer allows multiple Virtual Machines (VMs) to run simultaneously on the same physical hardware, with each VM hosting its own operating system and applications independently. Resources such as CPU, memory, Network Interface Cards (NIC), and disk space are dynamically allocated and shared among these VMs, which enhances hardware

utilization. As a result, different operating systems, such as Windows, macOS, and Linux, can coexist on a single machine.

Virtualization significantly reduces the need for multiple physical servers, lowers energy costs, increases scalability, and improves flexibility by enabling VMs to be easily created, modified, or relocated without disrupting other systems.

Characteristics of Virtualization

Virtualization offers several important features that contribute to its widespread adoption in modern IT environments. Key characteristics of virtualization include:

Partitioning

Virtualization enables a single physical system to be segmented into several virtual environments by allocating hardware resources like CPU, memory, and storage. Each segment functions as an individual Virtual Machine (VM) capable of running its own operating system and applications. This method promotes better use of hardware resources, enabling several workloads to run simultaneously on a single physical machine, which improves efficiency and reduces hardware costs.

Isolation

Each VM is entirely independent of the physical host system and from other virtual machines that are operating on the same host. This isolation ensures that processes, applications, and even failures within one VM do not impact others. It also improves security, ensuring that any breach or failure within one virtual machine does not propagate to others, thereby maintaining system stability and protecting data integrity.

Encapsulation

A virtual machine is contained within a single file or a collection of files, which include all its elements, operating system, applications, and virtual hardware. This structure simplifies the management, transfer, or backup of entire virtual machines as straightforward files. Encapsulation also safeguards each VM from interference by other VMs, ensuring that alterations or problems in one VM do not affect others and preserving the integrity of each virtual environment.

Emulation

Guest applications run in an environment managed by the virtualization layer, which is essentially a program itself. Furthermore, it is possible to emulate an entirely different environment compared to the host, enabling the execution of guest applications that demand specific features absent in the physical host.

Resource Sharing

Virtualization enables several virtual machines to utilize the resources of one physical machine, including CPU, memory, storage, and network bandwidth. This enhances hardware usage and minimizes the necessity for extra physical servers.

Aggregation

Sharing physical resources across multiple guests is achievable, but virtualization enables aggregation as well, which works oppositely. Separate hosts can be combined and presented to guests as one unified virtual host. This capability is realized through cluster management software, which utilizes the physical resources of a uniform group of machines and portrays them as a single resource.

Benefits of Virtualization

Virtualization is an important technique that makes efficient use of physical resources by creating many virtual instances. Some key benefits that virtualization offers are:

Resource Efficiency

Virtualization enhances hardware usage by enabling several Virtual Machines (VMs) to operate on one physical machine. This improves resource distribution and decreases the necessity for extra hardware, which ultimately boosts the Return on Investment (ROI) by optimizing the use of current infrastructure.

Reduced Disk Space Consumption

By enabling efficient sharing of storage resources, virtualization minimizes disk space consumption. Virtual machines can dynamically use storage space as needed, allowing better utilization of available disk space and reducing the need for unnecessary physical storage expansion.

Business Continuity

Virtualization supports seamless business continuity and enhances disaster recovery capabilities. It allows for rapid backups, quick failovers, and easy restoration of virtual machines in the event of hardware failure, ensuring minimal downtime and data loss.

Migration

One of the most powerful features of virtualization is its ability to migrate data, applications, operating systems, and processes from one machine to another with minimal disruption. Live migration features even allow these transfers while systems remain operational, minimizing downtime.

Increase in Uptime

Virtualization improves uptime by offering redundancy and failover mechanisms within the same physical system. If one VM fails, another can automatically take over, reducing service interruptions and improving overall system availability.

Increased Flexibility

With virtualization, deployment becomes more flexible, allowing organizations to quickly scale resources up or down. It also enables network resource multiplexing, letting multiple VMs share networking hardware more efficiently.

Improved Quality of Services (QoS)

Virtualization enhances QoS by efficiently distributing network loads across multiple VMs. This reduces bottlenecks, improves performance, and ensures better allocation of computing resources based on priority and need.

Environmental Benefits

By combining workloads on a smaller number of physical servers, virtualization minimizes the need for hardware, which in turn reduces power usage and CO_2 emissions. This leads to considerable energy savings and supports a more environmentally friendly and sustainable IT ecosystem.

Common Virtualization Vendors

Virtualization vendors are companies that develop and provide virtualization software, platforms, and solutions. These vendors create tools that enable businesses to generate virtual versions of physical hardware, such as servers, storage devices, networks, and operating systems. This allows multiple Virtual Machines (VMs) to operate on a single physical machine.

Their solutions assist organizations in optimizing resource utilization, improving scalability, reducing hardware costs, and enhancing flexibility by allowing various operating systems and applications to run independently on the same hardware.

Figure 4-03: Common Virtualization Vendors

VMware

VMware (https://www.vmware.com) provides advanced virtualization solutions encompassing networking, storage, and security, thereby facilitating the creation of virtual data centers that enhance the provisioning and management of IT resources.

Its applications, such as vSphere and ESXi, enable organizations to consolidate workloads, increase operational efficiency, and diminish hardware expenditures by enabling the execution of multiple Virtual Machines (VMs) on a single physical server.

Citrix

Citrix (https://www.citrix.com) specializes in desktop and application virtualization by transforming Windows apps and desktops into secure, on-demand services. It focuses on meeting the mobility, security, and performance needs of both IT professionals and end users. Solutions like Citrix Virtual Apps and Desktops are widely used for remote desktop access and virtual application delivery.

Oracle

Oracle (https://www.oracle.com) offers a complete suite of virtualization tools for managing both hardware and software stacks, ranging from desktops to enterprise data centers. Solutions like Oracle VM enable organizations to virtualize servers, networks, and storage while maintaining tight integration with Oracle applications and databases.

Microsoft

Microsoft (https://www.microsoft.com) offers virtualization products like Hyper-V, which supports managing both physical and virtual assets through a single platform. These solutions serve both data centers and desktop environments, providing businesses with tools for server virtualization, desktop virtualization, and integration with Azure for hybrid cloud management.

Virtualization Security and Concerns

Virtualization security encompasses a range of measures, procedures, and processes aimed at safeguarding the virtualization infrastructure and environment from various threats and vulnerabilities. Since virtualization enables multiple Virtual Machines (VMs) to operate on a single physical system, implementing effective security becomes crucial to mitigate risks such as data leakage, unauthorized access, and potential system compromises.

Virtualization Security Processes

Virtualization security processes involve safeguarding virtualized environments from threats, ensuring the integrity, confidentiality, and availability of Virtual Machines (VMs), hypervisors, and network resources.

Securing the Virtual Environment

Securing the virtual environment involves protecting key components like the hypervisor and management console, as they control all virtual machines on a host. Important measures include enforcing strong access controls, implementing role-based access, and ensuring only authorized users have admin privileges. Regular updates and patches for hypervisors and management software are crucial to fix vulnerabilities. Additionally, deploying Intrusion Detection Systems (IDS) and real-time monitoring tools can detect and respond to suspicious activities effectively.

Securing Each Virtual Machine (VM) at the System Level

Each virtual machine operates as an independent system and must be secured individually to prevent unauthorized access or exploitation. Security at this level focuses on hardening the VM's operating system and applications. Installing anti-malware and firewall solutions helps block malicious software and unauthorized network traffic. Keeping operating systems and applications up to date with patches and updates ensures that vulnerabilities are addressed promptly. Implementing the least privilege principle, which gives users the minimum access required for their roles, reduces the risk of insider threats. Additionally, disabling unnecessary services and closing unused ports reduces the attack surface accessible to potential attackers.

Securing the Virtual Network

Securing a virtual network involves protecting communication between virtual machines and external networks. Key strategies include deploying virtual firewalls and intrusion prevention systems to monitor traffic, using VLANs for network segmentation to isolate sensitive VMs, and encrypting data during operations like live VM migrations to prevent interception. Continuous monitoring with tools like SIEM helps detect anomalies and respond to threats in real time.

Virtualization Security Concerns

While virtualization offers numerous benefits, it comes with some security concerns also, which include:

Increased Complexity

The additional layer of virtualization infrastructure makes it challenging to monitor unusual events and detect anomalies, as activities may be hidden across various virtual layers.

Offline VM Exploitation

Offline virtual machines can serve as gateways for attackers to obtain access to a company's systems if not properly secured, as they may bypass standard monitoring and security controls.

Dynamic Workload Movement

The flexible nature of virtual machines allows workloads to move easily between hosts. If a workload is transferred to a less secure VM, it could introduce vulnerabilities and increase the risk of a security breach.

Virtual Firewall

A virtual firewall is a software-based security solution designed to monitor, control, and filter network traffic between Virtual Machines (VMs) within a virtualized environment. Unlike traditional hardware firewalls, virtual firewalls operate entirely within the virtual infrastructure, protecting communication between VMs without relying on physical hardware. These firewalls enforce security policies and rulesets to ensure that only legitimate and authorized data packets are transmitted across the network.

Virtual firewalls filter data packets based on predefined security policies, similar to traditional firewalls but tailored for virtual environments. They monitor the traffic flow between VMs on the same host or across different virtual networks, preventing malicious activity and unauthorized access.

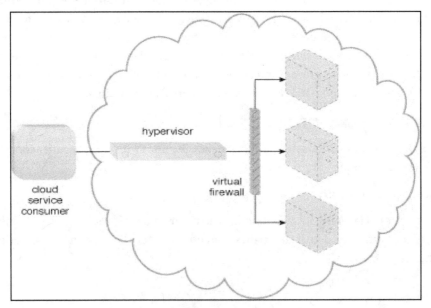

Figure 4-04: Virtual Firewall Illustration

Modes of Operation

The virtualized firewalls function in two modes, including the bridge-mode and hypervisor-mode.

Bridge-Mode

In bridge-mode, the virtual firewall operates at the level of the inter-network virtual switch. It filters traffic as it moves between VMs and different virtual networks, ensuring that data packets comply with the organization's security rules. This mode primarily focuses on traffic between VMs and the external network or between different virtual network segments. It is useful for isolating different virtual networks and enforcing strict communication boundaries.

Hypervisor-Mode

In hypervisor-mode, the firewall is integrated directly into the Virtual Machine Monitor (VMM), commonly referred to as the hypervisor. This enables it to oversee all VM activities at a more profound level, including access to hardware resources, software operations, storage interactions, services, and even memory usage. By operating at the hypervisor layer, it offers a comprehensive level of security that can identify threats impacting the foundational virtual infrastructure, such as resource misuse or unauthorized access attempts within the virtual environment.

Virtual Operating Systems

A Virtual Operating System (Virtual OS) is an operating system that runs within a virtualized environment instead of being directly installed on physical hardware. It functions as a guest operating system within virtualization software that operates on a host operating system. This enables various operating systems to run concurrently on one physical machine, enhancing flexibility and optimizing the utilization of available resources.

The key element that enables this functionality is the hypervisor. This software layer manages the allocation of system resources, including CPU, memory, storage, and networking. There are two types of hypervisors: Type 1 (Bare-Metal), which runs directly on the hardware without needing a host operating system, and Type 2 (Hosted), which operates on top of an existing operating system.

Advantages of Virtual Operating System

The advantages of the virtual operating system include:

- **Multi-OS Support:** Run multiple operating systems (e.g., Windows, Linux, macOS) simultaneously on a single machine.

- **Resource Optimization:** Efficiently utilizes system resources by allowing shared access across multiple virtual OS instances, reducing the need for additional hardware.

- **Easy Switching between Oss:** Seamlessly switch between virtual OS environments without rebooting or reconfiguring hardware.

- **Isolation and Security:** Each virtual OS operates in its own isolated environment, decreasing the risk of system-wide failures or security breaches.

- **Testing and Development Environment:** Developers can test applications across different operating systems without needing separate physical machines.

- **Backup and Recovery:** Snapshots allow quick backups of virtual OS states and easy restoration if issues occur.

Limitations of Virtual Operating System

Besides several advantages, Virtual operating systems also have some limitations, which include:

- **Performance Overhead:** Virtualization can lead to a reduction in performance because of resource sharing.

- **Resource Contention:** Several virtual operating system instances may vie for scarce physical resources.

- **Complexity:** Administering virtual environments demands specific expertise and tools.

- **Licensing Costs:** Operating multiple OS instances might incur extra licensing expenses.

Virtual Databases

A Virtual Database is a type of Database Management System (DBMS) that enables users to access and query multiple databases simultaneously as if they were a single, unified entity. Instead of physically merging data from various sources, a virtual database creates a logical layer that integrates data from different databases, allowing seamless access without altering the underlying structure of each database. This approach allows organizations to retrieve and analyze data from disparate sources—such as SQL, NoSQL, or cloud-based databases—without needing to replicate or move the data. Virtual databases are particularly useful for businesses with distributed data systems, as they simplify data management, improve efficiency, and reduce the complexity involved in handling multiple databases individually.

A Virtual Database (VDB) serves as a metadata repository for components that facilitate the integration of data from various sources. This configuration allows for the data to be accessed cohesively through a singular, uniform Application Programming Interface (API).

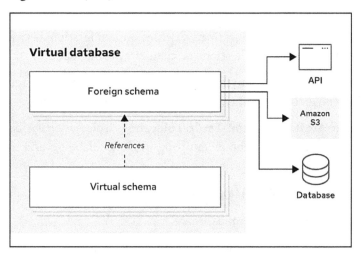

Figure 4-05: Virtual Database

A virtual database generally consists of various schema components, commonly referred to as models, with each schema holding the metadata (tables, procedures, functions). There are two distinct categories of schemas:

- Foreign schema

- Virtual schema

How a Virtual Database Works

A virtual database establishes an abstraction layer over one or more data sources (including SQL databases, NoSQL databases, or external APIs) by employing a method called "data virtualization" to generate a logical data model aligned with their data structures. This resulting framework enables users to query information from different subsystems utilizing a shared set of data definitions and commands.

Use Cases of Virtual Database

- Organizations often utilize virtual databases to attain a consolidated view of data for business analysis and reporting purposes.

- IT professionals leverage virtual databases to assist with data migration — for instance, by linking source and target databases.

- Virtual databases facilitate seamless access to data from various sources for management and IT applications.

Advantages of Virtual Databases

Virtual Database advantages are as follows:

- **Load Sharing across Databases**: Distributes workloads across multiple databases, improving performance and preventing overload.

- **Simplified Database Migration:** Enables easy migration between servers without reconfiguring applications or manually moving data.

- **Dynamic Resource Deployment:** Automatically allocates resources based on demand, enhancing flexibility, especially in cloud environments.

- **Increased Availability and Fault Tolerance**: Isolates virtual databases to prevent system-wide failures, ensuring high availability and minimizing downtime.

Disadvantages of Virtual Databases

The disadvantages of Virtual Databases are:

- **High Resource Consumption:** Running multiple virtual databases demands significant CPU, memory, and storage, potentially causing performance bottlenecks.

- **Increased Complexity for DBAs:** Administrators must manage both databases and the virtualization layer, adding complexity and requiring broader skills.

- **Troubleshooting Challenges:** Identifying issues can be difficult due to multiple layers (VM, virtualization software, hardware), leading to longer resolution times.

Domain 05: Web Markup and Programming Languages

Introduction

The development of modern web applications relies on a combination of markup languages, programming languages, and application frameworks to deliver dynamic, interactive, and scalable solutions. Web markup languages such as HTML and XML define the structure and content of web pages, while CSS enhances their visual presentation. Programming languages like JavaScript, Python, PHP, and Ruby enable client-side and server-side functionalities, making web applications responsive and interactive.

However, with the increasing complexity of web development, application development frameworks—such as J2EE, Ruby on Rails, and Ajax—have become essential for streamlining development. While these frameworks provide efficiency and scalability, they also introduce security vulnerabilities, including remote code execution, Cross-Site Scripting (XSS), SQL injection, and authentication bypass attacks. Understanding these risks is critical for securing web applications.

Web applications consist of multiple subcomponents, including web browsers, web servers, and database servers, each playing a crucial role in processing and delivering content. This domain explores the fundamental technologies of web development, security vulnerabilities in application frameworks, and the architecture of web components, providing a comprehensive overview of the web ecosystem and its associated security challenges.

Web Markup and Programming Languages

Markup languages define the structure and presentation of web content. These are presentational languages that do not execute logic but provide the framework for displaying web pages, such as HTML. HTML does not perform logical operations, comparisons, or computations. Instead, it is used to structure and present content inside a web browser. It tells the browser how to organize data for a specific page layout, including headings, titles, tables, and styling elements. Essentially, it formats data or controls its presentation. Examples of markup languages include HTML and XML, which are widely used in website design.

Programming languages consist of a set of instructions or code that tell a computer what to do. They provide logic and commands to perform tasks and generate desired outputs. For example, when writing or burning a CD, copying files to a USB drive, or executing software functions, instructions are processed through code that interacts with hardware.

Programming languages are high-level languages that must be converted into machine-level language (binary: 0s and 1s) because computers can only understand machine code. Developers write instructions in a human-readable format, and then a compiler converts the code into machine language. The compiler scans the entire codebase at once and reports any errors. Examples of programming languages include Java, C, C++, and C#, which are widely used for software development and driver programming.

HTML

HyperText Markup Language (HTML) is the primary markup language used to create web pages and structure content that can be displayed in a web browser. It provides the foundation for web development by defining the elements that make up a webpage, such as headings, paragraphs, images, links, tables, and forms. HTML uses a system of tags and attributes to organize and format content. Tags, enclosed within angle brackets (e.g., <h1>, <p>, <img>), define elements, while attributes provide additional information about these elements, such as specifying an image source (src) or setting a hyperlink reference (href). HTML works alongside Cascading Style Sheets (CSS) for styling and JavaScript for interactivity, forming the backbone of modern web development.

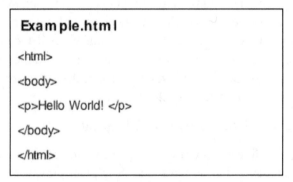

Figure 5-01: Basic HTML Code Structure

Extensible Markup Language (XML)

Extensible Markup Language (XML) is a markup language that defines a structured set of rules for encoding data in a format that is both human-readable and machine-readable. Derived from the Standard Generalized Markup Language (SGML), XML is primarily designed for storing and transporting data rather than displaying it. Unlike HTML, which focuses on presentation, XML carries data without specifying how it should be displayed. This flexibility makes it widely used for data exchange between different systems and applications.

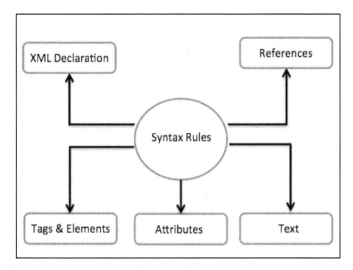

Figure 5-02: XML Syntax Rules

XML has several key characteristics that make it a powerful tool for data storage and exchange:

- **Extensible:** XML allows users to define their custom tags, making it highly flexible and adaptable to various data structures. Unlike predefined markup languages such as HTML, XML is not limited to a fixed set of tags.

- **Carries, but does not present, the data:** XML is purely a data container and does not dictate how the data should be displayed. Unlike HTML, which focuses on formatting and presentation, XML organizes and transports information, allowing different applications to process and display it as needed.

- **A public standard:** XML is an open standard maintained by the World Wide Web Consortium (W3C), ensuring compatibility across different platforms, programming languages, and systems. Its public nature makes it widely adopted for data exchange in various industries.

XML is a preferred choice for data management and communication due to its flexibility and interoperability. It enables seamless data exchange between organizations, applications, and platforms, making it widely used in web services, APIs, and enterprise applications. XML is also useful for database backups, migrations, and synchronization, allowing efficient offloading and reloading of large datasets. Its structured format facilitates customized data storage and handling, making it easy to organize, search, and manipulate information. Additionally, XML integrates with XSLT and CSS to transform raw data into various formats, such as HTML and PDF, ensuring adaptability for different display and processing needs.

Java

Java is a powerful, object-oriented programming language that was developed by Sun Microsystems in 1995 and was later acquired by Oracle Corporation. It is designed with platform independence in mind, following the principle of "Write Once, Run Anywhere" (WORA). This principle ensures that Java applications can be executed on any system equipped with a compatible Java Virtual Machine (JVM), making it an ideal choice for building applications in distributed environments, such as enterprise systems, cloud computing, and network-based platforms. Due to its robustness, reliability, and scalability, Java has been widely adopted by developers worldwide.

One of Java's early features was its ability to create applets, which were small application modules embedded within web pages to provide interactive functionalities. Through these applets, web applications were enhanced with dynamic content and features, such as animations and real-time data processing. However, with the rise of modern web technologies such as JavaScript, HTML5, and WebAssembly, the use of Java applets has declined, and they are no longer widely adopted. Despite this, Java continues to be used extensively in web application development through frameworks such as Spring Boot, Jakarta EE (formerly Java EE), and Apache Struts.

A comprehensive security model is also provided by Java, making it one of the most secure programming languages for application development. A vast set of protocols, mechanisms, tools, APIs, and security algorithms is included to protect the application code from vulnerabilities and attacks. Features such as bytecode verification ensure that strict security guidelines are adhered to before execution, preventing unauthorized operations. Security policies that restrict access to system resources can be defined using the Security Manager and Access Control mechanisms. Additionally, cryptographic libraries are provided through the Java Cryptography Architecture (JCA) to support encryption, hashing, and digital signatures, while Java Secure Socket Extension (JSSE) is used to ensure secure network communication via SSL/TLS. The Java Authentication and Authorization Service (JAAS) provides a framework for authentication and access control, ensuring that sensitive data is accessible only to authorized users.

Overall, Java remains one of the most widely used programming languages due to its platform independence, strong security features, and extensive ecosystem of libraries and frameworks. It continues to be implemented in enterprise applications, banking systems, cloud computing, and mobile development, solidifying its role as a fundamental language in modern computing.

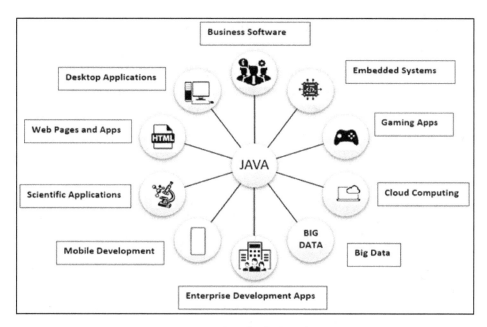

Figure 5-03: Standard Uses of Java

Java is widely recognized for its versatility, making it suitable for various computing environments, including Personal Digital Assistants (PDAs) and smart cards. The ability of the language to operate on resource-constrained devices is derived from its platform independence, security features, and efficient memory management. Due to these attributes, Java has been preferred for embedded systems, financial transactions, and mobile computing.

Some key features of Java are as follows:

Platform Independence

One of the most significant advantages of Java is its platform independence, which is achieved through the Java Virtual Machine (JVM). Java applications are compiled into bytecode, which is executed on any device equipped with a compatible JVM. Because of this feature, Java-based applications can be run seamlessly on PDAs, smart cards, mobile phones, and embedded systems without requiring modifications.

Multithreaded Programming

Support for multithreading is provided by Java, enabling applications to execute multiple tasks concurrently. This capability is particularly beneficial for PDAs and smart card systems, where efficient processing is required for handling user interactions, security checks, and background operations without performance bottlenecks.

Built-in Support for Computer Networks

Java was designed with networking capabilities in mind and built-in libraries such as java.net are provided for communication over TCP/IP, HTTP, and sockets. Because of this, Java is considered ideal for PDAs, which rely on wireless communication, web services, and remote data synchronization.

Automatic Garbage Collection

Automatic memory management (garbage collection) is included in Java to optimize resource usage and prevent memory leaks. This feature is particularly crucial for smart cards and PDAs, which have limited processing power and memory capacity. By ensuring the automatic reclamation of unused memory, the stability and longevity of applications on such constrained devices are enhanced.

Secure Execution of Remote Code

Security has been emphasized in Java's design. Applications running on PDAs and smart cards are often required to process sensitive data, such as financial transactions or identity verification. Strict security mechanisms—including sandboxing, bytecode verification, encryption, and role-based access control—are enforced to prevent unauthorized access and the execution of malicious code from remote sources.

Exception Handling

Java provides a robust exception-handling mechanism, allowing errors to be detected and managed gracefully. This feature is essential in smart cards and PDAs, where unexpected failures—such as invalid user inputs, failed transactions, or connectivity issues—must be handled without causing application crashes.

Portability

The portability of Java allows applications to be executed on various hardware and software environments without requiring modifications. This feature is particularly advantageous for embedded systems, PDAs, and smart cards, where different manufacturers use varying architectures. The use of a standardized execution environment ensures compatibility across different devices.

Java Security Platform

The Java Security Platform is designed to provide a secure execution environment for Java applications by incorporating multiple layers of security mechanisms. It is composed of two primary components: Core Java Security Architecture and Java Cryptography Architecture (JCA). These components are integrated to enforce security policies, protect against unauthorized access, and ensure the confidentiality, integrity, and authenticity of data.

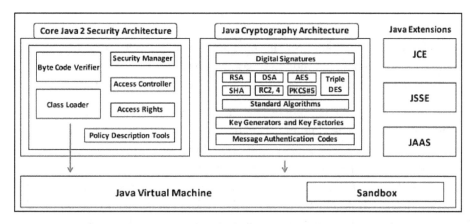

Figure 5-04: Java Security Platform

Core Java Security Architecture

The Core Java Security Architecture, also known as the Java 2 Security Architecture, is responsible for defining and enforcing security policies at runtime. Several critical components are included in this architecture. The Bytecode Verifier is used to ensure that Java bytecode adheres to strict security rules before execution, preventing unauthorized operations from being performed by malicious code. The Class Loader is responsible for managing the dynamic loading of Java classes while ensuring namespace separation and preventing conflicts between trusted and untrusted code. The Security Manager and Access Controller are utilized to restrict access to system resources, such as the file system, network, and memory, based on predefined security policies. These components collectively contribute to the creation of a sandbox environment, where untrusted Java applications, such as applets and downloaded code, are isolated and securely executed.

Java Cryptography Architecture

The Java Cryptography Architecture (JCA) is implemented to provide a robust framework for cryptographic operations, ensuring secure communication and data protection within Java applications. A wide range of cryptographic algorithms, including RSA, DSA, AES, Triple DES, SHA, and RC4, are supported and used for encryption, hashing, and digital signatures. Additionally, mechanisms for secure key generation, key management, and Message Authentication Codes (MACs) are included, allowing security features such as authentication, data integrity verification, and secure data storage to be implemented. The cryptographic framework of Java is designed to be extensible, enabling integration with third-party security providers while maintaining compliance with industry security standards.

.Net

Microsoft .NET is a software programming architecture developed by Microsoft for building internet-enabled and web-based applications. It provides a unified framework for developing web, desktop, cloud, and mobile applications.

.NET consists of several technologies that enable developers to build internet-based distributed systems. The Common Language Runtime (CLR) manages execution, memory, and security, while the .NET Class Library offers prebuilt functionalities for file handling, networking, and cryptography. ASP.NET and ASP.NET Core facilitate web application development, supporting both server and client-side logic. Windows Communication Foundation (WCF) and google Remote Procedure Call (gRPC) enable secure communication between distributed services.

.Net Implementations

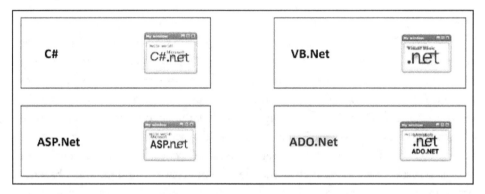

Figure 5-05: .Net Implementations

- **C-Sharp (C#):** A modern, object-oriented programming language designed for building high-performance applications across web, desktop, and cloud environments. It supports asynchronous programming, memory management, and strong type safety.

- **Visual Basic .NET (VB.NET):** A language that simplifies Rapid Application Development (RAD) with a focus on readability and ease of use. It is widely used in enterprise solutions and integrates seamlessly with .NET libraries.

- **ASP.NET:** A web framework for creating dynamic, interactive, and scalable web applications. It supports Model-View-Controller (MVC) architecture, RESTful APIs, and Razor Pages for efficient web development.

- **ADO.NET:** A data access technology that enables applications to interact with databases like SQL Server, MySQL, and Oracle. It provides connected and disconnected data access models for optimized performance in enterprise applications.

.Net Framework Architecture

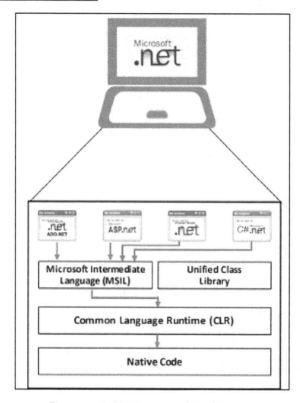

Figure 5-06: .Net Framework Architecture

The .Net Framework Architecture consists of multiple layers that work together to provide a runtime environment for building and executing applications. It is designed to support multiple programming languages and application models, ensuring seamless interoperability and performance.

The key components of the .Net Framework Architecture are as follows:

- **Programming Languages (C#, VB.NET, ASP.NET, ADO.NET):** .NET supports multiple programming languages such as C#, Visual Basic .NET (VB.NET), ASP.NET (for web applications), and ADO.NET (for database access). These languages allow developers to write applications that target different platforms, including desktop, web, and enterprise applications.

- **Microsoft Intermediate Language (MSIL):** Code written in .NET languages is compiled into Microsoft Intermediate Language (MSIL) instead of directly to machine code. This intermediate representation allows portability and security, enabling execution across different operating systems with the .NET runtime.

- **Unified Class Library**: The .NET Class Library provides a comprehensive set of reusable classes and APIs for file handling, database access, web services, cryptography, and more. It offers a standardized way to perform common programming tasks across all .NET applications.

- **Common Language Runtime (CLR):** The CLR is the heart of the .NET Framework, responsible for executing MSIL code. It provides essential services such as memory management (garbage collection), exception handling, security enforcement, and Just-In-Time (JIT) compilation to convert MSIL into native code.

- **Native Code Execution:** At runtime, the CLR translates MSIL into native machine code specific to the host operating system and hardware. This ensures optimized performance and security while executing .NET applications.

C#

C#, known as "C sharp", is a contemporary, object-oriented, and type-safe programming language created by Microsoft within the .NET ecosystem. It is designed to provide a balance between simplicity, productivity, and performance, making it suitable for a wide range of applications, including desktop, web, mobile, and cloud-based solutions.

C# shares a syntax similar to C and C++, making it familiar to programmers with experience in these languages. However, unlike C++, C# includes built-in memory management through garbage collection, reducing the risk of memory leaks and pointer-related errors. It also enforces type safety, preventing unintended type conversions that could lead to runtime errors.

One of C#'s strengths is its combination of Rapid Application Development (RAD) productivity and the power of C++. It offers high-level abstractions that simplify development while still allowing fine-grained control over system resources when needed. Features such as Language Integrated Query (LINQ), asynchronous programming with async/await, and automatic memory management enable rapid development without sacrificing performance.

Additionally, C# is tightly integrated with the .NET Framework and .NET Core, providing access to a vast standard library for networking, data access, cryptography, and user interface development. Its versatility allows developers to build applications for Windows, macOS, and Linux, as well as mobile platforms through frameworks like Xamarin.

Figure 5-07 illustrates two examples that show different ways of writing the C# "Hello World" program.

Example 1	Example 2

// Hello1.cs
 	
public class Hello1
 	
{
 	
public static void Main()
 	
{
 	
System.Console.WriteLine("Hello, World!");
 	
}
 	
}
 	
Output:
Hello, World!
	• To avoid fully qualifying classes throughout a program, use the using directive shown:
	
	// Hello2.cs
	
	using System;
	
	public class Hello2
	
	{
	
	public static void Main()
	
	{
	
	Console.WriteLine("Hello, World!");
	
	}
	
	}
	
	Output:
	Hello, World!

Figure 5-07: Examples of C# Programs

JavaServer Pages (JSP)

JavaServer Pages (JSP), also known as Jakarta Server Pages is a Java-based technology that enables the creation of dynamic and interactive web pages. It is built on top of the Java Servlet API, allowing developers to embed Java code directly within HTML to generate dynamic content. Unlike static HTML pages, JSP pages can process user input, interact with databases, and generate customized web responses, making them ideal for developing web applications.

JSP runs within a server-side component called a JSP container, which is part of a Java-based web server or application server, such as Apache Tomcat, JBoss, or GlassFish. The JSP container translates JSP pages into Java Servlets, which are then compiled and executed to generate dynamic content. This makes JSP similar to other server-side scripting technologies like Active Server Pages (ASP) and PHP, but it has the advantage of leveraging the Java programming language's robustness, portability, and scalability.

JSP Model 2 Architecture

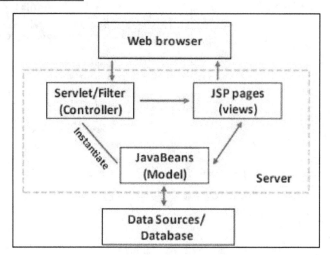

Figure 5-08: JSP Model 2 Architecture

JSP Model 2 Architecture is a design pattern based on the Model-View-Controller (MVC) architecture used to develop Java-based web applications. It divides an application into three separate components:

1. **Model (JavaBeans or Enterprise JavaBeans):** Manages business logic and data, often interacting with databases.

2. **View (JSP Pages):** Handles the presentation layer, displaying data received from the Model.

3. **Controller (Servlets or Filters):** Manages user requests, processes them, and determines which view to display.

This architecture improves maintainability, scalability, and separation of concerns in JSP-based web applications.

Fundamental JSP Tags

JSP provides several types of tags to structure dynamic content and Java code within web pages:

- **Scriptlets (<% … %>):** These allow embedding Java code within JSP pages. The code inside a scriptlet is executed each time the page is requested.

- **Declarations (<%! … %>):** Used to declare class-level variables and methods that can be accessed within the JSP page.

- **Directives (<%@ … %>):** These provide global configuration settings for the JSP page, such as importing Java classes or defining page encoding.

- **Expressions (<%= ... %>):** Used to output values directly into the HTML response, similar to embedding variables in print statements.

Advantages of JSP

- **Supports HTML and Java Code:** JSP allows seamless integration of Java logic within HTML, making it flexible for web development

- **Compatible with Standard Web Development Tools:** JSP can be developed using widely used IDEs such as Eclipse, IntelliJ IDEA, and NetBeans

- **Simplified Tag-Based Syntax:** JSP provides custom tags and JavaServer Faces (JSF) support, reducing the need for extensive Java coding in UI components

Disadvantages of JSP

- **Difficult to Debug:** Since JSP pages are first converted into Servlets before execution, debugging errors can be challenging, requiring a deeper knowledge of Java Servlets

- **Complex Database Connectivity:** Unlike modern frameworks like Spring Boot and Hibernate, connecting JSP with databases requires manual JDBC implementation, making it more complex

- **Servlet Engine Selection Challenges:** Choosing the right JSP container or servlet engine can be difficult due to compatibility and performance considerations across different application servers

Active Server Pages (ASP)

Active Server Pages (ASP) is Microsoft's server-side scripting framework designed for building dynamic and interactive web pages. It enables developers to create web applications that process user inputs, interact with databases, and generate dynamic content in real time. ASP executes on the server before the page is sent to the user's browser, ensuring a seamless and responsive user experience.

ASP supports multiple scripting languages, including VBScript and JScript, allowing developers to embed logic directly within HTML pages. It integrates with databases such as Microsoft SQL Server and Access, simplifying the development of data-driven web applications. ASP provides built-in objects like Request, Response, Session, and Application, which facilitate handling form submissions, managing user sessions, and controlling application-wide settings.

Despite being an older technology, ASP laid the foundation for more advanced frameworks like ASP.NET, which offer improved performance, security, and

scalability. However, classic ASP is still used for legacy applications and remains supported by Internet Information Services (IIS).

Processing of an ASP page

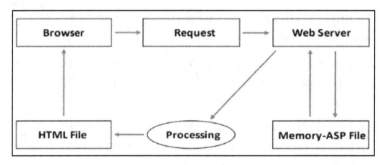

Figure 5-09: Processing of an ASP Page

Figure 5-09 illustrates the request-response process in an ASP-based web application. When a user accesses a web page through a browser, a request is sent to the web server. The server processes the request by retrieving the corresponding ASP file from memory. The ASP script is then executed on the server, generating an HTML response. This processed HTML file is sent back to the browser, where it is displayed to the user. Since ASP runs on the server, only the resulting HTML is sent to the client, ensuring security and enabling dynamic content generation.

Advantages of ASP

- **3-Tier Architecture:** Supports a structured approach by separating the presentation, business logic, and data layers, improving maintainability

- **Multi-Language Compatibility:** Works with around 55 programming languages, including VBScript and JScript, offering flexibility

- **Consistent Programming Model:** Ensures uniformity across applications, making development more efficient

- **Built-in Security:** Provides direct security features such as authentication and authorization mechanisms

Disadvantages of ASP

- **Limited Client-Side Control:** Since ASP runs on the server, it has a restricted ability to manage client-side events dynamically

- **Interpreted and Loosely-Typed:** Lacks strong type-checking, leading to potential runtime errors

- **Mixes HTML and Scripting Code:** Embedding logic within HTML can make code difficult to maintain

- **Limited Debugging Tools:** ASP does not provide advanced debugging capabilities compared to modern frameworks

- **No Real State Management:** Requires additional mechanisms like cookies or session variables to maintain state across requests

Hypertext Preprocessor (PHP)

Hypertext Preprocessor (PHP) is an open-source, server-side scripting language designed for developing dynamic and interactive web applications. It is widely used in web development due to its simplicity, flexibility, and compatibility with various databases and operating systems.

PHP scripts execute on a web server, generating dynamic content before delivering it to the client's browser. It is cross-platform compatible, running on Windows, Linux, and macOS. Additionally, PHP seamlessly integrates with databases like MySQL, PostgreSQL, and SQLite, making it ideal for data-driven applications. One of its key advantages is its ability to be embedded directly within HTML, enabling easy integration with web pages. As an open-source and freely available technology, PHP benefits from a large community that provides support, continuous updates, and enhancements, making it a reliable choice for web developers.

```
<html>
        <head>
                <title>Hello World</title>
        </head>
        <body>
                <?php echo "Hello, world!";?>
        </body>
</html>
```

Figure 5-10: PHP Script to Print "Hello World"

Advantages of PHP

- **Easy to Use:** PHP has a simple and intuitive syntax, making it easy for beginners to learn and use. Its resemblance to C and JavaScript further simplifies adoption for developers familiar with these languages.

- **Fast Performance:** PHP is lightweight and optimized for web applications, ensuring quick execution of scripts. When used with caching mechanisms like OPcache, it significantly improves response times.

- **Open Source and Powerful Library Support:** Being an open-source language, PHP is freely available, with an extensive collection of built-in

functions and third-party libraries for various tasks, such as image processing, PDF generation, and email handling.

- **Stable:** With over two decades of development, PHP has matured into a stable and well-maintained language, ensuring reliability for long-term projects.

- **Supports Both Procedural and Object-Oriented Programming (OOP):** PHP allows developers to write both procedural and OOP code, offering flexibility in programming styles and enabling code reusability through classes and objects.

- **Built-in Database Connection Module:** PHP has native support for database connectivity, allowing seamless integration with databases like MySQL, PostgreSQL, and SQLite without requiring additional configuration.

Disadvantages of PHP

- **Security Concerns:** Being open-source, PHP is more susceptible to security vulnerabilities if not properly maintained. Developers must implement best practices such as input validation, prepared statements, and proper error handling to secure applications.

- **Open Source:** Since PHP is open source, attackers can analyze its source code for potential vulnerabilities. This makes it crucial to keep PHP and its associated libraries up to date.

- **Not Suitable for Large-Scale Applications:** PHP lacks a strict modular structure, making it less efficient for building highly complex enterprise applications. While frameworks like Laravel and Symfony improve scalability, PHP alone is not the best choice for large-scale, distributed applications compared to languages like Java or C#.

Practical Extraction and Report Language (Perl)

Perl is a high-level, general-purpose, interpreted, and cross-platform programming language known for its flexibility and dynamic capabilities. Initially designed for text processing, it has evolved into a widely used tool for web development, system administration, and network programming. Perl is particularly effective for text editing and manipulation, making it a popular choice for scripting and automation tasks.

One of Perl's key strengths is its compatibility with various markup languages, including HTML and XML, allowing seamless integration with web applications. It supports Unicode, ensuring proper handling of multilingual text, and is Y2K-

compliant, making it reliable for date-related operations. Perl accommodates both procedural and object-oriented programming paradigms, providing developers with the flexibility to structure their code according to their needs.

Perl can interface with external C and C++ libraries using XS or SWIG, enhancing its functionality and enabling performance optimizations. Its extensibility, supported by a vast repository of modules available through Comprehensive Perl Archive Network (CPAN), makes it highly adaptable for diverse programming tasks, including image processing, database management, and networking.

Advantages of Perl

- **Powerful Text Handling:** Perl is one of the most powerful languages for text handling and parsing, making it ideal for tasks such as data extraction, report generation, and log analysis.
- **Faster Execution in Development:** Since Perl scripts are interpreted rather than compiled, they execute faster in development environments, reducing the time required for code execution.
- **Simple and Flexible:** The language is simple, easy to learn, and highly flexible, allowing developers to write concise yet powerful scripts.
- **Object-Oriented Support:** Perl supports object-oriented programming, providing structured development capabilities.
- **Web Development and Security:** It is widely used in web development, particularly in payment gateways, where its text-processing efficiency and security features are highly beneficial.

Disadvantages of Perl

- **Limited GUI Support:** Despite its strengths, Perl has minimal Graphical User Interface (GUI) support compared to other modern programming languages, making it less suitable for developing desktop applications.
- **Learning Curve for Regular Expressions:** While Perl excels in handling complex text patterns, mastering its powerful regular expressions and scripting techniques requires significant experience, which may present a learning curve for beginners.

JavaScript

JavaScript is a dynamic, high-level scripting language that plays a crucial role in modern web development. It is supported by all major web browsers, including Google Chrome, Mozilla Firefox, Microsoft Edge, Safari, and Opera, making it one of the most widely used programming languages. JavaScript enables developers to create interactive and engaging web experiences by enhancing webpage design,

validating user input in forms, detecting browser types, and managing cookies for personalized content.

One of the key strengths of JavaScript is its ability to run directly within a web browser without needing additional plugins or installations. This makes it an essential tool for client-side development, where it is used to dynamically manipulate HTML and CSS, handle events, and create smooth animations. Additionally, JavaScript serves for server-side programming with platforms like Node.js, enabling full-stack development.

Furthermore, JavaScript supports modern web technologies, including AJAX for asynchronous data loading, APIs for interacting with external services, and frameworks such as React, Angular, and Vue.js for building sophisticated web applications. Its versatility, ease of use, and widespread adoption make JavaScript an indispensable language in web development.

Advantages of JavaScript

- **Less Server Interaction:** JavaScript executes on the client side, reducing the need for frequent server requests. This improves performance and reduces server load, making applications faster and more efficient.

- **Immediate Feedback for Visitors:** JavaScript allows real-time validation and instant user feedback, such as form validation before submission. This enhances the user experience by reducing unnecessary page reloads.

- **Richer Interfaces:** JavaScript enables the creation of dynamic, visually appealing interfaces with features like animations, sliders, interactive menus, and drag-and-drop functionality. This improves the overall usability and engagement of web applications.

- **Increased Interactivity:** JavaScript enhances web pages by enabling interactive elements such as dropdowns, pop-ups, and real-time updates without requiring a page refresh.

Disadvantages of JavaScript

- **Lacks Multithreading or Multiprocessing Capabilities:** JavaScript is single-threaded by default, meaning it cannot efficiently handle complex computations or tasks that require concurrent processing. This can limit performance in highly intensive applications.

- **Cannot Be Used for Networking Applications:** Unlike languages like Python or Java, JavaScript alone cannot handle low-level networking tasks such as direct file transfers, socket programming, or building standalone

network applications. It relies on additional technologies like WebSockets or server-side JavaScript (e.g., Node.js) to handle networking functionality.

Bash Scripting

Bourne Again Shell (Bash) is a powerful command-line shell and scripting environment that comes pre-installed with most Linux distributions. It is widely used in penetration testing for automating tasks, managing system processes, and executing complex sequences of commands efficiently. Since many security tools and exploits are Linux-based, understanding Bash scripting is essential for penetration testers to streamline their workflow and execute tasks more effectively.

Bash scripting allows penetration testers to automate repetitive tasks such as network scanning, privilege escalation, and log analysis, significantly reducing manual effort. It enables chaining multiple commands, creating loops, and handling conditions, making it ideal for automating attack sequences. For example, scripts can be written to automate brute-force attacks, extract system information, or execute payloads on compromised systems.

Bash provides seamless integration with security tools like Nmap, Metasploit, and Netcat, allowing testers to execute commands efficiently and manipulate outputs for further analysis. Understanding Bash scripting enhances a penetration tester's ability to interact with Linux-based systems, develop custom exploits, and execute reconnaissance and post-exploitation tasks with precision.

Creating Bash File

You can create a Bash script file as shown in Figure 5-11. To do this, open any text editor and create a new text file with the *.sh* extension (e.g., *script.sh*). At the beginning of the file, include the shebang line *#!/bin/bash* to specify that the script should be run in the Bash shell. You can then add your desired commands below it. For example, one script uses the *dig* and *whois* commands to gather IP information, another runs an *nmap* scan on a domain, and another simply prints a message. Once you've written your script, save the file and make it executable using the *chmod +x script.sh* command in the terminal.

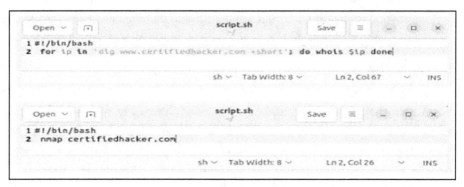

Figure 5-11(a): Bash File Creation

Figure 5-11(b): Bash File Creation

PowerShell

PowerShell is an object-oriented command-line shell and scripting language developed by Microsoft to assist system administrators in configuring systems and automating administrative tasks. Unlike traditional command-line interfaces, PowerShell is built on the .NET Framework Common Language Runtime (CLR), allowing it to handle and manipulate .NET objects instead of just plain text. This makes it a powerful tool for system management, automation, and task scheduling.

One of PowerShell's key features is its set of cmdlets (command-lets)—lightweight commands designed to perform specific functions, such as retrieving system information, managing processes, and configuring network settings. PowerShell provides a consistent syntax and structure for executing commands, making automation scripts more efficient and scalable.

PowerShell can execute four different types of commands:

1. **PowerShell functions:** Custom-defined, reusable blocks of code that perform specific tasks.

2. **Executable programs:** External applications such as ipconfig, ping, or notepad.exe.

3. **Cmdlets:** Built-in PowerShell commands like Get-Process, Set-Service, and Restart-Computer.

4. **PowerShell scripts:** .ps1 script files that combine multiple commands for automation.

With its deep integration into Windows environments, PowerShell enables system administrators to manage Active Directory, configure Windows services, automate security policies, and perform remote management tasks efficiently. It is also extensible through PowerShell modules, making it a versatile tool for IT professionals.

C

C is a procedure-oriented programming language widely used for writing computer programs due to its efficiency, portability, and control over system resources. It provides low-level access to memory while maintaining the flexibility of high-level languages, making it a powerful tool for software development.

One of C's key advantages is that it gives programmers total control over system resources, allowing efficient reading and writing of code across different platforms. This includes applications in scientific computing, operating system development, embedded systems, and microcontroller programming. Due to its lightweight and performance-oriented nature, C is commonly used for developing system-level software, such as compilers, drivers, and real-time operating systems.

C is classified as a middle-level programming language because it combines features of both high-level and low-level languages. It supports abstraction and structured programming like high-level languages while providing direct access to hardware, memory management, and efficient execution, similar to assembly language. This balance makes C an essential language for programmers who require performance, portability, and precise system control.

C is a powerful and versatile programming language that blends low-level and high-level features, making it ideal for system programming and application development. It supports direct hardware manipulation, portability across compilers, and efficient control structures. With bit manipulation capabilities, modular programming, and robust memory management through pointers and dynamic allocation, C ensures performance and flexibility. Additionally, its rich standard library provides functions for string handling, I/O operations, and mathematical computations, making it widely used in various applications.

Figure 5-12 illustrates the basic C program syntax.

```
#include <stdio.h>
int main(void)
{
printf("Example program in C");
return 0;
}
```

Figure 5-12: C Program Syntax

C++

C++ is an Object-Oriented Programming (OOP) language that extends the capabilities of the C language by introducing concepts such as classes and objects, which allow for better abstraction and modular code design. By encapsulating data and functions within objects, C++ enhances code reusability, maintainability, and security, making it widely used in software development.

As a superset of C, C++ retains all the core functionalities of C while adding object-oriented features, including inheritance, encapsulation, and polymorphism. It supports both static and dynamic polymorphism, enabling developers to create flexible and scalable applications. Static polymorphism is achieved through function overloading and templates, allowing multiple functions or classes to share the same name but with different parameters. Dynamic polymorphism, on the other hand, is implemented using virtual functions, enabling runtime method overriding and enhancing extensibility.

C++ is widely used in system programming, game development, high-performance applications, and real-time simulations due to its speed, efficiency, and control over system resources. It also supports both procedural and object-oriented programming paradigms, giving developers the flexibility to structure their code based on project requirements.

C++ offers a rich set of Object-Oriented Programming (OOP) features that improve code organization, reusability, and efficiency. It supports classes, allowing developers to create user-defined data types, and inheritance, enabling one class to acquire the properties of another for better code reuse. Data abstraction hides complex implementation details, focusing only on essential functionalities, while encapsulation ensures data security by bundling data and functions within a single entity. Polymorphism allows a single interface to support multiple implementations, with dynamic binding ensuring function calls are resolved at runtime. Message passing enables communication between objects, while function and operator overloading provide flexibility by allowing multiple definitions with varying parameters. C++ also includes robust error handling through exception

handling (try-catch-throw), stricter type checking, and versatile access control mechanisms, making it a powerful and reliable programming language for various applications.

Figure 5-13 illustrates the basic C++ program syntax.

```
#include <iostream>
using namespace std;

int main()
{
        cout << "Hello World!";
        return 0;
}
```

Figure 5-13: C++ Program Syntax

CGI

Common Gateway Interface (CGI) is a standard protocol that enables web servers to interact with external applications, allowing them to generate dynamic content for web pages. When a user requests a webpage that requires processing, the web server executes a CGI script, which can be written in languages like Python, Perl, or C, to process the request and return the output to the browser. CGI acts as a bridge between the client and the server-side applications, enabling functionalities such as form processing, database interactions, and dynamic content generation. Although CGI was widely used in early web development, it has been largely replaced by more efficient alternatives like FastCGI, PHP, and server-side scripting frameworks due to performance limitations, as CGI spawns a new process for each request, which can be resource-intensive. However, it remains a foundational concept in web server communication.

Figure 5-14 illustrates CGI-based architecture.

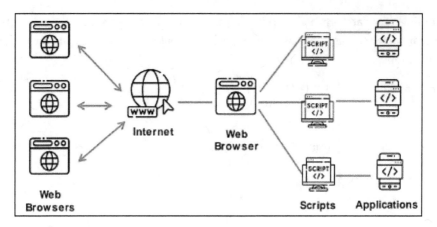

Figure 5-14: CGI-Based Architecture

Common Gateway Interface (CGI) acts as a mediator between web browsers, web servers, and external programs, enabling dynamic content generation. As shown in Figure 5-15, when a user submits a request, such as filling out a form or clicking a button, the web browser sends data to the web server. The server then passes this data to a CGI script or program, which processes the request—such as retrieving database information, performing calculations, or executing other operations. Once the external program generates a response, CGI forwards the output back to the web server, which then delivers it to the user's browser as an HTML page or other content format. This interaction allows web applications to handle user input dynamically, making web pages more interactive. However, due to performance concerns, modern alternatives like FastCGI and server-side scripting frameworks are now more commonly used.

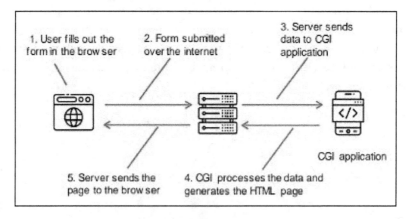

Figure 5-15: CGI Request Processing

Application Development Frameworks and Their Vulnerabilities

Application development frameworks, like J2EE, Ruby on Rails, ColdFusion, and Ajax, simplify web application development but introduce security risks. Common vulnerabilities include remote code execution, XSS, SQL injection, authentication bypass, and DoS attacks. Secure coding, regular updates, and proper configurations help mitigate these threats.

.NET Framework

The .NET Framework is a software development platform designed by Microsoft that provides a comprehensive environment for building and running applications. Its architecture is primarily based on three core components: the Common Language Runtime (CLR), the Framework Class Library (FCL), and Just-In-Time (JIT) compilation technology.

The Common Language Runtime (CLR) is the execution engine that manages code during runtime, providing services such as memory management, security enforcement, exception handling, and garbage collection. It enables developers to write code in multiple languages while ensuring interoperability between them.

The Framework Class Library (FCL) is a vast collection of reusable classes, functions, and APIs that simplify application development by offering built-in support for tasks such as file handling, networking, data access, and user interface design. This library ensures consistency and efficiency across .NET applications.

Just-In-Time (JIT) Compilation enhances performance by compiling intermediate code (MSIL – Microsoft Intermediate Language) into native machine code just before execution. This allows applications to run efficiently across different system architectures.

.NET also supports multi-language development, meaning developers can use languages like C#, VB.NET, and F# within the same application. Additionally, with the introduction of .NET Core and .NET 5+, .NET has become cross-platform, enabling applications to run seamlessly on Windows, Linux, and macOS. This flexibility makes .NET a powerful framework for building modern web, desktop, cloud, and mobile applications.

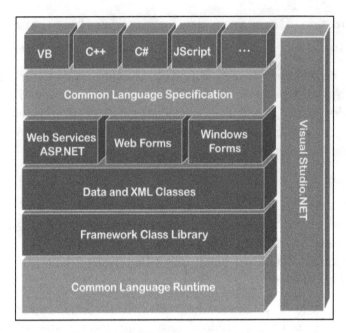

Figure 5-16: .NET Framework Architecture

.NET Framework Vulnerabilities

The .NET Framework, like any other software platform, is susceptible to various security vulnerabilities that can be exploited by attackers if not properly mitigated. Some common vulnerabilities in the .NET Framework include:

- **Remote Code Execution (RCE) Vulnerability:** This critical vulnerability allows an attacker to execute arbitrary code on a target system remotely. It is often exploited through malicious documents, crafted input, or specially designed applications that exploit weaknesses in .NET components. If successful, an attacker can gain unauthorized control over the system, potentially leading to data theft, malware deployment, or further exploitation.

- **Denial-of-Service (DoS) Vulnerability:** Attackers can exploit DoS vulnerabilities in .NET applications by sending maliciously crafted web requests that overload the application, causing service disruption or unavailability. This prevents legitimate users from accessing the service, leading to downtime and potential financial or reputational damage.

- **Feature Bypass Vulnerability:** This vulnerability occurs when an attacker can circumvent security mechanisms, such as Enhanced Security Usage (ESU) tagging, by presenting an invalid or malicious certificate. By bypassing these security checks, attackers can exploit weaknesses in

authentication, encryption, or authorization processes, potentially leading to unauthorized access or privilege escalation.

- **.NET Assembly Tampering (Framework Core Modification):** Attackers may modify the core .NET framework components (DLL files) to alter the application's behavior. This type of attack can introduce malicious code, disable security checks, or modify application logic, leading to data manipulation, unauthorized access, or system compromise. Ensuring the integrity of .NET assemblies through digital signatures and integrity checks is crucial to preventing such attacks.

J2EE Framework

Java 2 Platform, Enterprise Edition (J2EE), now known as Jakarta EE, is a platform-independent environment designed for building and deploying Java-based enterprise applications. It follows a multi-tiered, distributed architecture, enabling scalable and efficient development of web applications and enterprise solutions.

J2EE provides a structured framework for developing modular, reusable, and secure applications. It is built on Java SE (Standard Edition) and extends its capabilities with additional APIs and services tailored for enterprise-level development. The multi-tier architecture consists of the client tier (user interface), web tier (servlets and JSPs handling requests), business tier (EJBs and business logic), and data tier (database and persistence management). This separation ensures better scalability, maintainability, and flexibility.

J2EE supports various enterprise technologies, including Servlets, JavaServer Pages (JSP), Enterprise JavaBeans (EJB), Java Persistence API (JPA), and Java Messaging Service (JMS), allowing developers to create robust web applications, distributed systems, and cloud-based solutions.

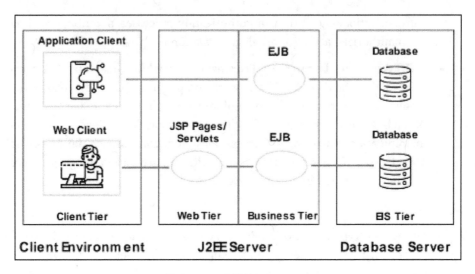

Figure 5-17: J2EE Components

The J2EE architecture consists of multiple tiers, each serving a specific function in enterprise application development:

- **Client Tier (Client Environment):** Includes Application Clients (standalone Java applications) and Web Clients (browsers interacting with JSP/Servlets).

- **Web Tier (J2EE Server):** Handles client requests using JavaServer Pages (JSP) and Servlets for dynamic content generation.

- **Business Tier (J2EE Server):** Contains Enterprise JavaBeans (EJBs) that manage business logic and transactions.

- **Enterprise Information System (EIS) Tier (Database Server):** Stores and retrieves data using relational databases connected through JDBC or ORM frameworks.

J2EE Framework Vulnerabilities

The J2EE framework is a widely used platform for developing enterprise applications, but like any technology, it has vulnerabilities that can be exploited if not properly secured. Below are some notable J2EE security vulnerabilities:

- **Bypassing Cross-Site Scripting (XSS) Protections:** Some J2EE applications fail to properly sanitize input, allowing attackers to bypass XSS filters by using non-canonical encoding techniques, such as overlong Unicode representations or inserting encoded null bytes (%00). This can enable the execution of malicious scripts, leading to session hijacking, data theft, or phishing attacks.

- **Arbitrary Code Execution:** The PointBase 4.6 database component, part of the J2EE 1.4 reference implementation, is vulnerable to SQL injection attacks that allow remote attackers to execute arbitrary system commands. Exploiting this vulnerability can lead to unauthorized access, data modification, and Remote Code Execution (RCE) on the server.

- **Denial-of-Service (DoS) Attacks:** The PointBase database component can be exploited to execute SQL statements that cause excessive resource consumption, leading to service disruption. Attackers can flood the system with malicious queries, overwhelming the server and making the application unavailable to legitimate users.

- **Sensitive Information Disclosure:** Poor security controls in the J2EE reference implementation may expose sensitive data, such as database connection strings, user credentials, or application logs. Attackers can exploit misconfigured access controls or vulnerabilities in the PointBase component to leak critical business information, which can be used for further attacks.

ColdFusion

ColdFusion is a rapid web application development platform that simplifies building dynamic websites and enterprise applications. It is built on Java and runs within the Apache Tomcat J2EE container, leveraging Java's scalability and cross-platform compatibility. ColdFusion uses ColdFusion Markup Language (CFML) to enable fast development with minimal coding. It supports database integration, RESTful APIs, security features, and Java interoperability, making it ideal for high-performance web applications.

ColdFusion Framework Vulnerabilities

Some key security risks associated with ColdFusion are as follows:

- **Directory Traversal:** This vulnerability allows attackers to manipulate file paths and access restricted directories on the server. By using specially crafted requests, an attacker may gain unauthorized access to sensitive files outside the web root.

- **ColdFusion CSRF Vulnerability:** Cross-Site Request Forgery (CSRF) attacks exploit the trust between users and a web application by tricking authenticated users into executing unintended actions, such as changing settings or deleting records, without their consent.

- **Unvalidated Browser Input:** If ColdFusion applications do not properly validate and sanitize user input, they become vulnerable to attacks like

Cross-Site Scripting (XSS) and SQL Injection, allowing attackers to execute malicious scripts or gain unauthorized access to databases.

- **CFFILE, CFFTP, and CFPOP Vulnerability:** ColdFusion provides powerful file-handling and FTP-related functions (CFFILE, CFFTP, CFPOP), but improper implementation can allow attackers to upload malicious files, gain unauthorized access to FTP servers, or exploit email-based vulnerabilities.

- **ColdFusion DoS Attack Vulnerability:** ColdFusion applications may be susceptible to Denial-of-Service (DoS) attacks, where attackers overwhelm the server with a high number of requests, leading to performance degradation or downtime.

Ruby On Rails

Ruby on Rails (RoR) is a server-side web application framework designed to simplify and accelerate the development of web applications. Built using the Ruby programming language, it follows the Model-View-Controller (MVC) architectural pattern, which promotes organized and maintainable code.

Model (ActiveRecord)

The Model layer is responsible for maintaining the relationship between objects and the database. It provides an abstraction layer that allows developers to interact with databases using Ruby code instead of raw SQL queries. ActiveRecord simplifies data manipulation, offering built-in support for validation, associations, and database migrations.

View (ActionView)

The View layer handles the presentation of data to the user. It utilizes template-based systems, similar to Java Server Pages (JSP), Active Server Pages (ASP), and PHP, to render dynamic content efficiently. Views ensure that user interfaces remain separate from the application logic, improving code modularity and maintainability.

Controller (ActionController)

The Controller acts as the intermediary between the Model and the View. It processes incoming requests, retrieves relevant data from the model, and organizes that data for display in the view. The controller directs application logic, ensuring efficient request handling and routing within the framework.

Rails emphasizes convention over configuration, reducing the need for boilerplate code, and follows the Do not Repeat Yourself (DRY) principle, promoting code reusability and maintainability.

Ruby On Rails Framework Vulnerabilities

While Ruby on Rails (RoR) is a powerful and secure framework, it is still susceptible to several vulnerabilities if not properly configured or updated. Here are some common security risks associated with Rails applications:

- **Remote Code Execution (RCE):** Any Ruby on Rails application with the XML parser enabled is susceptible to RCE. Attackers can exploit this to execute arbitrary code, retrieve sensitive data from the database, or take control of the system.

- **Authentication Bypass Vulnerability:** The basic authentication mechanism in Ruby on Rails does not use a constant-time algorithm for credential verification, making it susceptible to timing attacks. Attackers can measure response times to infer valid credentials, potentially bypassing authentication mechanisms.

- **Denial-of-Service (DoS) Attack:** RoR applications can be vulnerable to cache and memory exhaustion attacks. Exploiting wildcard controller routes or improper Multipurpose Internet Mail Extensions (MIME) type cache handling can lead to excessive memory consumption, causing performance degradation or service outages.

- **Directory Traversal Vulnerability:** The Action View component can be exploited to read arbitrary files when an application improperly uses the render method. Attackers can provide .. (dot dot) in the pathname to navigate outside the intended directory and access sensitive files.

- **Cross-Site Scripting (XSS) Vulnerability:** Action View allows attackers to inject malicious web scripts or HTML when improperly handling text marked as "HTML safe." If such unsafe data is used as attribute values in tag handlers, it can lead to session hijacking, credential theft, or phishing attacks.

AJAX

Asynchronous JavaScript and XML (AJAX) frameworks facilitate the development of dynamic web applications by enabling real-time data exchange between the client and the server without requiring a full page reload. These frameworks rely on several web technologies, each playing a crucial role in the implementation of AJAX-based applications:

- **HTML/XHTML, CSS (Presentation):** Defines the structure and styling of the web page, ensuring a visually appealing user interface.

- **Document Object Model (DOM) (Dynamic Display and Interaction):** Allows for real-time updates and interaction with webpage elements without reloading the entire page.

- **JSON, XML (Data Interchange):** Used for exchanging structured data between the client and server, with JSON being widely preferred due to its lightweight nature.

- **XSLT (Data Manipulation):** Transforms and processes XML data to be displayed in a structured format.

- **XMLHttpRequest Object (Asynchronous Communication):** Enables background requests to the server, allowing web applications to send and receive data asynchronously.

- **JavaScript (Integration & Functionality):** Acts as the core scripting language that integrates all AJAX technologies, managing asynchronous calls, handling responses, and updating the webpage dynamically.

AJAX Workflow

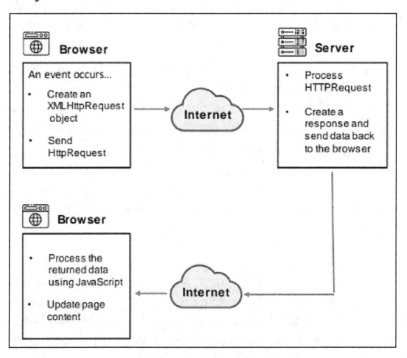

Figure 5-18: AJAX Workflow

Figure 5-18 illustrates the AJAX workflow, demonstrating how a web browser interacts with a server to update content dynamically without requiring a full page reload. When an event occurs in the browser (e.g., a user action), an

XMLHttpRequest object is created and an HTTP request is sent to the server over the internet. The server processes the request, generates a response, and sends the data back to the browser. The browser then processes the returned data using JavaScript and updates the page content accordingly. This process enables seamless, real-time updates and improves user experience.

AJAX Framework Vulnerabilities

AJAX frameworks introduce several security risks due to their dynamic and asynchronous nature. The vulnerabilities primarily arise from increased attack surfaces, browser-based attacks, Cross-Site Scripting (XSS), and data stream manipulations.

- **Increased Attack Surface:** AJAX applications rely on multiple hidden server requests and scattered endpoints, making them more susceptible to security threats. The complexity of handling numerous asynchronous calls increases the risk of unauthorized access, data leaks, and unmonitored security loopholes.

- **Browser-Based Attacks:** The traditional browser security model is inadequate to address AJAX security concerns. Since AJAX depends heavily on JavaScript, it is inherently vulnerable to various browser-based attacks, including malicious script injections, session hijacking, and unauthorized data access.

- **Cross-Site Scripting (XSS):** AJAX applications dynamically build the Document Object Model (DOM), allowing scripts to execute based on untrusted responses. Attackers can inject malicious JavaScript, leading to self-propagating XSS attacks. User-controlled data is present in multiple locations, making it easier for attackers to manipulate and exploit.

- **Data Stream Manipulation (JSON, XML, etc.):** Since AJAX relies on JSON, XML, and other data formats for communication, attackers can inject malicious content into these streams. This includes sending harmful payloads disguised as legitimate requests, resulting in security breaches such as SQL injection and remote code execution.

- **Mashup and Widget Hacks:** Mashups integrate data and services from multiple sources, but they lack strict security boundaries. A mashup XSS attack occurs when malicious code is injected into third-party components, affecting all integrated services. Additionally, third-party widgets inherit the same security privileges as the host site, making them a potential entry point for attackers.

- **Cross-Site Request Forgery (CSRF):** AJAX introduces cross-domain access workarounds that can be exploited to launch Dynamic CSRF attacks. Attackers craft malicious AJAX requests that trigger unauthorized actions on behalf of an authenticated user, leading to data modification, session hijacking, or privilege escalation.

- **XML and JSON-Based Attacks:** Attackers can exploit AJAX's reliance on XML and JSON by injecting harmful payloads, including SQL Injection, XPATH Injection, and JavaScript-based malware. Since GET requests retrieving JSON data often lack proper security validation, they can be leveraged for unauthorized data extraction.

- **Injection Attacks (SQL, XPATH, and SWF Injection):** AJAX-driven applications often process user inputs dynamically, making them susceptible to SQL Injection in backend databases. Similarly, XPATH Injection manipulates XML queries to access or alter sensitive data. Attackers may also inject malicious Shockwave Flash (SWF) files, leading to malware distribution and the exploitation of client-side vulnerabilities.

Different Web Subcomponents

Web subcomponents include the web browser (client), web application server, and database server.

Web Subcomponents

Web applications are structured into three main components: the Web Browser (Client), Web Application Server, and Database Server. Each plays a distinct role in ensuring smooth communication between the user and the backend systems.

Web Browser (Client)

The web browser acts as the front-end interface for users to interact with the web application. It is responsible for:

- **Rendering the UI:** Displays web pages using HTML, CSS, and JavaScript.

- **Handling Presentation Logic:** Controls the look and feel of the application, ensuring a smooth user experience.

- **Validating User Input:** Implements client-side validation (e.g., checking for valid email formats or preventing empty form submissions) before sending data to the server.

Web Application Server

The web application server is responsible for processing user requests, executing business logic, and rendering dynamic content. It acts as the bridge between the client (browser) and the database server. Key functions include:

- **Request Handling:** The server receives HTTP requests and processes them using server-side technologies such as PHP, ASP.NET, Java (J2EE), Python (Django/Flask), or Node.js.

- **Executing Business Logic:** Ensures that all application rules and workflows are executed correctly (e.g., checking user credentials and processing payments).

- **Rendering Output:** Generates dynamic responses (HTML, JSON, or XML) and sends them back to the client.

Database Server

The database server manages data storage, retrieval, and business logic execution for the web application. It ensures that application data remains secure and accessible.

- **Data Storage**: Stores structured and unstructured data in databases like MySQL, PostgreSQL, Microsoft SQL Server, or MongoDB.

- **Data Retrieval:** Executes SQL queries to fetch data requested by the web application.

- **Business Logic in Stored Procedures:** Some business logic can be implemented at the database level using stored procedures and triggers to optimize processing.

Thick and Thin Clients

In a Client/Server architecture, the client is an application that runs on a user's machine and interacts with a server to request services, process data, or retrieve resources. The client handles user interactions and sends requests to the server, which processes these requests and returns responses. This model enables centralized management, better resource sharing, and improved scalability.

Clients can be categorized into thin clients, which rely heavily on the server for processing; thick clients, which handle most processing locally while still communicating with the server; and smart clients, which can work offline and sync with the server when needed. Servers, on the other hand, can host databases, web applications, or APIs, ensuring that clients receive the necessary data or services.

This architecture is widely used in web applications, cloud services, and enterprise networks.

Thin Clients

A thin client is a lightweight application that relies on a server for most of its processing power and data storage. It has minimal computing capabilities and primarily serves as an interface to interact with a remote system. Since most of the logic and computation occur on the server, thin clients require a continuous network connection to function efficiently. Examples include web browsers accessing cloud applications like Google Docs or virtual desktop environments where the server handles all heavy processing.

Thick Clients

A thick client (also known as a fat client) is an application that performs most of its processing locally on the client machine while still communicating with a server for specific functions like data storage or synchronization. Unlike thin clients, thick clients do not require a constant network connection to operate and can function independently to a certain extent. These applications offer better performance and richer functionality since they leverage local hardware resources. Examples include desktop applications like Microsoft Office, Adobe Photoshop, or standalone email clients like Outlook.

Smart Clients

A smart client combines the best of both thin and thick client architectures by allowing applications to function offline while still syncing with a server when needed. These clients dynamically determine whether to process tasks locally or delegate them to a server based on network availability and workload distribution. Smart clients are commonly used in mobile applications and hybrid cloud-based software that can operate seamlessly across online and offline environments. Examples include Microsoft OneDrive, Evernote, and modern Progressive Web Applications (PWAs) that function even with limited connectivity.

Applet

An applet is a small Java program embedded within a webpage that runs inside a web browser on the client side. It leverages the entire Java API, providing access to a wide range of functionalities while maintaining security within a controlled execution environment (sandbox). Since applets execute on the client side, they offer fast performance by reducing server-side processing. Additionally, they are platform-independent, running seamlessly on various operating systems such as Linux, Windows, and Mac. However, applets have significant drawbacks, primarily requiring a browser plugin to function, which has led to compatibility and security

concerns. Due to declining browser support for Java plugins, applets have largely been replaced by modern web technologies like JavaScript, HTML5, and WebAssembly.

Life Cycle of an Applet

The life cycle of an applet consists of several key methods that manage its execution within a web browser.

1. **init:** Used to initialize the applet.

2. **start:** Automatically called after the browser calls the init method.

3. **stop:** Automatically called on exiting from the applet page.

4. **destroy:** Called when the browser shuts down normally.

5. **paint:** Invoked immediately after the start() method.

Advantages of Applet

- **Platform Independence:** It runs on any operating system with a Java-compatible browser

- **Security:** It executes in a restricted environment (sandbox) to prevent unauthorized access

- **Lightweight:** It uses minimal system resources compared to standalone applications

- **Fast Execution:** It is compiled into bytecode, making it efficient for web-based applications

- **Rich User Interface:** It supports graphics, animations, and interactive UI components

- **Automatic Updates:** IT always loads the latest version from the server, eliminating manual updates

- **Seamless Integration:** It can be embedded in web pages for interactive content

Disadvantages of Applet

- **Requires Java Plugin:** Needs a Java-enabled browser, which is not always available

- **Security Restrictions:** Runs in a sandbox, limiting access to system resources

- **Slow Loading:** Takes time to initialize, especially for large applets

- **Compatibility Issues:** May not work in modern browsers that have dropped Java support
- **Limited Functionality:** Restricted access to local files and system resources
- **Deprecated Technology:** Java applets are outdated and replaced by modern web technologies like JavaScript and HTML5
- **Higher Resource Consumption:** Can be resource-intensive compared to native web applications

Servlet

A servlet is a Java-based server-side program that processes client requests and generates dynamic web content. It is robust, scalable, and platform-independent, inheriting all the features of Java while enabling seamless communication between the client and the server. Servlets are widely used for creating dynamic web pages and are portable across different web servers. However, they come with challenges such as complex design, reduced performance in large applications, and difficulty in implementing intricate business logic. Additionally, servlets require a Java Runtime Environment (JRE) on the server, adding to deployment overhead.

Life Cycle of a Servlet

The lifecycle of a Servlet ensures efficient request handling and resource management in Java-based web applications.

1. **init():** Initialize the servlet instance.
2. **service():** Invoked after every service request.
3. **destroy():** Remove the servlet out of service.

Advantages of Servlet

- **Platform Independent:** Runs on any server with a Java-enabled environment
- **Efficient and Scalable:** Handles multiple requests using multithreading, improving performance
- **Secure:** Provides built-in security features like authentication and encryption
- **Robust and Stable:** Eliminates memory leaks and crashes common in CGI-based applications
- **Lightweight:** Requires fewer resources compared to traditional CGI processes

- **Easy to Maintain:** Supports reusability and modular development
- **Supports Session Management:** Allows tracking of user interactions efficiently

Disadvanatages of Servlet

- **Complex Development:** Writing and managing servlets can be more complicated than scripting languages
- **Hard to Debug:** Debugging servlets in a server environment can be challenging
- **Requires Java Knowledge:** Developers must be proficient in Java and its libraries
- **No Built-in Presentation Support:** Unlike JSP, servlets require explicit HTML handling
- **Server Dependency:** Needs a servlet container or web server to execute

ActiveX

ActiveX is a Microsoft technology based on the Component Object Model (COM) that enables seamless integration and reuse of software components across applications, including web browsers and Windows programs. It supports component-based development and allows ActiveX components to run anywhere using COM/DCOM.

Key Features of ActiveX include:

- **ActiveX Controls:** Reusable software components that can be visually manipulated using GUI tools
- **Java VM & Java Components:** Java-based components can function as ActiveX elements for better compatibility
- **ActiveX Scripting:** Supports various scripting languages like VBScript, JScript, Perl, PowerScript, and Tcl/Tk, allowing automation and integration within Windows applications

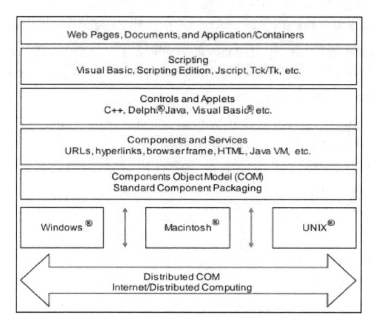

Figure 5-19: Elements of ActiveX

Flash Application

Flash technology was widely used to enhance web applications by enabling animations, interactive content, desktop and mobile applications, games, and video players. It allowed developers to create rich and engaging user experiences with cross-browser compatibility. However, Flash had several limitations, including slow loading times, the need for a dedicated Flash Player, and poor Search Engine Optimization (SEO).

Developers utilized tools like Adobe Animate, Flash Builder, FlashDevelop, and Apache Flex for designing applications while viewing required Flash Player, Adobe AIR, or third-party players like Scaleform. ActionScript was the primary programming language used for Flash development.

Despite its popularity, Flash was eventually phased out due to security vulnerabilities, performance issues, and the rise of modern web technologies like HTML5, JavaScript, and WebGL, which offer a more secure and efficient alternative for interactive web applications.

Advantages of Flash Application

- **Rich Multimedia Support:** Enables animations, videos, and interactive content

- **Cross-Platform Compatibility:** Runs on multiple operating systems with a Flash plugin

- **Smooth Animations:** Provides high-quality vector graphics and animations

- **Browser Integration:** Works across different browsers with minimal compatibility issues

- **Interactive User Experience:** Supports games, interactive media, and dynamic content

- **Lightweight Files:** Uses vector graphics, reducing file size and improving load times

Disadvanatages of Flash Application

- **Requires Flash Plugin:** Needs Adobe Flash Player, which is no longer supported on modern browsers

- **Security Vulnerabilities:** Frequently targeted by hackers due to its outdated architecture

- **Performance Issues:** High CPU usage can slow down devices

- **Limited Mobile Support:** Not supported on iOS and many Android devices

- **Depreciated Technology:** Phased out in favor of HTML5, CSS3, and JavaScript

- **SEO Limitations:** Flash content is difficult for search engines to index

Domain 06: Database Connectivity

Introduction

In modern computing environments, applications need to efficiently store, retrieve, and manage data. Database connectivity plays a crucial role in enabling seamless communication between applications and databases, ensuring smooth data exchange and integration. This domain explores key concepts related to database connectivity, focusing on two important aspects: Network File System (NFS) and database connectivity.

Network File System (NFS)

Network File System (NFS)

The Network File System (NFS) is a distributed file system protocol that enables users to read, write, store, and access files across multiple devices connected through a network. It is designed to function seamlessly on all IP-based networks and utilizes both TCP and UDP for efficient data access and delivery.

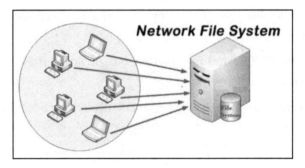

Figure 6-068: Network File System

When it comes to security, NFS provides two key levels of protection.

Host-Level Security

Host-level security in NFS restricts access to specific devices within the network. This is typically enforced through IP-based access control, where only authorized hosts are allowed to mount and interact with NFS shares. Administrators can define access permissions using configuration files like /etc/exports, ensuring that only trusted systems can connect.

File-Level Security

File-level security in NFS controls how users interact with files and directories. It is managed through standard Unix file permissions, Access Control Lists (ACLs), and authentication mechanisms like Kerberos. These controls ensure that only

authorized users can read, write, or execute files, providing an additional layer of protection beyond host-level restrictions.

NFS Access Control Mechanisms

NFS enforces access controls using several methods.

Root Squashing

Root squashing, limits superuser privileges by mapping the root user's UID to an anonymous user within the NFS RPC credential structure. This prevents unauthorized root-level access to shared files.

nosuid

nosuid disables SUID and SGID permissions on the filesystem, preventing user identity executables from running in an NFS-mounted directory.

noexec

noexec enhances security by blocking the execution of binary files from a specific partition, restricting unauthorized execution of programs.

Database Connectivity

SQL Server

Web applications use different methods to connect with an SQL Server database. These methods include Connection Strings, OLE DB Files (.UDL), and ODBC Data Source Names (DSN).

Connection String

A connection string is a string of parameters used by an application to establish a direct connection with an SQL Server database. It typically contains details like the server address, database name, authentication credentials, and other configuration settings. Connection strings are commonly used in web applications and programming languages like C#, Java, and Python to interact with databases efficiently.

OLE DB File (.UDL)

Object Linking and Embedding Database (OLE DB) files, commonly known as Universal Data Link (.UDL) files, provide a way to store and manage database connection settings outside of the application code. These files contain configuration details that allow applications to connect with SQL Server using OLE DB providers. UDL files help simplify database connections and make it easier to modify settings without changing the application's source code.

ODBC Data Source Name (DSN)

Open Database Connectivity (ODBC) Data Source Name (DSN) is another method used to connect web applications with SQL Server. It requires configuring a DSN on the operating system, which acts as a reference for database connection settings. Applications can use the DSN to establish a connection without specifying details like the server address and authentication credentials in the code, enhancing security and manageability.

To successfully connect to an SQL Server database, it is essential to know the server name, security information, database name, data interface or API to use, and connection procedure. By choosing the appropriate connection method, web applications can efficiently communicate with the database while maintaining flexibility and security.

Authentication Modes

When connecting to an SQL Server, web applications can use either Windows authentication mode or mixed mode.

Windows Authentication Mode

Windows authentication mode is the default security mode for SQL Server. In this approach, Windows users and groups are trusted to log in without requiring separate credentials. Authentication is handled using a series of encrypted messages, ensuring a secure exchange between the user and the server. This mode is typically used when both the database and the application are hosted on the same server, leveraging Windows-based authentication for seamless and secure access.

Mixed Mode

Mixed mode allows user credentials to be maintained within the SQL Server itself. This mode is useful when users connect from different, non-trusted domains, such as in web applications accessible over the internet. By supporting both SQL Server authentication and Windows authentication, mixed mode provides flexibility in managing database access for a broader range of users.

Data Controls Used for SQL Server Connection

To establish a connection with an SQL Server database, applications must provide specific details. These controls determine the efficiency and compatibility of the connection method.

Data Controls

Data controls provide an interface for applications to interact with databases. They primarily use Data Access Object (DAO), which is designed for JET databases,

making it an efficient choice for handling local databases. However, DAO does not natively support direct connections to SQL Server, requiring alternative approaches for connectivity.

ADO Data Controls

ActiveX Data Objects (ADO) provide a flexible way to connect applications with SQL Server. ADO Data Controls allow developers to set connection properties using a connection string and define the RecordSource property to retrieve and manipulate data from the database. This method simplifies database interaction without requiring complex programming.

ADO Data Controls (DSN)

This approach leverages ADO with a Data Source Name (DSN) to establish a connection with SQL Server. By using DSN, applications can avoid hardcoding connection parameters in the code, improving security and manageability. The DSN configuration allows applications to set connection strings dynamically and utilize the RecordSource property for querying data.

ADO Data Controls (UDL)

Universal Data Link (UDL) files provide another method for configuring ADO connections. ADO Data Controls using UDL rely on a separate configuration file that stores connection details, making it easier to manage database connections externally. Like DSN-based connections, this approach allows developers to modify connection settings without altering application code, improving flexibility and maintainability.

ADO Programmatically

This method involves manually writing code to handle database connections using ADO. Developers declare an ADO connection object, set the connection string, open the connection, and instantiate a recordset to fetch and manipulate data. This approach provides greater control over database interactions, allowing for customized data retrieval and transaction handling.

Others

Apart from ADO, other methods exist for connecting to SQL Server. Remote Data Objects (RDO) function similarly to ADO and support both DSN-based and DSN-less connections. ODBCDirect uses RDO for direct database connectivity, bypassing the JET Engine for improved performance. Additionally, Open Database Connectivity (ODBC) provides an API to access databases, offering a standardized way to interact with SQL Server and other database systems.

MS ACCESS

To establish a web application connection with an underlying MS Access database, certain components and steps are required to ensure smooth communication between the application and the database. The connection relies on an OLE DB connection manager and an appropriate data provider to facilitate data exchange.

OLE DB Connection Manager

The OLE DB Connection Manager is responsible for establishing and managing connections between applications and databases, including MS Access. It facilitates communication by providing an interface for executing queries, retrieving data, and managing transactions.

Data Provider

A Data Provider acts as a bridge between the application and the database, enabling the application to interact with data sources. In the case of MS Access, the OLE DB Data Provider ensures smooth data retrieval, updates, and execution of commands while maintaining compatibility with the database system.

Steps to connect to MS Access from the application

To connect an application to an MS Access database, the process begins with creating an OLE DB connection manager. Once the connection manager is set up, the next step is selecting the appropriate data provider. This can be done using tools like the Connection Managers area in SSIS Designer or the SQL Server Import and Export Wizard, which simplify the integration process and streamline data transfer between the web application and the database.

This approach ensures that applications can efficiently interact with MS Access while leveraging the capabilities of SQL Server Integration Services (SSIS) for data management.

MySQL

When connecting a web application to a MySQL database, MySQL provides a variety of connectors that enable seamless integration with different platforms. These connectors include standards-based drivers such as JDBC, ODBC, .NET, and native C, allowing applications to establish a reliable connection with the database.

MySQL Pluggable Authentication

MySQL supports Pluggable Authentication, which allows authentication mechanisms to be added dynamically without modifying the core MySQL server. This feature enhances security and flexibility by enabling external authentication providers and proxy users.

External Authentication

External authentication allows clients to connect to MySQL using third-party authentication methods such as Pluggable Authentication Modules (PAM), Windows login IDs, Lightweight Directory Access Protocol (LDAP), or Kerberos. This eliminates the need for MySQL to store user credentials, reducing security risks while integrating seamlessly with existing authentication frameworks.

Proxy Users

Proxy users enable role-based authentication in MySQL by allowing an externally authenticated user to act on behalf of another user. This allows the authenticated user to assume the second user's identity and privileges, making it useful for role delegation, application user management, and secure access control.

External User

An external user is a MySQL user who is authenticated using an external authentication provider. This user can be granted the ability to act as a proxy user, allowing them to impersonate another MySQL user and inherit their permissions and privileges.

Second User

The second user, also known as the proxied user, is the actual MySQL user whose identity and privileges are assumed by the proxy user. This mechanism is useful in cases where applications require temporary or controlled access to MySQL resources without sharing direct credentials.

The following are MySQL standards-based drivers used to build and connect a database from applications: JDBC, ODBC, .NET, and native C.

Developed by MySQL

- ADO.NET Driver for MySQL (ConneC API for MySQL (mysqlclient)ctor/NET)
- ODBC Driver for MySQL (Connector/ODBC)
- JDBC Driver for MySQL (Connector/J)
- C++ Driver for MySQL (Connector/C++)
- C Driver for MySQL (Connector/C)
- C API for MySQL (mysqlclient)

Developed by Community

- ADO.NET Driver for MySQL (ConneC API for MySQL (mysqlclient)ctor/NET)
- Perl Driver for MySQL (DBD::mysql)
- Ruby Driver for MySQL (ruby-mysql)
- C++ Wrapper for MySQL C API (MySQL++)

ORACLE

Oracle provides various drivers that enable web applications to connect to its databases. These drivers facilitate seamless integration between applications and Oracle databases across different platforms and programming environments.

List of Oracle Drivers to Connect to Web Applications

1. Oracle ODBC Driver

The Oracle ODBC Driver allows ODBC-based applications to connect to Oracle databases. It supports multiple operating systems, including:

- Microsoft Windows
- Linux
- Solaris
- IBM Advanced Interactive eXecutive (AIX)

This driver is commonly used for applications that require SQL-based access to Oracle databases.

2. Oracle Data Provider for .NET (ODP.NET)

ODP.NET enables ADO.NET applications to connect and interact with Oracle databases. It provides efficient data access for .NET-based applications.

There are two types of ODP.NET Managed Drivers:

- **ODP.NET:** A fully managed driver designed for enhanced performance
- **Unmanaged Driver:** Allows direct interaction with Oracle's native libraries for additional flexibility

3. Oracle JDBC Driver for Java

The Oracle JDBC Driver enables Java applications to establish connections with Oracle databases. It is commonly used in Java-based enterprise applications that require efficient database interaction.

4. Oracle OCI8 (Oracle Call Interface 8)

OCI8 is an Oracle PHP extension that allows PHP applications to connect to Oracle databases. It provides high-performance connectivity and supports advanced Oracle database features like connection pooling and caching.

Domain 07: Information Security

Introduction

Information security protects sensitive data, systems, and networks from unauthorized access, use, disclosure, disruption, modification, or destruction. Organizations implement security measures to safeguard their assets against cyber threats, data breaches, and compliance risks.

This domain explores key aspects of information security, starting with different security controls that help prevent, detect, and respond to threats. It also covers network segmentation, a crucial strategy for limiting unauthorized access and containing security incidents. Governance principles play a vital role in establishing security policies, ensuring compliance, and managing risks effectively. Finally, asset management ensures organizations track and protect their valuable resources, reducing vulnerabilities and improving overall security posture.

By understanding these concepts, organizations can build a strong security framework to protect their data, infrastructure, and operations.

Information Security Controls

Information Security Management Program

An Information Security Management Program (ISMP) consists of structured initiatives designed to help businesses operate with minimized security risks. It integrates all organizational and operational processes, ensuring that every participant plays a role in maintaining and enhancing information security. This program provides a systematic approach to identifying, assessing, and mitigating security threats, ultimately safeguarding sensitive information and maintaining business continuity.

An essential component of this program is the Information Security Management Framework, which combines well-defined policies, processes, procedures, standards, and guidelines. This framework establishes the required level of information security by providing a structured methodology for managing security risks, ensuring compliance with regulatory requirements, and promoting a culture of security awareness within the organization.

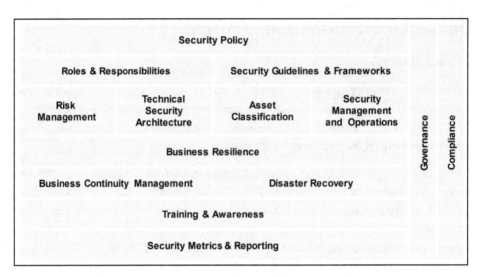

Figure 07-069: Information Security Management Program

Enterprise Information Security Architecture (EISA)

Enterprise Information Security Architecture (EISA) is a structured framework comprising requirements, processes, principles, and models that define the structure and behavior of an organization's information systems. It provides a strategic approach to managing security risks by aligning security initiatives with business objectives.

The primary goals of EISA include enabling real-time monitoring and detection of network behaviors to address both internal and external security risks. It enhances an organization's ability to detect and recover from security breaches while prioritizing resources and monitoring various threats effectively. Additionally, EISA contributes to cost efficiency by integrating security measures into incident response, disaster recovery, event correlation, and other security provisions. It also aids in analyzing essential IT procedures, ensuring the IT department functions efficiently while identifying critical assets. Furthermore, EISA supports risk assessment efforts by facilitating collaboration between IT staff and security teams to safeguard an organization's IT infrastructure.

Information Security Controls

Information Security Controls are measures and safeguards implemented to protect data, systems, and networks from unauthorized access, breaches, or cyber threats. These controls help ensure the Confidentiality, Integrity, and Availability (CIA) of information by preventing, detecting, and responding to security incidents. Controls can be classified into three main types as shown in Figure 07-02:

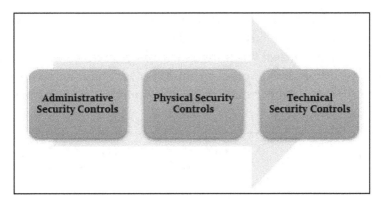

Figure 07-070: Types of Information Security Controls

Administrative Security Controls

Administrative Security Controls are management-implemented measures designed to regulate access and ensure the overall security of an organization. These controls focus on establishing policies, procedures, and guidelines to protect sensitive information and maintain compliance with security standards. By enforcing administrative controls, organizations can mitigate risks, enhance security awareness, and create a structured approach to information protection.

Key examples of administrative security controls include:

- Adherence to regulatory framework compliance, ensuring that the organization meets industry standards and legal requirements
- Establishing a comprehensive information security policy helps define security expectations and guidelines for employees
- Employee monitoring and supervision play a crucial role in detecting suspicious activities and ensuring compliance with security protocols
- Information classification categorizes data based on sensitivity levels, enabling organizations to implement appropriate security measures
- The separation of duties principle prevents conflicts of interest by dividing critical tasks among multiple employees
- The principle of least privilege restricts user access to only the necessary resources required for their roles, minimizing security risks
- Security awareness and training programs educate employees about potential threats and best practices, fostering a culture of security within the organization

Regulatory Frameworks Compliance

Regulatory Framework Compliance involves a collaborative effort between governments and private organizations to establish and enforce security standards. These frameworks are designed to encourage voluntary improvements in cybersecurity by providing guidelines that help organizations protect sensitive data,

manage risks, and maintain operational resilience. Compliance with these regulations ensures that businesses follow best practices, adhere to legal requirements, and enhance their overall security posture. By aligning with established regulatory frameworks, organizations can mitigate security threats, build customer trust, and demonstrate their commitment to data protection and cybersecurity.

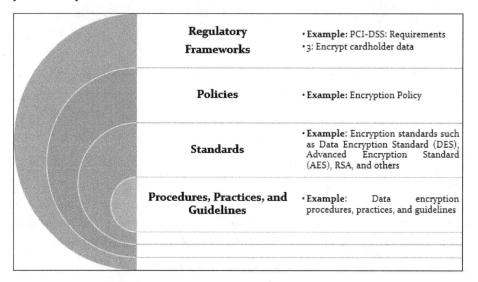

Regulatory Frameworks	• **Example:** PCI-DSS: Requirements • 3: Encrypt cardholder data
Policies	• **Example:** Encryption Policy
Standards	• **Example:** Encryption standards such as Data Encryption Standard (DES), Advanced Encryption Standard (AES), RSA, and others
Procedures, Practices, and Guidelines	• **Example:** Data encryption procedures, practices, and guidelines

Figure 07-071: Role of Regulatory Frameworks Compliance in an Organization's Administrative Security

Information Security Policies

Information Security Policies serve as the foundation of an organization's security infrastructure. These policies define the essential security requirements and rules necessary to safeguard information systems from potential threats. By establishing a structured approach to security, organizations can ensure consistency in managing and protecting sensitive data while minimizing vulnerabilities.

The primary goals of security policies include:

1. **Maintain an outline for the management and administration of network security**: Security policies help in establishing a structured approach to managing and administering network security. They define roles, responsibilities, and procedures to ensure that security measures are consistently applied throughout the organization.

2. **Protect an organization's computing resources**: Ensuring the security of computing resources is crucial for business continuity. Security policies safeguard systems, networks, and data from unauthorized access, malware, and other cyber threats that could compromise the organization's infrastructure.

3. **Eliminate legal liabilities arising from employees or third parties**: Security policies help organizations mitigate legal risks by setting clear guidelines on acceptable use, compliance with regulations, and data protection. This reduces the chances of facing legal consequences due to security breaches or policy violations.

4. **Prevent waste of the company's computing resources**: Security policies also ensure that computing resources are utilized efficiently. By preventing misuse or unnecessary consumption of resources, organizations can optimize system performance and reduce operational costs.

5. **Prevent unauthorized modifications of data**: Unauthorized data modifications can lead to integrity issues, data loss, or security breaches. Security policies enforce access controls and change management procedures to prevent unauthorized alterations to critical information.

6. **Reduce risks caused by illegal use of system resources**: Organizations must prevent the illegal use of system resources, such as unauthorized software installations, data theft, or hacking attempts. Security policies help in detecting, preventing, and addressing such risks effectively.

7. **Differentiate the users' access rights**: Not all users require the same level of access to systems and data. Security policies define Role-Based Access Controls (RBAC) to ensure that employees only have access to the information and systems necessary for their job roles.

8. **Protect confidential, proprietary information from theft, misuse, and unauthorized disclosure**: Confidential and proprietary information is a valuable asset for any organization. Security policies ensure data protection measures such as encryption, access restrictions, and monitoring to prevent theft, misuse, or unauthorized exposure of sensitive information.

These goals collectively strengthen an organization's security framework and help in maintaining a secure and compliant IT environment.

Types of Security Policies

Types of security policies define the level of access and control applied to an organization's system resources. These policies vary in their approach to security, ranging from highly permissive to extremely restrictive, depending on the organization's risk tolerance and security requirements.

Promiscuous Policy

A promiscuous policy imposes no restrictions on system resource usage, allowing unrestricted access. This approach is generally not recommended as it leaves the organization vulnerable to security threats.

Permissive Policy

A permissive policy starts with an open approach, blocking only known dangerous services, attacks, and behaviors. To remain effective, it must be regularly updated to address emerging threats and vulnerabilities.

Prudent Policy

A prudent policy prioritizes maximum security while allowing essential but potentially risky activities. It follows a restrictive approach by blocking all services and enabling only those deemed safe and necessary. Additionally, all activities are logged for monitoring and auditing purposes.

Paranoid Policy

A paranoid policy enforces the highest level of security by forbidding all activities. Internet access is either highly restricted or entirely prohibited, ensuring no external threats can compromise the system. This approach is typically used in environments that require extreme security measures, such as classified government networks or highly sensitive corporate systems.

Examples of Security Policies

Security policies are essential guidelines that define how an organization manages, protects, and controls access to its IT resources. Different types of security policies serve various aspects of security management.

Access Control Policy

An access control policy specifies the resources that need protection and the rules governing access to them. It ensures that only authorized users can interact with critical assets.

Remote-Access Policy

A remote-access policy defines who is permitted to access the organization's network remotely, the access medium they can use, and the security controls required to protect remote connections.

Firewall-Management Policy

A firewall-management policy focuses on the management, monitoring, and access control of an organization's firewalls. It ensures that firewalls are properly configured to prevent unauthorized access while allowing legitimate traffic.

Network-Connection Policy

A network-connection policy establishes guidelines for installing new resources on the network, approving the installation of new devices, documenting network modifications, and performing other administrative tasks to maintain a secure network environment.

Password Policy

A password policy provides instructions for using strong passwords to protect an organization's resources. It includes rules on password complexity, expiration, and storage to prevent unauthorized access.

User-Account Policy

A user-account policy defines the process of creating user accounts, assigning account authority, and specifying the rights and responsibilities of users. It helps in managing user access securely.

Information-Protection Policy

An information-protection policy determines the sensitivity levels of information, specifies who may access it, outlines how data should be stored and transmitted, and sets guidelines for securely deleting information from storage media.

Special-Access Policy

A special-access policy establishes the terms and conditions for granting special access privileges to system resources. This policy ensures that special access is only provided when necessary and under strict controls.

Email-Security Policy

An email-security policy governs the proper use of corporate email systems. It includes guidelines on email security, phishing protection, and restrictions on unauthorized email usage to prevent data breaches.

Acceptable-Use Policy

An acceptable-use policy defines the acceptable use of system resources within the organization. It ensures that employees use company assets responsibly and in compliance with security protocols.

These security policies collectively contribute to an organization's cybersecurity framework by ensuring data protection, preventing unauthorized access, and maintaining compliance with regulatory standards.

Privacy Policies at the Workplace

Employers have access to employees' personal information, which may be confidential and something they wish to keep private. To ensure proper handling of such information, workplaces must follow essential privacy rules.

It is important to inform employees about what information is collected, why it is being collected, and how it will be used. Employers must also keep employees' personal information accurate, complete, and up-to-date to maintain its integrity.

The collection of information should be limited and gathered only through fair and lawful means. Employees should also have access to their personal information to review and ensure its correctness.

Organizations must inform employees about the potential collection, use, and disclosure of personal information to ensure transparency. Furthermore, employers are responsible for keeping employees' personal information secure to prevent unauthorized access or misuse.

> **Note:** Employee privacy rules in workplaces may vary from country to country.

Steps to Create and Implement Security Policies

Developing strong security policies is essential for protecting an organization's assets and ensuring compliance with security standards.

1. Perform a Risk Assessment

The first step in creating security policies is conducting a thorough risk assessment. This process helps identify potential risks and vulnerabilities that could threaten the organization's assets. By understanding these risks, organizations can develop policies that effectively mitigate security threats.

2. Refer to Standard Guidelines

Learning from standard security guidelines and best practices followed by other organizations is essential. Adopting industry-recognized frameworks ensures that policies are comprehensive, effective, and aligned with regulatory requirements.

3. Involve Senior Management and Staff

Security policies should not be developed in isolation. Involving senior management and other employees ensures that policies are practical, relevant, and

enforceable across different levels of the organization. Their input can also help in achieving better compliance and acceptance.

4. Define and Enforce Clear Penalties

Policies must include well-defined penalties for non-compliance. Clear consequences help reinforce accountability and ensure that employees take security measures seriously. Enforcing these penalties consistently strengthens the overall security culture within the organization.

5. Make the Final Version Accessible

Once the security policy is finalized, it should be made readily available to all employees. Ensuring accessibility allows staff members to review and understand their responsibilities, reducing the chances of accidental security breaches.

6. Ensure Staff Reads, Signs, and Understands the Policy

Every employee must acknowledge the policy by reading, signing, and confirming their understanding of its contents. This step ensures that all staff members are aware of security expectations and their role in protecting organizational assets.

7. Deploy Tools to Enforce Policies

Implementing security policies requires the right tools and technologies. Organizations should deploy automated enforcement mechanisms, such as access controls, monitoring tools, and compliance tracking systems, to ensure adherence to security measures.

8. Train Employees on Security Policies

Employee training is crucial for effective policy implementation. Regular security awareness sessions educate staff on best practices, potential threats, and their responsibilities, helping to minimize security risks.

9. Regularly Review and Update Policies

Security policies must evolve to keep up with changing threats and business needs. Conducting periodic reviews and updates ensures that the policies remain relevant and effective in addressing new security challenges.

These steps, when followed diligently, help in building a strong security framework, ensuring compliance, and safeguarding organizational data.

HR or Legal Implications of Security Policy Enforcement

HR Implications of Security Policy Enforcement

The HR department plays a crucial role in ensuring employees are aware of security policies. It is responsible for making employees aware of security policies and

training them on best practices outlined in the policy. Additionally, HR collaborates with management to monitor policy implementation and address any violations or concerns related to compliance. This ensures that employees adhere to security policies while also fostering a culture of security awareness within the organization.

Legal Implications of Security Policy Enforcement

Security policies must be developed in consultation with legal experts to ensure compliance with local laws and regulations. Organizations must carefully enforce policies to avoid violating users' rights. Failure to comply with legal requirements can lead to lawsuits and reputational damage. Therefore, enterprises must ensure that security enforcement aligns with the legal framework to protect both the organization and its employees.

Security Awareness and Training

Employees are one of the primary assets of an organization, but they can also be part of the organization's attack surface. To mitigate risks, organizations must provide formal security awareness training when hiring employees and periodically thereafter. This training helps employees understand how to defend themselves and the organization against threats, follow security policies and IT procedures, identify the appropriate personnel to contact in case of a security issue, classify data correctly, and protect the organization's physical and informational assets.

Additionally, organizations must conduct security awareness training to comply with regulatory frameworks. Various methods can be used to train employees, including classroom-style training, online courses, roundtable discussions, security awareness websites, hints and reminders, short films, and seminars. These approaches help reinforce security best practices and ensure employees stay informed about potential risks.

Security Policy

Security policy training ensures that employees understand how to perform their duties while complying with security policies. Organizations should train new employees before granting full network access or, alternatively, restrict their access until training is complete.

Advantages of Security Policy Training:

- Ensures effective implementation of security policies
- Creates awareness of compliance requirements
- Strengthens overall network security

Employee Awareness and Training

Physical Security

Proper training is essential to educate employees on physical security measures. Increasing awareness helps prevent breaches, protect hardware, and safeguard sensitive data.

Key Aspects of Physical Security Training

1. Strategies to Minimize Security Breaches: Employees should follow security protocols like badge authentication, restricted access, and device locking to prevent unauthorized access. Awareness of threats such as tailgating and social engineering is crucial.

2. Identifying Elements That Are Prone to Hardware Theft: High-risk items like laptops, storage drives, and mobile devices should be secured using locks, proper storage, and vigilance in shared spaces.

3. Assessing Risks When Handling Sensitive Data: Employees must classify, encrypt, and securely dispose of sensitive data while ensuring safe transmission and storage practices.

4. Ensuring Physical Security at the Workplace: Access control, surveillance, clean desk policies, and emergency response training help maintain a secure workplace.

Social Engineering

Employees should be trained to recognize and counteract social engineering tactics used by cybercriminals to manipulate individuals into divulging sensitive information as outlined in Table 07-01.

Area of Risk	Attack Technique	Train Employee or Help Desk on
Phone	Impersonation	• Not providing any confidential information
Dumpsters	Dumpster Diving	• Not throwing sensitive documents in the thrash • Shredding document before throwing out • Erasing magnetic data before throwing out
Email	Phishing or Malicious Attachments	• Differentiating between legitimate emails and a targeted phishing email • Not downloading malicious attachments

Data Classification

Organizations should train employees to distinguish between different levels of information sensitivity and understand how to handle data accordingly.

Area of Risk	Attack Technique	Train Employee or Help Desk on
Office	Stealing sensitive information	How to classify and mark document-based classification levels and keep sensitive document in a secure place

Table 07-014: Employee Awareness and Training Guidelines for Data Classification

Typical Information Classification Levels:

- **Top Secret (TS):** Highest level of security; unauthorized disclosure could cause severe damage
- **Secret:** Information that requires protection against significant threats
- **Confidential:** Sensitive data that could harm the organization if exposed
- **Restricted:** Limited access due to potential risks of misuse
- **Official:** Internal use only; not for public distribution
- **Unclassified:** Publicly available information
- **Clearance:** Access granted based on an individual's authorization level
- **Compartmented Information:** Data segmented into specific categories, restricting access even among those with clearance

Security labels help enforce these classifications by marking information assets and controlling access based on clearance levels. Organizations implement these labels to ensure proper data protection and compliance.

Separation of Duties (SoD) and Principle of Least Privileges (POLP)

Separation of Duties (SoD)

Separation of Duties (SoD) is a security principle that ensures no single individual has complete control over all critical security functions. By distributing responsibilities among multiple employees, organizations can prevent conflicts of interest and reduce risks such as security breaches, information theft, and unauthorized access. SoD is particularly effective in minimizing insider threats, as certain security breaches require collusion between multiple parties. Additionally, regulatory frameworks like GDPR emphasize the need for clear role definitions and responsibilities within security teams to prevent unauthorized actions.

Principle of Least Privileges (POLP)

The Principle of Least Privileges (POLP) operates on the idea that employees should be granted only the minimum level of access required to perform their job functions. By restricting excessive permissions, organizations can limit insider threats and reduce the potential impact of security breaches. POLP also contributes to system stability, as it prevents unauthorized or accidental modifications to critical systems. Furthermore, by enforcing strict access controls, organizations can strengthen overall security, ensuring that sensitive data and vital infrastructure remain protected from both internal and external threats.

Physical Security

Physical security serves as the first layer of protection in any organization. It focuses on safeguarding organizational assets from both environmental and man-made threats. Ensuring robust physical security measures helps organizations prevent unauthorized access, data theft, and potential damage to critical infrastructure.

Importance of Physical Security

Physical security is crucial for multiple reasons:

- It prevents unauthorized access to system resources, ensuring only authorized personnel can interact with critical infrastructure.
- It helps prevent tampering or stealing of data from computer systems, reducing the risk of cyber and physical breaches.
- It safeguards against espionage, sabotage, damage, and theft, protecting sensitive business information.
- It ensures the safety of personnel and helps prevent social engineering attacks, which exploit human interactions to gain access to systems and data.

Physical Security Threats

Organizations face various physical security threats, categorized into environmental and man-made risks:

- **Environmental Threats:** These include natural disasters such as floods, earthquakes, fires, and dust, which can damage infrastructure and disrupt operations.
- **Man-Made Threats:** These threats result from human actions and include terrorism, wars, explosions, dumpster diving (data scavenging), theft, and vandalism, all of which can compromise an organization's security.

By implementing strong physical security measures, organizations can mitigate these risks and ensure a safer working environment for both personnel and assets.

Physical Security Controls

Physical security controls are essential for preventing unauthorized access to physical devices some examples include:

- Locks secure doors and restrict access to authorized personnel
- Fences create physical barriers to deter intrusions
- Badge systems authenticate and track individuals entering a restricted area
- Security guards provide human surveillance and respond to potential threats
- Mantrap doors control access by allowing only one person at a time through a secured space
- Biometric systems use unique biological traits like fingerprints or retina scans for identification
- Lighting enhances visibility and deters unauthorized activities
- Motion detectors identify movement and trigger alerts for suspicious activity
- Closed-Circuit TVs (CCTVs) provide continuous monitoring and recording of security-sensitive areas
- Alarms notify security personnel of unauthorized access or breaches

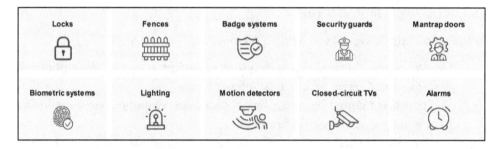

Figure 07-04: Examples of Physical Access Controls

Types of Physical Security Controls

Physical security controls play a crucial role in safeguarding assets by preventing, detecting, deterring, recovering from, or compensating for security breaches.

Preventive Controls

Preventive controls are the first line of defense, designed to prevent security violations by enforcing strict access control mechanisms. These include physical barriers such as door locks, security guards, and surveillance checkpoints that restrict unauthorized access and ensure a secure environment.

Detective Controls

Detective controls are responsible for identifying security breaches and recording any intrusion attempts, allowing for timely responses. These controls rely on motion detectors, alarm systems, sensors, and video surveillance to continuously monitor and alert security teams about potential threats.

Deterrent Controls

Deterrent controls work by discouraging attackers before they attempt a breach, often through visual warnings like security signs, posted policies, or even the presence of surveillance cameras, which create a perception of high risk for intruders.

Recovery Controls

Recovery controls are implemented to restore information and systems to their original state after a security violation, minimizing downtime and ensuring business continuity. These include well-structured disaster recovery plans, business continuity strategies, and reliable backup systems that help organizations quickly recover from disruptions.

Compensating Controls

Compensating controls serve as alternative measures when the primary security controls fail or cannot be applied. These include hot sites, backup power systems, and redundant security mechanisms that ensure operations continue smoothly even in the face of unexpected failures. Together, these security controls provide a layered defense strategy to protect physical assets from unauthorized access, damage, or disruptions.

Categories of Physical Security Controls

Physical security controls are essential for protecting an organization's assets, including personnel, infrastructure, and sensitive information. These controls help prevent unauthorized access, theft, and damage caused by physical threats. The Table 07-03 outlines different categories of physical security measures that organizations can implement to ensure a secure environment.

Category	Security Measures
Premises and company surroundings	Fences, gates, walls, guards, alarms, CCTV cameras, intruder systems, panic buttons, burglar alarms, windows and door locks, deadlocks, and other methods.
Reception area	Lock up important files and documents. Lock equipment when not in use.
Server and workstation area	Lock the systems when not in use, disable or avoid having removable media and DVD-ROM drives, CCTV cameras, and workstation layout design.

Other equipment such as fax, modem, and removable media	Lock fax machines when not in use, file received faxes properly, disable modems' auto-answer mode, do not place removable media in public places, and physically destroy corrupted removable media.
Access control	Separate work areas, implement biometric access controls (fingerprinting, retinal scanning, iris scanning, vein structure recognition, facial recognition, voice recognition), entry cards, man traps, faculty sign-in procedures, identification badges, and other means.
Computer equipment maintenance	Appoint a person to look after computer equipment maintenance.
Wiretapping	Routinely inspect all wires carrying data, protect the wires using shielded cables, and never leave any wires exposed.
Environmental control	Humidity and air conditioning, HVAC, fire suppression, EMI shielding, and hot and cold aisles.

Table 07-015: Physical and Technical Security Measures

Technical Security Controls

A collection of security measures implemented to safeguard data and systems from unauthorized access, ensuring confidentiality, integrity, and availability.

Examples of Technical Security Controls

- **Access Control:** Restricts user access to systems and data based on predefined policies
- **Authentication:** Verifies user identity through passwords, biometrics, or multi-factor authentication
- **Authorization:** Determines the level of access granted to authenticated users
- **Auditing:** Tracks and records system activities to detect and investigate security incidents
- **Security Protocols:** Establish encrypted communication and secure data transmission (e.g., TLS, SSL, IPsec)
- **Network Security Devices:** Includes firewalls, intrusion detection/prevention systems, and VPNs to safeguard networks

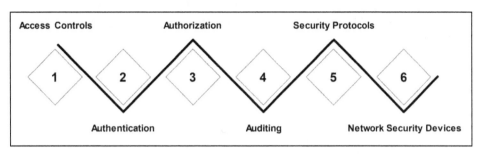

Figure 07-05: Examples of Technical Security Controls

Access Control

Access control is the selective restriction of access to a system, network resource, or physical location. It safeguards information assets by determining who can and cannot access them. This process involves four key components: user identification, authentication, authorization, and accountability.

In access control terminology:

- **Subject:** Refers to a user or process requesting access to a resource
- **Object:** Represents the resource being accessed, such as a file or hardware device
- **Reference monitor:** Enforces security policies by verifying access control rules and ensuring compliance with restrictions
- **Operation:** Signifies the specific action a subject performs on an object, such as reading, writing, or executing a file

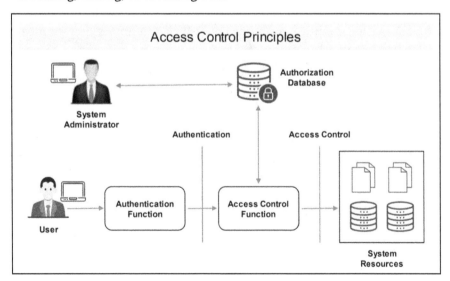

Figure 07-06: Access Control Principles

Types of Access Controls

There are several types of access control mechanisms used to regulate and restrict access to information and resources.

Discretionary Access Control (DAC)

Discretionary Access Control (DAC) allows users who have been granted access to decide how to protect the information and determine the level of sharing. Access to files is restricted based on user identity and group membership.

Mandatory Access Control (MAC)

Mandatory Access Control (MAC) does not allow end users to decide who can access information or transfer their privileges to others, preventing unauthorized access from being circumvented.

Role-Based Access Control (RBAC)

Role-Based Access Control (RBAC) assigns users access to systems, files, and fields based on their roles rather than granting individual permissions. This simplifies the assignment of privileges and ensures users have the necessary access to perform their duties efficiently.

Identity and Access Management (IAM)

Identity and Access Management (IAM) is a comprehensive framework that includes users, procedures, and software solutions to manage digital identities and control access to an organization's resources. It ensures that the right users gain access to the right information at the right time, enhancing security and operational efficiency. IAM services are categorized into four key components: Authentication, which verifies user identities; Authorization, which determines user permissions; User Management, which handles user accounts and access policies; and Enterprise Directory Services, which serve as a central repository for managing user identities across the organization.

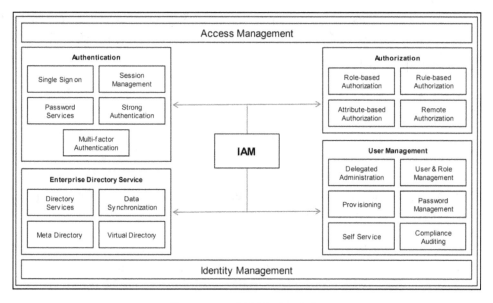

Figure 07-07: IAM Framework

User Identification, Authentication, Authorization, and Accounting

Identification

Identification is the process of verifying that an individual holds a valid identity within a system. It involves using unique identifiers such as usernames, account numbers, or other forms of identifying data to establish a user's presence in a network or application.

Authentication

Authentication follows identification by validating the authenticity of the provided identity. This is achieved through credentials such as passwords, PINs, biometrics, or multi-factor authentication, ensuring that the user is genuinely who they claim to be before granting access.

Authorization

Authorization determines the level of access a user has within a system. It enforces security policies by specifying what actions a user can perform on resources. For example, a user may be permitted to read a file but may not have permission to modify or delete it, ensuring data integrity and security.

Accounting

Accounting involves tracking and recording user activities on a network. It logs details such as who accessed the system, when they did so, and how they interacted

with resources. This process helps in monitoring user behavior, detecting unauthorized actions, and maintaining compliance with security policies.

Types of Authentication

Password Authentication

Password authentication is a common authentication method that uses a combination of a username and password to verify a user's identity. The entered password is checked against a stored database, granting access if it matches. However, this method is vulnerable to attacks such as brute force and dictionary attacks, making it necessary to use strong passwords and additional security measures.

Two-factor Authentication

Two-Factor Authentication (2FA) enhances security by requiring two different authentication factors out of three possible categories: knowledge (something the user knows), possession (something the user has), and inherence (something the user is). Common combinations include a password with a smart card or token, a password with biometrics, or a password with a One-Time Password (OTP). Among these, biometrics is considered the most secure factor as it is difficult to forge. Common biometric authentication methods include fingerprints, palm patterns, voice and face recognition, iris scanning, keyboard dynamics, and signature analysis.

Biometrics

Biometric authentication uses an individual's unique physical characteristics for identification and authentication.

Various biometric identification techniques include:

- Fingerprint recognition, which analyzes the ridges and furrows of a fingertip
- Vein structure recognition, which examines the thickness and positioning of veins
- Retinal scanning, which assesses the blood vessel layer at the back of the eye
- Face recognition, which analyzes facial feature patterns
- Iris scanning, which examines the colored part of the eye
- Voice recognition, which identifies an individual's vocal patterns. These techniques provide high security and are difficult to replicate

Smart Card Authentication

Smart card authentication utilizes a small computer chip embedded in a card to store personal authentication information securely. Users must insert their smart card into a reader and enter a Personal Identification Number (PIN) to complete

the authentication process. This method is based on cryptographic techniques and offers stronger security compared to traditional password authentication.

Single Sign-On (SSO)

Single Sign-On (SSO) allows users to authenticate once and gain access to multiple systems or applications without the need to re-enter their credentials. This improves user convenience by eliminating the need to remember multiple passwords and reduces the time spent entering login details. Additionally, SSO decreases network traffic to the authentication server and enhances overall system efficiency by requiring users to authenticate only once across multiple platforms.

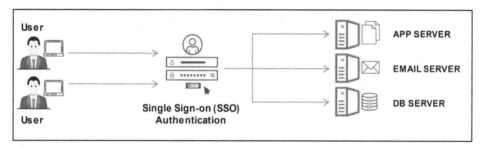

Figure 07-08: SSO Authentication

Types of Authorization

Authorization is the process of controlling an individual's access to information and resources within a system. It determines what actions a user can perform on a specific resource. For example, a user may have permission to read a file but not overwrite or delete it. Authorization ensures that users can access only the resources they are permitted to, thereby enhancing security and preventing unauthorized modifications.

Centralized Authorization

Centralized authorization is a system where a single centralized authorization unit controls access to network resources and applications. It maintains a unified database that stores authorization details, simplifying access management. This approach is cost-effective and easy to implement, as all authorization decisions are made from a single point, ensuring consistency and reducing administrative overhead.

Decentralized Authorization

Decentralized authorization allows each network resource to manage its own authorization independently, providing more flexibility but requiring additional administrative efforts. This approach is useful in distributed environments where different departments or systems need to enforce their own access policies.

Implicit Authorization

Implicit authorization allows users to access a requested resource on behalf of others. The access request first passes through a primary resource, which then grants access to the final resource. This method is commonly used in systems where delegation of access is required, such as service accounts or applications acting on behalf of users.

Explicit Authorization

Explicit authorization, in contrast to implicit authorization, requires a separate authorization process for each requested resource. It explicitly defines access permissions for each object, ensuring that authorization is granted only when specific conditions are met. This approach provides stricter security control and is often used in highly sensitive systems where precise access management is necessary.

Accounting

Accounting is a method of tracking user actions on a network to ensure security and accountability. It records details such as who accessed the network, when they accessed it, and how they interacted with its resources. By maintaining logs of user activities, accounting helps identify both authorized and unauthorized actions, ensuring compliance with security policies.

The collected accounting data is valuable for various purposes, including trend analysis, detecting potential data breaches, and conducting forensic investigations in case of security incidents. Organizations use this data to monitor network usage, improve security measures, and ensure that users adhere to access policies.

Network Segmentation Concepts

Network Segmentation

Network Segmentation is the practice of dividing a network into smaller, isolated segments to enhance security and performance. Unlike traditional flat networks, where all resources such as servers and workstations exist on the same network, segmentation separates different systems and applications, limiting access between them. In a flat network, if an attacker breaches the perimeter defense, they can easily navigate through the entire network. However, in a segmented network, systems or applications that do not need to interact are placed in separate segments, preventing unauthorized access to other parts of the network even if an attacker gains entry.

The key security benefits of network segmentation include improved security, as attackers are restricted from moving laterally; better access control, ensuring only

authorized users can reach specific resources; enhanced monitoring, making it easier to track network activity; improved performance, as traffic is better managed within smaller network segments; and better containment, which helps isolate security incidents and minimize their impact on the entire network.

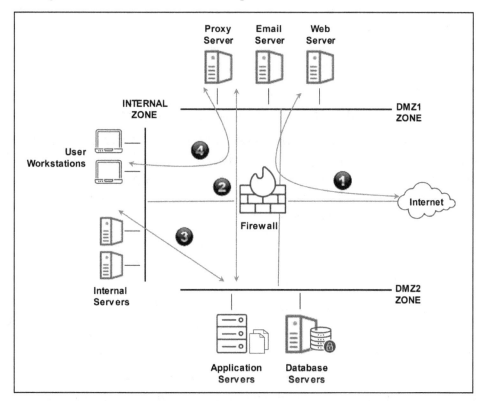

Figure 07-09: Network Segmentation

Network Security Zoning

Network Security Zoning is a mechanism that enables organizations to create a secure network environment by defining different security levels for various zones within their internet and intranet networks. This approach allows for effective monitoring and control of both inbound and outbound traffic, ensuring that sensitive areas of the network remain protected while still allowing necessary communication between different zones.

Examples of Network Security Zones include:

- **Internet Zone:** An uncontrolled zone outside the organization's security boundaries, where no security measures are enforced by the company.
- **Internet DMZ:** A controlled zone that acts as a buffer between internal networks and the public internet, often used for hosting public-facing services.

- **Production Network Zone:** A highly restricted zone that strictly limits direct access from uncontrolled networks to protect sensitive business applications and data.
- **Intranet Zone:** A controlled zone within the organization with moderate security restrictions, typically used for internal communication and resource sharing.
- **Management Network Zone:** A highly secure zone with strict access control policies, ensuring only authorized personnel can manage critical network resources.

Network Segmentation Example: Demilitarized Zone (DMZ)

A Demilitarized Zone (DMZ) is a specialized subnetwork that acts as an additional security layer between an organization's private network (such as a LAN) and an external public network (such as the internet). The primary purpose of a DMZ is to enhance security by isolating external-facing services from the internal network, reducing the risk of unauthorized access.

The DMZ typically contains servers that need to be accessed from external networks, such as:

- Web servers for hosting websites and applications
- Email servers to handle external email communication
- DNS servers for domain name resolution services

DMZ Configurations

- Both internal and external networks can connect to the DMZ
- Hosts within the DMZ can establish connections with external networks
- Hosts in the DMZ cannot directly connect to internal networks, ensuring an additional security barrier to protect sensitive internal resources

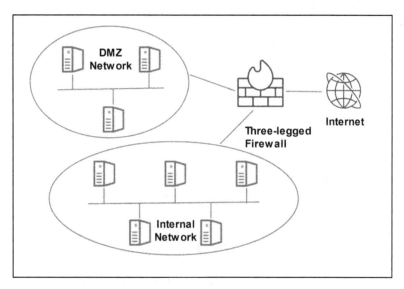

Figure 07-10: Demilitarized Zone (DMZ)

Secure Network Administration Principles

Network Virtualization (NV)

Network Virtualization (NV) is the process of consolidating all available network resources and enabling network administrators to allocate these resources efficiently among users through a single administrative unit. This is achieved by dividing the network bandwidth into independent channels, which can be dynamically assigned or reassigned to specific servers or devices in real-time.

Network virtualization enhances flexibility and efficiency, allowing users to access shared network resources such as files, folders, computers, printers, hard drives, and other assets from their devices. By virtualizing the network infrastructure, organizations can improve resource utilization, streamline management, and enhance security by isolating different network segments as needed.

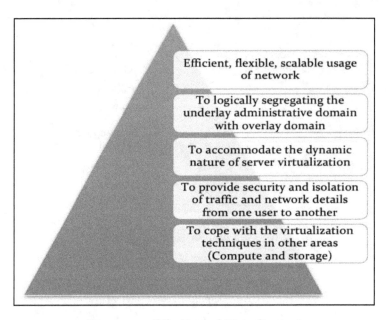

Figure 07-72: Why Network Virtualization?

Virtual Networks

Virtual networks are the outcome of network virtualization, allowing multiple isolated networks to operate over the same physical infrastructure. These networks enable efficient resource allocation, improved security, and simplified management.

Virtual networking is facilitated through specialized software, which can be deployed either externally, outside a virtual server, or internally, within a virtual server. The choice of placement depends on the size and type of the virtualization platform. By leveraging virtual networks, organizations can enhance flexibility, optimize network performance, and implement better security controls.

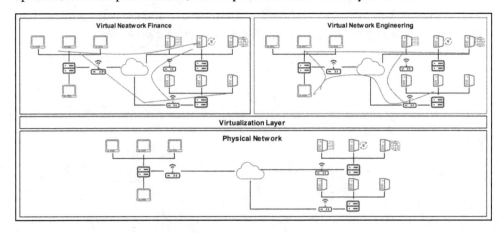

Figure 07-12: Virtual Networks

VLANs

Virtual Local Area Networks (VLANs) are logical groupings of workstations, servers, and network devices that function as if they are on a single, isolated LAN, regardless of their physical location. VLANs help in segmenting network traffic, reducing congestion, and enhancing security by restricting communication between different groups of devices.

The primary purpose of VLANs is to simplify network management while improving security and traffic control. By isolating network segments, VLANs prevent unauthorized access and ensure efficient data flow within an organization's infrastructure.

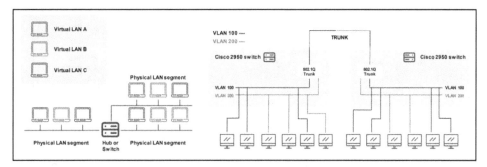

Figure 07-13: VLANs

Security Governance Principles

Corporate Governance Activities

Corporate governance encompasses a framework of rules and practices established by a board of directors to ensure accountability, fairness, and transparency in an organization's relationships with its stakeholders. It plays a crucial role in maintaining ethical business conduct, regulatory compliance, and strategic oversight.

The key areas of corporate governance include:

1. **IT Governance:** Focuses on aligning IT strategies with business objectives, ensuring optimal use of technology resources, managing IT risks, and maintaining regulatory compliance in digital operations.

2. **Information Security Governance:** Establishes policies and controls to protect an organization's sensitive data, ensuring confidentiality, integrity, and availability of information while mitigating cybersecurity threats.

3. **Financial Governance:** Involves financial planning, risk management, compliance with financial regulations, and maintaining transparency in financial reporting to support the organization's long-term stability.

4. **Project Governance:** Ensures that projects align with corporate objectives, are executed efficiently, and adhere to organizational policies, budgets, and risk management strategies.

By implementing strong governance practices in these areas, organizations can enhance operational efficiency, reduce risks, and foster trust among stakeholders.

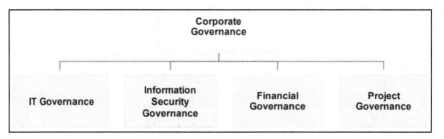

Figure 07-14: Key Areas of Corporate Governance

Critical Areas for Corporate Governance Effectiveness

For an organization to maintain strong governance, effectiveness in the following areas is essential:

1. **Risk Oversight:** Ensures that potential risks, including financial, operational, and cybersecurity threats, are proactively identified, assessed, and managed to protect the organization's assets and reputation.

2. **Enterprise Architecture:** Establishes a structured framework to align IT infrastructure and business strategy, optimizing processes, technology, and resource utilization for long-term success.

3. **Asset Management:** Involves tracking, maintaining, and optimizing physical and digital assets to ensure they deliver maximum value while complying with regulatory and financial requirements.

4. **Change Management:** Provides a structured approach for transitioning individuals, teams, and processes to new strategies, systems, or technologies while minimizing disruptions and ensuring stakeholder alignment.

5. **Business Continuity Management:** Develops and implements plans to ensure that essential operations continue during and after unexpected disruptions, such as cyberattacks, natural disasters, or system failures.

Effective governance in these areas strengthens an organization's resilience, ensures compliance, and enhances overall operational efficiency.

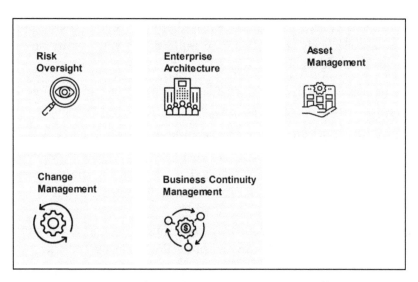

Figure 07-73: Critical Areas for Corporate Governance Effectiveness

Information Security Governance Activities

Information security governance activities are an essential subset of corporate governance that define the structure and order of security-related practices within an organization. These activities ensure that information security and risk management strategies are effectively implemented, aligning with business objectives and regulatory requirements. A strong governance framework helps in establishing policies, controls, and procedures to protect sensitive data and mitigate security risks. Moreover, these activities require active participation from the Board of Directors or the highest level of leadership to drive a culture of security, ensuring that cybersecurity measures are integrated into the organization's overall strategic direction.

The National Association of Corporate Directors (NACD) highlights four essential practices for effective information security governance.

- First, organizations must prioritize information security by ensuring it is a key agenda item for the Board of Directors. This establishes a strong foundation for security-driven decision-making at the highest level.
- Second, it is crucial to identify information security leaders, hold them accountable for their roles, and provide them with the necessary support to implement security measures effectively.
- Third, organizations should regularly review and approve the corporation's information security policies to ensure their effectiveness and alignment with business objectives and regulatory requirements.
- Lastly, assigning information security responsibilities to a dedicated key committee with adequate support ensures continuous oversight and

enforcement of security policies across the organization. These governance activities collectively strengthen an organization's cybersecurity posture and risk management framework.

Information security governance activities are carried out across three distinct areas: program management, security engineering, and security operations.

- Program management focuses on establishing security policies, frameworks, and strategies to align with organizational goals and regulatory requirements.
- Security engineering involves designing, developing, and implementing security controls, ensuring that systems and applications are built with security best practices in mind.
- Security operations is responsible for monitoring, detecting, and responding to security threats, ensuring continuous protection against cyber risks.

Together, these areas form a comprehensive approach to managing and safeguarding an organization's information assets.

Figure 07-74: Key Areas for Information Security Governance Activities

Program Management

Program management plays a crucial role in information security governance by overseeing and coordinating various security-related activities to align with organizational goals. One of its key responsibilities is the development and maintenance of formal documentation, which includes security policies, procedures, and frameworks that provide clear guidelines for securing information assets. Additionally, education, training, and awareness initiatives are essential components, ensuring that employees and stakeholders understand security best practices, threats, and compliance requirements.

Another vital aspect of program management is the Information Security Steering Committee, which serves as a governing body to guide strategic security decisions, assess risks, and ensure that security measures align with business objectives. Lastly, metrics and reporting are integral to measuring the effectiveness of security initiatives. By tracking Key Performance Indicators (KPIs) and analyzing security

trends, organizations can make data-driven decisions to enhance their security posture.

Security Engineering

Security engineering is a structured approach to defining an organization's protection strategy, ensuring that security is embedded at every stage of its operations. It involves integrating security principles into the design, development, and deployment of software, systems, solutions, and controls. By proactively incorporating security measures, organizations can build resilient infrastructures that safeguard critical assets from potential threats. Security engineering focuses on establishing a robust security framework that aligns with business objectives while maintaining compliance with industry standards and regulations.

Security Operations

Security operations define an organization's ability to detect security events and provide a timely response. The effectiveness of security operations depends on three key factors: people, processes, and technology.

Key Components of Security Operations:

- **People:** Skilled professionals responsible for monitoring, detecting, and responding to security threats
- **Processes:** Well-defined security policies, procedures, and workflows to manage incidents effectively
- **Technology:** Tools and systems that support threat detection, incident response, and continuous monitoring

By integrating these components, organizations can enhance their security posture and ensure a proactive approach to threat management.

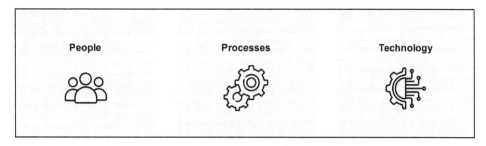

Figure 07-75: Security Operations

Corporate Governance and Security Responsibilities

Every person and role in an organization has responsibilities related to information security. Organizations should clearly define the security expectations associated with each role to ensure a secure and well-governed environment.

- The Board of Directors must have a clear understanding of the organization's IT needs and the role of IT systems in achieving business success. Their awareness and strategic oversight help align IT with business objectives, ensuring that security measures support the organization's long-term goals.

- The Chief Executive Officer (CEO) is responsible for supporting information security initiatives, ensuring adequate funding, and holding the business's security policies and procedures accountable for compliance. By prioritizing security at the executive level, the CEO fosters a culture of security awareness and ensures that necessary resources are allocated for effective risk management.

- The Chief Information Officer (CIO) oversees IT governance and service delivery, ensuring that IT systems effectively support business processes and operational needs. The CIO plays a critical role in implementing security strategies, maintaining compliance, and integrating security best practices into the organization's technological framework.

- The Chief Risk Officer (CRO) is responsible for overseeing enterprise risk management, ensuring that information security risks are addressed alongside operational, financial, strategic, and reputational risks. By managing these risks, the CRO helps protect the organization from potential threats and vulnerabilities that could impact business continuity.

- The Chief Technology Officer (CTO) plays a crucial role in linking information security policies to the organization's network, systems, and data. They oversee system administrators and ensure that security protocols are properly implemented across the IT infrastructure.

- The Enterprise Architect possesses a deep understanding of the organization's overall business strategy and the broader IT landscape. Their role is to align IT systems and solutions with business goals while staying updated on emerging trends and technological advancements.

- Enterprise Administrators are key players in protecting the organization's assets. They ensure that security measures are in place and actively contribute to maintaining a secure IT environment.

- Database Administrators manage and maintain database repositories, ensuring that data is accessible only to authorized individuals. Their role is critical in safeguarding sensitive information and ensuring data integrity.

Asset Management Process

Asset Management

Asset Management defines the policies and procedures for managing assets within an organization. An asset refers to any item of value to the organization, while an information asset specifically represents an item containing valuable information.

Asset management encompasses several key aspects, including ownership, classification, inventory, value, and protection.

- Ownership ensures accountability by assigning responsibility for assets
- Classification involves categorizing assets based on their importance and sensitivity
- Inventory refers to maintaining an organized record of assets to track and manage them efficiently
- Value assessment helps in understanding the significance and impact of assets on the organization
- Protection ensures that assets are safeguarded against risks and potential threats to maintain their integrity and availability

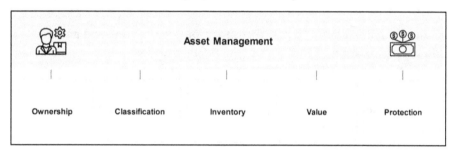

Figure 07-18: Asset Management

Asset Ownership

Asset ownership plays a crucial role in effective asset management by ensuring accountability and proper oversight. An engaged asset owner must be assigned to support essential functions such as asset classification, inventory management, valuation, and protection. Ideally, the asset owner should be a business unit leader who directs daily operations and manages business processes that rely on technology or information assets. Additionally, the asset owner is responsible for selecting and implementing a suitable protection strategy based on recommendations from security professionals. If the chosen strategy is ignored or proves ineffective, the asset owner must accept responsibility for any resulting compromises.

Asset Classification

Asset classification is a structured process that categorizes assets based on specific attributes defined by an organization. This classification helps in organizing and managing assets efficiently, ensuring that they are handled according to their value, sensitivity, and importance. By mapping a defined set of expectations and activities to each category, asset classification ensures that appropriate security measures,

management practices, and compliance requirements are applied consistently across different types of assets.

Category	Severity/Impact		
	High	**Moderate**	**Low**
Defense	Top-Secret	Secret	Confidential
Qualitative	High	Moderate	Low
Corporate	Restricted	Confidential	Public

Table 07-016: Asset Classification

Asset Inventory

Asset inventory serves as a central repository for documenting and tracking assets within an organization. It records essential details about each asset, including its existence, location, significance, and ownership. By maintaining an up-to-date asset inventory, organizations can effectively manage their resources, ensure accountability, and implement appropriate security and compliance measures. This process helps in optimizing asset utilization, reducing risks, and improving overall operational efficiency.

Asset Value

Asset value plays a crucial role in determining the importance of an item and the level of protection it requires. Tangible assets are easier to value, as organizations can directly map their monetary worth based on procurement costs. However, valuing intangible assets is more complex since there is no direct financial mapping. Instead, organizations must assess the potential impact of compromise or data loss to understand the true value of such assets. Proper asset valuation helps in prioritizing security measures and resource allocation to protect critical business components effectively.

Protection Strategy and Governance

Protection strategy and governance in asset management involve the collaboration of corporate governance and information security governance to safeguard an organization's assets effectively.

Corporate Governance

Corporate governance establishes expectations and protection measures in advance, ensuring that the organization's approach to asset protection is codified in policies.

Security Governance

On the other hand, security governance plays a critical role in providing recommendations based on insights from asset owners. It also documents both accepted and rejected recommendations, ensuring transparency and accountability in asset protection decisions. This combined approach helps organizations maintain a structured and well-documented security framework.

Domain 08: Network Security

Introduction

In today's interconnected digital landscape, network security is essential for protecting sensitive data, systems, and infrastructure from cyber threats. Organizations rely on robust security measures to prevent unauthorized access, data breaches, and system disruptions.

This domain explores key aspects of network security, including Network Security Solutions, which cover various technologies such as SIEM, UBA, UTM, NAC, VPNs, and secure router configurations to enhance network protection. It also delves into Data Leakage Concepts, highlighting the risks of unauthorized data exposure and strategies to mitigate data loss. Additionally, the Data Backup Process is discussed, highlights the importance of creating secure copies of critical information to ensure business continuity in case of data corruption, cyberattacks, or hardware failures.

Network Security Solutions

Network security solutions are technologies and practices designed to protect an organization's network infrastructure, data, and connected devices from cyber threats, unauthorized access, and data breaches. These solutions ensure the confidentiality, integrity, and availability of network resources.

Some technologies to protect networks from cyber threats and unauthorized access include Security Information and Event Management (SIEM), User Behavior Analytics (UBA), Unified Threat Management (UTM), Load balancers, Network Access Control (NAC), and Virtual Private Networks (VPNs).

Security Incident and Event Management (SIEM)

A Security Information and Event Management (SIEM) system plays a crucial role in real-time Security Operations Center (SOC) functions, enabling organizations to identify, monitor, record, audit, and analyze security incidents. By continuously collecting and processing security data from various sources, SIEM helps security teams detect and respond to potential threats before they escalate. Its ability to provide a centralized view of an organization's security posture allows analysts to correlate events and uncover suspicious activities that might otherwise go unnoticed.

A primary function of SIEM is tracking end-user behavior in real time to identify anomalies that may indicate security threats. By analyzing patterns of user activities, SIEM can detect unusual access attempts, privilege escalations, or unauthorized data transfers. These insights enable security teams to take proactive

measures, such as blocking malicious actions or launching investigations to determine the cause of suspicious behavior.

SIEM solutions integrate two essential components:

1. **Security Information Management (SIM):** SIM is responsible for the long-term storage, analysis, and reporting of log data collected from various sources, including servers, firewalls, and applications. This allows security professionals to conduct forensic investigations, ensure compliance reporting, and perform historical analysis of security events.

2. **Security Event Management (SEM):** SEM focuses on real-time monitoring, event correlation, alerting, and providing security teams with immediate insights into potential threats. By combining SIM and SEM capabilities, SIEM provides a comprehensive approach to security management.

In addition to detecting and analyzing security threats, SIEM helps organizations safeguard their IT assets from data breaches caused by both internal and external threats. Whether it is an insider threat attempting to exfiltrate sensitive data or an external attacker exploiting vulnerabilities, SIEM enables security teams to detect and mitigate risks on time. By leveraging advanced analytics, machine learning, and threat intelligence, SIEM enhances an organization's ability to effectively respond to emerging cyber threats.

Key Functions of SIEM

A Security Information and Event Management (SIEM) system provides a range of essential functions that help organizations enhance security monitoring, threat detection, compliance management, and incident response. Key functions of SIEM are as follows:

Log Collection

SIEM continuously collects logs from various sources, including firewalls, Intrusion Detection/Prevention Systems (IDS/IPS), servers, databases, endpoint devices, and cloud services. This centralized logging ensures that security teams have access to comprehensive data for monitoring and analysis.

Log Analysis

Once logs are collected, SIEM systems analyze them to detect anomalies, identify patterns, and recognize potential security threats. This involves parsing raw logs, normalizing data, and applying advanced analytics to uncover Indicators of Compromise (IoCs).

Event Correlation

SIEM correlates events across different systems to detect complex attack patterns. For example, failed login attempts from different locations followed by a successful login may indicate credential compromise. By correlating multiple data points, SIEM helps security teams uncover sophisticated threats.

Log Forensics

SIEM enables forensic investigations by allowing analysts to search historical logs, reconstruct security incidents, and identify attack vectors. This helps determine the root cause of an incident and aids in legal or compliance-related investigations.

IT Compliance and Reporting

Organizations must comply with industry regulations such as GDPR, HIPAA, PCI DSS, and ISO 27001. SIEM automates compliance reporting by generating audit logs, maintaining data integrity, and providing reports that meet regulatory requirements.

Application Log Monitoring

SIEM monitors logs generated by applications, including web servers, databases, and enterprise software. This helps detect application-layer attacks such as SQL injection, unauthorized API access, or abnormal user behavior.

Object Access Auditing

By tracking access to critical files, directories, and system objects, SIEM provides visibility into unauthorized access or modifications. This is crucial for detecting insider threats and ensuring data integrity.

Data Aggregation

SIEM aggregates logs and security events from multiple sources, normalizing them into a unified format for easier analysis. This eliminates data silos and provides security analysts with a holistic view of the organization's security posture.

Real-Time Alerting

SIEM generates real-time alerts when suspicious activities or security incidents occur. Alerts can be configured based on predefined rules, thresholds, or anomaly detection mechanisms, ensuring that security teams can respond quickly to threats.

User Activity Monitoring

By tracking user behavior across systems, SIEM helps detect unauthorized access, privilege escalations, and policy violations. User and Entity Behavior Analytics

(UEBA) enhances this capability by identifying deviations from normal behavior patterns.

Dashboards

SIEM provides visual dashboards that display security metrics, threat intelligence, and incident trends. These dashboards enable security teams to monitor the organization's security posture at a glance and make informed decisions.

File Integrity Monitoring (FIM)

SIEM tracks changes to critical files and system configurations. If unauthorized modifications occur, security teams are alerted to investigate potential security incidents such as malware infections or unauthorized access.

System and Device Log Monitoring

SIEM continuously monitors logs from network devices, security appliances, and endpoints. This helps detect misconfigurations, vulnerabilities, and attacks targeting infrastructure components.

Log Retention

To support forensic investigations and compliance, SIEM retains logs for extended periods. Long-term log storage ensures that historical data is available for auditing, trend analysis, and incident investigations.

SIEM Architecture

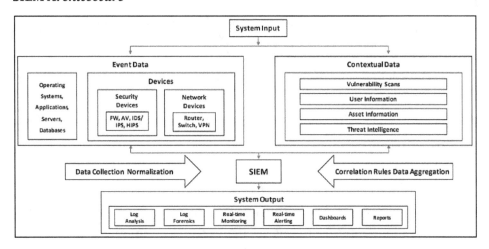

Figure 8-01: SIEM Architecture

The SIEM architecture consists of multiple components that work together to collect, process, correlate, and analyze security data. The key elements are:

System Input

SIEM collects data from various sources, categorized into:

- **Event Data:** Logs from operating systems, applications, servers, and databases
- **Devices:** Security devices (firewalls, antivirus, IDS/IPS, HIPS) and network devices (routers, switches, VPNs)
- **Contextual Data:** Enrichment sources like vulnerability scans, user and asset information, and threat intelligence

Data Collection and Normalization

The system processes and standardizes the collected Event Data and Contextual Data to ensure consistency across various sources. Normalization converts diverse log formats from different devices into a unified structure. This standardization enables seamless integration within the SIEM system, allowing for efficient correlation and analysis. As a result, security teams can identify and address threats with greater accuracy.

SIEM Processing (Correlation and Aggregation)

SIEM applies correlation rules and data aggregation to detect anomalies, threats, and security incidents by analyzing raw logs and contextual data.

System Output

SIEM provides actionable insights through:

- **Log Analysis and Forensics:** Enables deep investigation of incidents
- **Real-time Monitoring and Alerting:** Detects threats and generates alerts
- **Dashboards and Reports:** Provides security visibility and compliance reporting

This architecture ensures continuous security monitoring, threat detection, and compliance management.

User Behavior Analytics (UBA)

User Behavior Analytics (UBA) is a powerful security tool that tracks user activities to detect malicious attacks, potential threats, and fraudulent behavior. By analyzing behavioral patterns, UBA helps organizations identify security risks that may go unnoticed by traditional security tools. This proactive approach enables security teams to detect insider threats, compromised accounts, and unauthorized access attempts before they escalate into major incidents.

UBA provides advanced threat detection by continuously monitoring specific behavioral characteristics of employees and users within an organization. It examines various data points, including login patterns, access privileges, and system interactions, to detect deviations from normal behavior. If an employee suddenly attempts to access sensitive data or performs actions inconsistent with their usual behavior, UBA raises alerts, allowing security teams to investigate and respond promptly.

One of the key functions of UBA technologies is to analyze traffic patterns to identify unusual activities. These variations in user behavior can indicate threats from disgruntled employees attempting to exfiltrate data or external attackers who have gained unauthorized access. UBA helps distinguish between normal and suspicious actions, reducing false positives and improving threat detection accuracy.

Why User Behavior Analytics (UBA) is Effective

User Behavior Analytics (UBA) enhances cybersecurity by leveraging data-driven insights to detect threats that traditional security tools may overlook. It continuously monitors user activities, establishes behavioral baselines, and identifies anomalies that could indicate security risks. Here are the key reasons why UBA is an effective security solution:

Analyzes Different Patterns of Human Behavior and Large Volumes of User Data

UBA is designed to process vast amounts of user activity data and identify patterns that indicate normal and abnormal behavior. By leveraging machine learning and advanced analytics, it can differentiate between typical user actions and potentially malicious activities, reducing false positives and improving detection accuracy.

Monitors Geolocation for Each Login Attempt

UBA tracks the geolocation of every login attempt, helping to detect unauthorized access attempts from unusual locations. If a user usually logs in from one country but suddenly attempts to access the system from a different, high-risk location, UBA can flag the activity and trigger security alerts. This feature is especially useful in preventing credential theft and account compromise.

Detects Malicious Behavior and Reduces Risk

UBA helps organizations identify insider threats, compromised accounts, and external attacks by detecting behavioral anomalies. If an employee suddenly starts accessing large amounts of sensitive data or performing unauthorized actions, UBA can alert security teams, reducing the risk of data breaches and cyberattacks.

Monitors Privileged Accounts and Provides Real-Time Alerts

Privileged accounts, such as system administrators and executives, have elevated access that makes them prime targets for attackers. UBA continuously monitors these accounts and generates real-time alerts if suspicious behavior is detected. This includes unauthorized privilege escalations, unusual access requests, and excessive data transfers, helping organizations prevent insider threats and privilege abuse.

Provides Actionable Insights to Security Teams

UBA generates valuable insights that enable security teams to make informed decisions and improve their security posture. By analyzing user behavior trends, organizations can refine their access control policies, enforce least privilege principles, and enhance threat detection strategies. These insights help security teams respond proactively to emerging risks.

Produces Results Soon After Deployment

Unlike traditional security solutions that rely on predefined rules and require extensive fine-tuning, UBA begins delivering results quickly. Since it continuously learns from user activity and refines its detection models, it can start identifying threats soon after deployment. This enables organizations to improve threat detection and incident response without significant delays.

Unified Threat Management (UTM)

Unified Threat Management (UTM) is an all-in-one network security solution that allows administrators to monitor and manage an organization's security infrastructure from a centralized management console. It consolidates multiple security functions into a single appliance, reducing the need for separate security tools and streamlining network protection.

UTM solutions typically include firewall protection, Intrusion Detection and Prevention (IDS/IPS), antimalware scanning, spam filtering, load balancing, content filtering, Data Loss Prevention (DLP), and Virtual Private Network (VPN) capabilities. By integrating these security functions, UTM simplifies security operations and improves overall threat detection and response.

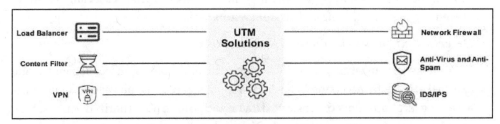

Figure 8-02: UTM Solutions

Figure 8-02 visually represents Unified Threat Management (UTM) solutions and the various security functions they provide.

Advantages of UTM

The advantages of UTM are as follows:

- **Reduced Complexity:** UTM combines multiple security functions into a single device, eliminating the need for separate solutions and reducing the complexity of managing different security tools. This consolidation simplifies security infrastructure, making it easier to maintain and troubleshoot.

- **Simplicity:** Since all security features are managed from a centralized console, administrators can easily configure policies, monitor network activity, and respond to threats efficiently. This simplicity is especially beneficial for Small and Medium-Sized Businesses (SMBs) that may lack dedicated security teams.

- **Easy Management:** UTM solutions provide an intuitive dashboard that allows IT teams to manage security policies, analyze logs, and monitor real-time network activity in one place. This centralized management reduces administrative overhead and enhances operational efficiency.

Disadvantages of UTM

The disadvantages of UTM are as follows:

- **Single Point of Failure:** Since UTM integrates multiple security functions into a single appliance, a hardware or software failure can disrupt all security services simultaneously. If the UTM device goes offline, firewall protection, intrusion detection, and other security functions may be compromised, leaving the organization vulnerable.

- **Single Point of Compromise:** A UTM appliance is a high-value target for attackers, as compromising it could expose all security defenses. If an attacker exploits a vulnerability in the UTM device, they may gain access to critical security controls, allowing them to bypass multiple layers of protection.

Load Balancer

A load balancer is a critical network device responsible that distributes incoming traffic across multiple servers in a distributed system. Its primary function is to ensure that no single server becomes overloaded, thereby improving the availability, reliability, and performance of applications. By evenly distributing network

requests, load balancers help optimize resource utilization, prevent bottlenecks, and enhance the user experience.

One of the significant advantages of a load balancer is its ability to mitigate rate-based attacks, such as Denial-of-Service (DoS) and Distributed Denial-of-Service (DDoS) attacks. These attacks overwhelm a server with excessive requests, leading to downtime and service disruptions. A load balancer helps in the following ways:

- **Traffic Throttling:** Limits the number of requests a single client or IP can send, preventing sudden traffic spikes.

- **Distributing Requests:** Spreads traffic across multiple servers, reducing the impact of an attack on a single target.

- **Filtering Malicious Requests:** Works in conjunction with Web Application Firewalls (WAFs) and Intrusion Prevention Systems (IPS) to detect and block suspicious traffic.

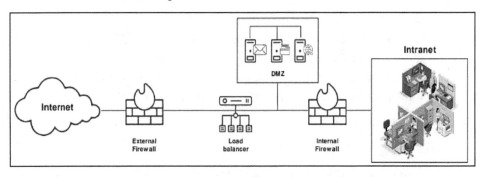

Figure 8-03: Network Security with Load Balancer

Figure 8-03 represents a network security architecture that incorporates firewalls, a load balancer, a Demilitarized Zone (DMZ), and an intranet to ensure secure communication and access control. The external firewall protects against threats from the internet. The load balancer distributes incoming traffic across multiple servers in the DMZ, ensuring high availability and preventing overload. The internal firewall secures the organization's intranet, restricting access to internal resources.

Network Access Control (NAC)

Network Access Control (NAC), also known as Network Admission Control, is a security solution designed to regulate and enforce security policies before allowing devices to connect to a network. NAC solutions work by authenticating users and verifying the security posture of connecting devices, ensuring that only compliant and authorized systems gain access. By implementing NAC, organizations can

minimize security risks such as unauthorized access, malware infections, and data breaches.

NAC solutions typically use a combination of authentication, authorization, and endpoint compliance checks. When a device attempts to connect to the network, the NAC system assesses it based on predefined security policies. This may include checking for updated antivirus software, security patches, endpoint configuration, or even verifying the device's identity. If the device does not meet security requirements, NAC can restrict access, quarantine the device, or enforce remediation before allowing full network access.

Key Functions of NAC

User Authentication

NAC ensures that only authorized users can connect to network resources. This is achieved through various authentication methods, such as passwords, Multi-Factor Authentication (MFA), and integration with identity management solutions like Active Directory or LDAP.

Device Identification and Profiling

NAC solutions identify and classify connected devices, determining their operating system, platform, and security posture. This helps organizations apply specific policies for different device types, such as corporate laptops, personal smartphones, or IoT devices.

Access Control and Policy Enforcement

NAC defines connection points for network devices, enforcing security policies based on user roles, device types, and network segments. For example, an employee using a company-issued laptop may receive full access, while a guest user is restricted to an isolated network segment.

Security Policy Implementation

Organizations can develop and apply customized security policies to control network access based on compliance checks. NAC can enforce policies that require up-to-date antivirus protection, proper firewall settings, and the latest operating system patches before granting network access.

Virtual Private Network (VPN)

A Virtual Private Network (VPN) is a security technology that establishes a secure, encrypted connection over an insecure network, such as the internet. It allows remote users, branch offices, or external partners to securely access a private

network while ensuring confidentiality, integrity, and data protection. VPNs are widely used by businesses and individuals to prevent unauthorized access and eavesdropping on sensitive communications.

VPNs function by encapsulating network traffic in an encrypted tunnel, protecting data from interception. When a user connects to a VPN, their device establishes a secure connection with a VPN server. The server assigns the user a new IP address, masking their real location and identity. The encrypted tunnel ensures that even if an attacker intercepts the traffic, they cannot decipher its contents.

VPN Architecture

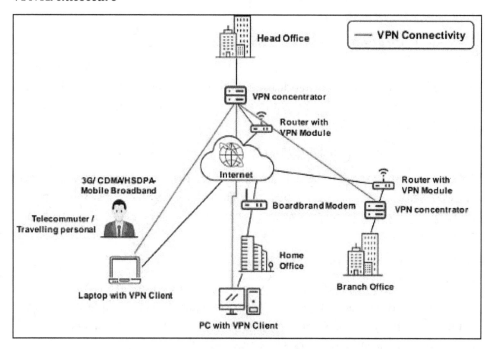

Figure 8-04: VPN Architecture

Figure 8-04 represents a VPN architecture, demonstrating how different locations and remote users securely connect to a corporate network over the internet. At the head office, a VPN concentrator and a router with a VPN module manage encrypted connections from remote offices and users. The branch office also has a VPN concentrator and router, ensuring secure communication between locations. Employees working from home connect via a broadband modem and VPN client while traveling personnel use mobile broadband and a VPN client to securely access corporate resources. This setup enhances security, ensures encrypted communication, and allows seamless remote access across the organization.

How VPN Works

A Virtual Private Network (VPN) ensures secure remote access by using encryption and authorization mechanisms to protect data transmissions over the internet. The process begins when a client device (such as a laptop, smartphone, or desktop) connects to the internet. The client then initiates a VPN connection to the organization's VPN server, which acts as an entry point to the internal network.

User authentication is required before access is granted. The VPN server verifies the client's identity using passwords, biometrics, security tokens, certificates, or Multi-Factor Authentication (MFA). This step ensures that only authorized users can connect, blocking unauthorized entities, such as hackers or cybercriminals.

Once authentication is successful, the VPN establishes a secure, encrypted tunnel between the client and the company's network. This encryption prevents eavesdropping and protects data from interception by attackers, ensuring confidentiality, integrity, and security of transmitted information.

Once the connection is established, the client can access internal company resources such as file servers, applications, databases, and email services, as if they were physically inside the corporate office. The VPN ensures sensitive data remains protected, even when the user connects from an untrusted or public network, such as a coffee shop or airport Wi-Fi.

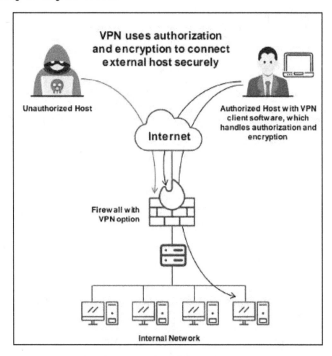

Figure 8-05: Working of VPN

Components of VPN

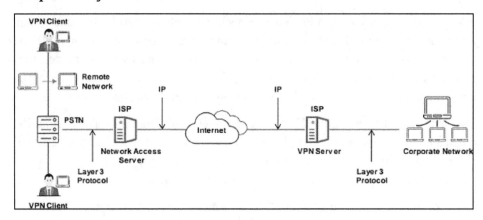

Figure 8-06: Components of VPN

Figure 8-06 represents the components of VPN which are elaborated below.

VPN Client

A VPN client is software or hardware that enables a device (laptop, smartphone, or workstation) to connect to a VPN server. It establishes a secure encrypted tunnel between the user and the corporate network, ensuring safe data transmission.

Network Access Server (NAS)

The NAS is an intermediary device that manages remote connections. It authenticates VPN users and forwards their traffic to the appropriate VPN server for secure network access.

Tunnel Terminating Device (VPN Server)

The VPN server is the endpoint of the VPN tunnel where encrypted data is decrypted and forwarded to the corporate network. It enforces security policies and ensures secure communication between VPN clients and internal resources.

VPN Protocol

VPN protocols define how data is encrypted and transmitted securely. Common protocols include IPsec, OpenVPN, SSL/TLS, and L2TP. These protocols ensure data confidentiality, integrity, and authentication during transmission over the Internet.

VPN Concentrators

A VPN concentrator is a specialized network device designed to establish and manage secure VPN connections. It serves as a central hub for handling multiple VPN tunnels, ensuring secure communication between remote users and corporate networks. By leveraging encryption and authentication mechanisms, it protects

data transmission over public networks, preventing unauthorized access or data breaches.

Functioning similarly to a VPN router, a VPN concentrator is commonly used for remote access and site-to-site VPNs. It enables remote employees, branch offices, and business partners to securely connect to an organization's internal network. Unlike traditional VPN routers, a VPN concentrator can handle hundreds or thousands of simultaneous VPN connections, making it ideal for enterprise-scale deployments.

The concentrator relies on tunneling protocols such as IPsec, SSL/TLS, L2TP, and GRE to establish encrypted communication channels. It negotiates security parameters, authenticates users, creates and manages VPN tunnels, and encapsulates or de-encapsulates packets as they travel through the VPN tunnel. Additionally, it ensures that only authorized users can access internal network resources by enforcing access control policies and security mechanisms like Multi-Factor Authentication (MFA).

Functions of a VPN Concentrator

A VPN concentrator functions as a bi-directional tunnel endpoint. Its main functions are:

- Encrypts and decrypts data
- Authenticates users
- Manages data transfer across the tunnel
- Negotiates tunnel parameters
- Manages security keys
- Establishes tunnels
- Assigns user addresses
- Manages inbound and outbound data transfers as a tunnel endpoint or router

Secure Router Configuration

Routers serve as the primary gateway to a network, directing data between internal and external systems. However, they are not designed as security devices, making them susceptible to various attacks. Threats can originate both externally, from cybercriminals attempting unauthorized access, and internally, from compromised or malicious insiders exploit vulnerabilities. If a router is not properly secured, attackers can take advantage of misconfigurations, weak credentials, or outdated firmware to compromise the network.

Securing, or hardening, a router involves implementing security measures that prevent unauthorized access and attacks. One major risk is information disclosure, where an attacker can gather details about the network's topology, connected devices, and routing configurations. By exploiting such information, attackers can disable routers, disrupt network communications, or reconfigure settings to reroute traffic for malicious purposes. This could lead to Man-In-The-Middle (MITM) attacks, data exfiltration, or even complete network outages.

Additionally, an unsecured router can be leveraged for both internal and external attacks. Internally, an attacker may escalate privileges, alter routing tables, or inject malicious configurations to facilitate further compromise. Externally, a compromised router can be used in botnets, DDoS attacks, or to pivot into more sensitive network areas.

Hardening a Router will enable the admins to prevent attackers from:

- Gaining information about the network
- Disabling routers and disrupting the network
- Reconfiguring routers
- Using routers to perform internal attacks
- Using routers to perform external attacks
- Rerouting network traffic

Router Security Measures

Securing a router is crucial for protecting a network from unauthorized access, misconfigurations, and cyber threats. Below are key security measures that administrators should implement to ensure the integrity, confidentiality, and availability of network infrastructure.

Establish a Router Security Policy

A well-documented, approved, and distributed router security policy ensures that all administrators follow standardized security best practices. It should include configuration guidelines, update schedules, and access control procedures.

Keep the Router's Firmware Updated

The Internetwork Operating System (IOS) version should always be checked and kept up to date. Vendors frequently release patches and updates to fix security vulnerabilities, so administrators must ensure that the latest stable firmware is installed.

Secure User Authentication and Passwords

To enhance security, user accounts should be configured with strong passwords while limiting administrative access to only essential personnel. Implementing Role-Based Access Control (RBAC) ensures that users have access only to the resources necessary for their roles, reducing the risk of unauthorized modifications to critical settings. Additionally, enabling password encryption prevents credentials from being stored or transmitted in plaintext, safeguarding them against potential breaches.

Access Restrictions and Console Security

Restricting access to the router's console and management interfaces is crucial to prevent unauthorized users from making critical changes. Only authorized personnel should have administrative access, enforced using Access Control Lists (ACLs) to limit entry based on specific IP addresses. To further enhance security, Secure Shell (SSH) should be used instead of Telnet for remote access, ensuring that administrative communications remain encrypted and protected from eavesdropping.

Disable Unnecessary Services and Interfaces

Disabling unused services, such as HTTP, FTP, or Cisco Discovery Protocol (CDP), helps minimize the attack surface and reduces the risk of exploitation. Additionally, unused interfaces should be shut down to prevent unauthorized entry points into the network. Proper configuration of essential services, such as Domain Name System (DNS), is necessary to mitigate risks like spoofing and cache poisoning attacks, which can compromise network integrity.

Implement Access Control Lists (ACLs)

Access Control Lists (ACLs) should be implemented to filter and restrict network traffic based on source and destination IP addresses, protocols, and ports. This prevents unauthorized access and ensures that only legitimate traffic is allowed through the network. Blocking reserved IP addresses and private IP ranges from being incorrectly routed further enhances security by preventing malicious actors from exploiting misconfigured routing settings.

Enable Logging and Time Synchronization

Enabling detailed logging of router activity is essential for monitoring security events and identifying potential threats. Network Time Protocol (NTP) should be used to synchronize the router's clock accurately, ensuring that log entries maintain correct timestamps for forensic investigations. A comprehensive log review policy should be established, ensuring that logs are regularly checked, analyzed, and archived for long-term security monitoring and incident response.

Key Components of a Router Security Policy

A Router Security Policy defines the rules and best practices that network administrators must follow to protect routers from unauthorized access, misconfigurations, and cyber threats.

Router Security Policy should consist of:

- Password Policy
- Authentication Policy
- Remote Access Policy
- Filtering Policy
- Backup Policy
- Redundancy Policy
- Documentation Policy
- Physical Access Policy
- Monitoring Policy
- Update Policy

Data Leakage Concepts

Data leakage refers to the unauthorized transmission of sensitive or confidential information outside an organization. It can occur through electronic means, such as email, malicious links, cloud storage, or external devices, as well as physical methods like theft, unauthorized access, or social engineering. Data leakage can result from insider threats, accidental disclosure, or external cyberattacks. To prevent data leakage, organizations implement Data Loss Prevention (DLP) solutions, access controls, encryption, and employee awareness programs to monitor and restrict unauthorized data transfers.

Data Leakage

Data leakage can result in financial losses, reputational damage, legal consequences, and security breaches. Organizations often store vast amounts of sensitive information, including customer data, financial records, intellectual property, and internal communications. When this data is leaked, it can be exploited for malicious purposes, including identity theft, corporate espionage, or financial fraud.

Data leakage can occur through electronic means. For example, employees may accidentally send sensitive information to the wrong recipient or fall victim to phishing attacks that deceive them into revealing confidential details.

Cybercriminals can also use malware, keyloggers, or exploit vulnerabilities in network security to gain unauthorized access to databases, leading to large-scale data breaches.

Physical methods of data leakage include device theft, unauthorized access to printed documents, or break-ins where hackers steal hard drives or other storage devices. Lost or stolen laptops, USB drives, and smartphones containing unencrypted sensitive data can expose an organization to significant risks. In some cases, insiders with malicious intent might deliberately extract confidential information and sell or leak it to competitors or cybercriminals.

Major Risks to Organizations

Data leakage poses severe risks to organizations, impacting financial stability, reputation, and competitive standing.

Some of the risks are as follows:

- **Loss of customer loyalty:** Customers lose trust in the organization, leading to decreased retention and engagement

- **Potential litigations:** Legal actions may be taken against the company for failing to protect sensitive data

- **Heavy fines:** Regulatory bodies impose financial penalties for non-compliance with data protection laws

- **Decline in share value:** Investor confidence drops, negatively impacting stock prices

- **Loss of brand name:** The company's image is damaged, reducing its market appeal

- **Loss of reputation:** Negative publicity affects credibility and trustworthiness

- **Reduction of sales and revenue:** Customer distrust leads to lower business performance and profitability

- **Unfavorable media attention:** Negative press coverage highlights security failures, further harming public perception

- **Unfavorable competitor advantage:** Competitors exploit leaked information to gain an edge

- **Insolvency or liquidation:** Severe financial losses may force the company to shut down

- **Loss of new and existing customers:** Both potential and current customers move to more secure alternatives

- **Monetary loss:** Expenses related to breach response, legal fees, and fines strain financial resources

- **Prone to cybercriminal attacks:** Once breached, companies become frequent targets for future attacks

- **Loss of productivity:** Employees shift focus to damage control instead of core business operations

- **Disclosure of trade secrets:** Competitors or malicious actors gain access to proprietary business strategies

- **Pre-release of latest technology:** Unauthorized exposure of newly developed innovations weakens competitive advantage

- **Loss of proprietary and customer information:** Sensitive business and client data is compromised

- **Ready-to-release projects get pirated:** Stolen intellectual property is leaked or sold before the official launch

Data Leakage Threats

Types of data leakage threats include:

Insider Threats

Insider threats pose a significant risk to organizations, as employees, whether intentionally or unintentionally, may leak sensitive data. Disgruntled employees may deliberately share confidential information to harm the company, while negligent employees may expose data due to a lack of awareness or careless behavior. Such leaks can result in financial losses, operational disruptions, and reputational damage. Employees may exploit techniques such as eavesdropping, shoulder surfing, or dumpster diving to access sensitive information that should remain confidential. These actions violate corporate policies and can lead to serious security breaches.

Reasons for Insider Threats

Several factors contribute to insider threats. One of the primary reasons is inadequate security awareness and training, which leaves employees unaware of best practices for handling sensitive data. Additionally, a lack of proper management controls prevents organizations from effectively monitoring employee activities, making it easier for insiders to exploit system weaknesses. The use of

insecure data transfer methods, such as sending unencrypted emails or using unauthorized cloud storage, further increases the risk of data leaks. Strengthening security training, implementing strict access controls, and monitoring user behavior are essential to mitigate insider threats.

External Threats

External threats come from cybercriminals who exploit vulnerabilities within an organization to gain unauthorized access to sensitive data. Attackers often target insiders through social engineering techniques, such as phishing, to steal credentials and impersonate legitimate employees. Once inside the network, they may gain unrestricted access to critical systems, allowing them to exfiltrate data, install malware, or disrupt operations. These external threats are particularly dangerous because attackers can remain undetected for long periods, causing significant harm before being discovered.

Examples of External Threats

Several attack vectors can be used to compromise an organization:

- Hacking or Code Injection Attacks
- Malware
- Phishing
- Corporate Espionage or Competitors
- Business Partners or Contractors

Data Loss Prevention (DLP)

Data Loss Prevention (DLP) is a security strategy that focuses on identifying, monitoring, and protecting sensitive data to prevent unauthorized access, transmission, or leakage. DLP solutions are designed to ensure that end users do not accidentally or intentionally send sensitive information outside the corporate network, thereby reducing the risk of data breaches, financial losses, and regulatory non-compliance.

DLP systems work by classifying and tracking sensitive data across various endpoints, including emails, cloud storage, and removable media. These solutions use predefined policies and rules to detect sensitive information such as Personal Identifiable Information (PII), financial records, intellectual property, and confidential corporate data. If a user attempts to share restricted data through unauthorized channels, the system can block, quarantine, or encrypt the transmission to prevent leakage.

Organizations implement DLP through network-based, endpoint-based, and cloud-based solutions. Network DLP monitors data in transit across company networks, Endpoint DLP protects data on devices such as laptops and USB drives, and Cloud DLP secures data stored and shared in cloud environments. These solutions help enforce compliance with regulations like GDPR, HIPAA, and PCI-DSS, ensuring that businesses meet legal and industry standards.

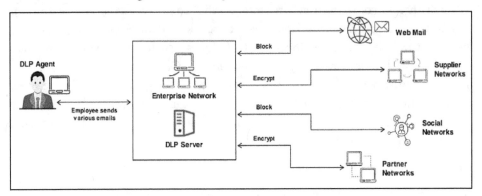

Figure 8-07: DLP Email Monitoring

Figure 8-07 illustrates a DLP system that monitors and controls the flow of emails sent by employees within an enterprise network. The DLP Agent on the employee's device ensures that emails pass through the DLP Server, where policies are enforced based on the destination. Emails addressed to webmail services and social networking platforms are blocked to prevent data leakage through unauthorized channels, while those sent to supplier and partner networks are encrypted to maintain confidentiality and safeguard against unauthorized access.

Data Backup Process

The data backup process involves creating a duplicate copy of critical data to ensure its availability in case of accidental deletion, corruption, or system failure. It includes identifying essential data, selecting an appropriate backup method, choosing storage locations, and scheduling regular backups. Organizations implement backup strategies using RAID configurations, encryption, and automated backup solutions to enhance data security and recovery efficiency.

Data Backup

Data is the backbone of any organization, and its loss can lead to financial losses, operational disruptions, reputational damage, and legal consequences. Organizations rely on data for daily operations, decision-making, and customer interactions. A loss of critical data due to cyberattacks, hardware failures, or accidental deletion can severely impact business continuity.

Backup is the process of creating a duplicate copy of critical data to ensure that it can be restored in case of corruption, accidental deletion, or cyber threats such as ransomware attacks. Backups play a key role in disaster recovery and business continuity, allowing organizations to recover from IT failures, application crashes, and security incidents. Without a proper backup strategy, organizations risk permanent data loss, financial penalties, and compliance violations.

Backup Strategy or Plan

A well-defined backup strategy ensures organizations can quickly restore lost data with minimal downtime. The key elements of a backup strategy include:

- **Identify Critical Business Data:** Determine which data is essential for operations, including customer records, financial transactions, intellectual property, and system configurations.

- **Select Backup Media:** Choose the appropriate storage medium such as hard drives, SSDs, magnetic tapes, optical discs, or cloud storage, considering cost, speed, and durability.

- **Select Backup Technology:** Implement backup solutions such as snapshot backups, Continuous Data Protection (CDP), and deduplication techniques to optimize storage and efficiency.

- **Select Appropriate RAID Levels:** Redundant Array of Independent Disks (RAID) configurations improve data redundancy and fault tolerance. For example:

  - RAID 1 (Mirroring): Provides data redundancy by duplicating data across multiple disks

  - RAID 5/6: Offers fault tolerance with distributed parity for recovery

  - RAID 10: Utilizes both mirroring and striping to enhance data redundancy and performance

- **Select an Appropriate Backup Method:** Organizations can choose between different backup methods based on their needs:

  - Full Backup: A complete copy of all data (high storage usage but fast recovery)

  - Incremental Backup: Only backs up data changed since the last backup (low storage usage, slower recovery)

  - Differential Backup: Backs up data changed since the last full backup (faster than incremental but larger storage needs)

- **Choose the Backup Location:** Backups can be stored on-site, off-site, or in the cloud. A combination of locations ensures redundancy and disaster recovery preparedness.

- **Select Backup Types:** Organizations may implement:
  - Local Backup: Stored within the enterprise network for quick recovery
  - Cloud Backup: Secure offsite storage for disaster recovery
  - Hybrid Backup: A mix of local and cloud backups for greater reliability

- **Choose the Right Backup Solution:** Selecting the right software and hardware is crucial. Options include enterprise-grade solutions such as Veeam, Acronis, and Commvault, and cloud-native backups like AWS Backup or Microsoft Azure Backup.

- **Conduct a Recovery Drill Test:** Regular testing of backup restoration ensures that the data can be successfully recovered when needed. Organizations should perform periodic disaster recovery drills to verify the integrity of their backups.

Redundant Array of Independent Disks (RAID) Technology

RAID is a data storage technology that combines multiple hard drives into a single logical unit to improve performance, enhance fault tolerance, and protect against data loss. By distributing or replicating data across multiple drives, RAID enables systems to continue operating even if one or more drives fail, ensuring high availability and data reliability.

RAID configurations help organizations enhance system performance, simplify storage management, and minimize the risk of data loss. Storing data across multiple drives allows Input/Output (I/O) operations to be processed in parallel, reducing latency and increasing efficiency. Additionally, RAID configurations provide a balance between performance, redundancy, and storage capacity, depending on the level implemented.

RAID represents a storage methodology that divides and replicates data across multiple drives, functioning as secondary storage for critical systems. It is widely used in enterprise environments, data centers, and server infrastructures to ensure continuous data availability and prevent system downtime in case of drive failures.

RAID has six levels—RAID 0, RAID 1, RAID 3, RAID 5, RAID 10, and RAID 50—each offering a balance of performance, redundancy, and storage efficiency for different use cases. All RAID levels rely on three fundamental storage techniques:

- **Striping:** Distributes data across multiple drives to enhance speed and performance

- **Mirroring:** Duplicates data onto two or more drives, ensuring redundancy
- **Parity:** Stores error correction information to reconstruct data in case of drive failure

Advantages of RAID

RAID provides several benefits, including enhanced system performance, fault tolerance, and data redundancy.

- **Hot-Swapping or Hot Plugging:** RAID supports hot-swapping, meaning faulty drives can be replaced without shutting down the system. This ensures that network operations remain unaffected, reducing downtime and enhancing business continuity.

- **Improved Read/Write Performance:** RAID supports disk striping, where data is divided across multiple disks, allowing the system to read and write simultaneously. This optimizes processor utilization and significantly boosts performance, particularly in RAID 0, RAID 5, and RAID 10 configurations.

- **Fault Tolerance and Data Redundancy:** Parity-based RAID levels (RAID 5, RAID 6, RAID 50) include built-in error detection and correction mechanisms, reducing the risk of system crashes and data loss. Mirroring techniques used in RAID 1 and RAID 10 ensure that if one drive fails, an identical copy remains available for recovery.

- **Increased System Uptime:** RAID minimizes downtime by allowing continuous operation even if a disk fails. With redundant storage mechanisms, systems can remain functional until the faulty drive is replaced.

Disadvantages of RAID

RAID also has certain limitations, such as compatibility issues, data loss risks, and complex configurations.

- **Hardware and Software Compatibility Issues:** Some older hardware components and software systems (such as system imaging programs) may not fully support RAID configurations, requiring additional setup, firmware updates, or specialized drivers.

- **Risk of Data Loss with Multiple Drive Failures:** While RAID provides redundancy, it does not eliminate the risk of failure. In RAID 5, if two drives fail simultaneously, data recovery becomes impossible because the parity disk cannot recreate the missing data. Similarly, in RAID 10, losing both mirrored drives in the same pair leads to complete data loss.

- **Not Suitable for All Applications:** oRAID does not guarantee performance improvements in all environments. Some applications with high random-access

workloads (such as databases or real-time analytics) may not experience significant performance boosts.

Complex Configuration and Maintenance: Setting up and managing a RAID array requires technical expertise, as it involves configuring multiple drives and understanding the specific RAID levels. Certain RAID levels that use parity, such as RAID 5 and RAID 6, require additional processing power, which can negatively impact system performance if not supported by adequate hardware. Moreover, recovering data in the event of a RAID failure can be both time-consuming and complex, particularly when multiple drives need to be rebuilt.

RAID Level 0: Disk Striping

RAID 0, also known as disk striping, distributes data into blocks and writes them evenly across multiple hard drives. This setup enhances Input/Output (I/O) performance by allowing multiple drives to read and write data simultaneously, significantly improving system speed.

However, RAID 0 does not provide data redundancy. Since there is no mirroring or parity, the failure of a single drive results in complete data loss, making recovery impossible. This makes RAID 0 highly vulnerable to hardware failures, despite its performance benefits.

A minimum of two drives is required to configure RAID 0. It is best suited for applications that prioritize speed over data protection, such as gaming, video editing, and high-performance computing where data loss is not a critical concern.

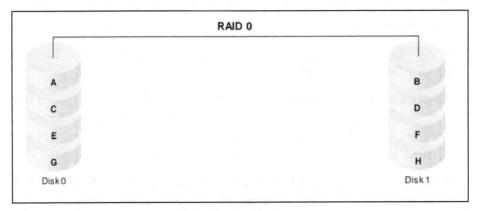

Figure 8-08: RAID 0

RAID Level 1: Disk Mirroring

RAID 1, also known as disk mirroring, ensures data redundancy by simultaneously writing identical copies of data to two or more drives. This setup enhances data

reliability since every piece of information is stored on multiple disks, reducing the risk of data loss in case of hardware failure.

One of the key benefits of RAID 1 is data recovery. If one drive fails, the system can continue operating using the mirrored copy, minimizing downtime and ensuring business continuity. However, since data is duplicated across drives, storage capacity is effectively halved, as each drive stores the same information.

RAID 1 requires a minimum of two drives and is best suited for applications where data integrity and fault tolerance are critical, such as database servers, financial systems, and business-critical applications.

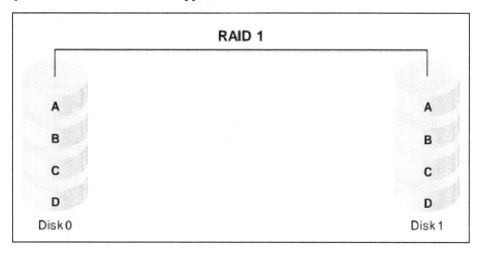

Figure 8-09: RAID 1

RAID Level 3: Disk Striping with Parity

RAID 3 uses disk striping with a dedicated parity drive, where data is divided at the byte level and spread across multiple drives, while one disk in the array is reserved for storing parity information. This configuration allows for fault tolerance, as the parity drive enables data recovery and error correction in case of a drive failure.

Since all drives except the parity disk are used simultaneously for reading and writing, RAID 3 delivers high throughput, making it well-suited for applications requiring sequential data access, such as video editing and streaming. However, the reliance on a single parity drive can create a bottleneck, reducing overall performance in high IOPS environments.

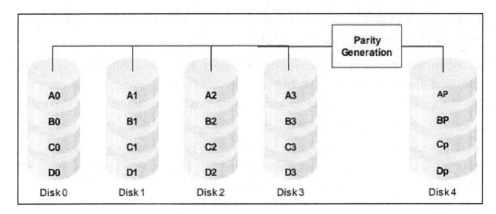

Figure 8-10: RAID 3

RAID Level 5: Block Interleaved Distributed Parity

RAID 5 utilizes block-level striping with distributed parity, meaning that data and parity information are spread across all drives in the array. This ensures fault tolerance, as the parity data enables the reconstruction of lost information if a single drive fails.

However, the data writing process is slower due to the additional step of calculating and writing parity information. Despite this, RAID 5 provides a good balance of performance, redundancy, and storage efficiency, making it ideal for file servers, databases, and general-purpose storage systems. A minimum of three drives is required for this RAID configuration.

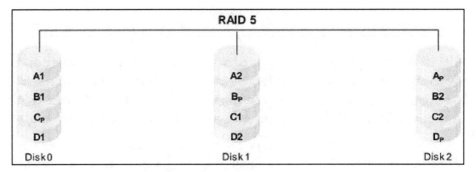

Figure 8-11: RAID 5

RAID Level 10: Blocks Striped and Mirrored

RAID 10, also known as striped mirroring, combines the advantages of RAID 0 (striping) and RAID 1 (mirroring) to enhance both performance and fault tolerance. Data is striped across multiple mirrored pairs, ensuring redundancy while maximizing read and write speeds.

Since each data block is mirrored, RAID 10 requires a minimum of four drives, effectively reducing usable storage by half. However, its high performance and resilience make it ideal for high-availability applications, such as databases, virtualization, and enterprise-level systems. Unlike RAID 5, RAID 10 does not suffer from slow parity calculations, allowing for faster recovery in case of drive failure.

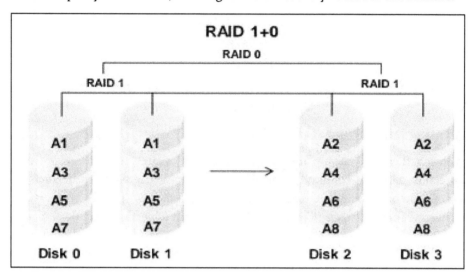

Figure 8-12: RAID 10

RAID Level 50: Mirroring and Striping Across Multiple RAID Levels

RAID 50 combines RAID 0 (striping) with RAID 5 (distributed parity) to enhance both performance and fault tolerance. By striping data across multiple RAID 5 arrays, RAID 50 improves read and write speeds while maintaining redundancy through distributed parity.

This setup requires a minimum of six drives, and can tolerate one drive failure per RAID 5 segment without data loss. However, if multiple drives fail within the same segment, the array becomes non-functional. While RAID 50 incurs higher parity overhead, it offers better fault tolerance and higher throughput than RAID 5, making it suitable for high-performance applications, large databases, and intensive workloads.

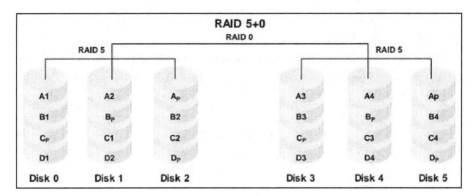

Figure 8-13: RAID 50

Selecting an Appropriate Backup Method

Choosing the right backup method is crucial for organizations to ensure data protection, business continuity, and disaster recovery. The selection depends on several factors, including organizational requirements, budget constraints, Recovery Time Objectives (RTO), and Recovery Point Objectives (RPO).

Hot Backup (Online Backup)

A hot backup is performed while the system, application, or database remains active and accessible to users. This method is crucial for organizations that require continuous availability and cannot afford downtime, such as financial institutions, healthcare systems, and e-commerce platforms. The primary advantage of a hot backup is that it allows immediate failover in case of system failure, ensuring minimal disruption. However, it is a costly solution due to the need for high-end infrastructure, additional storage resources, and advanced backup management tools.

Cold Backup (Offline Backup)

A cold backup is conducted when the system is shut down and completely unavailable to users. This method is typically used when scheduled downtime is allowed, making it ideal for periodic full backups of databases, archival systems, and applications that do not require real-time updates. The key advantage of cold backups is their lower cost compared to hot backups, as they do not require additional system resources. However, they come with the drawback of longer recovery times, as switching to a cold backup requires manually restoring the system before it becomes operational.

Warm Backup (Nearline Backup)

A warm backup is a hybrid approach that combines elements of both hot and cold backups. While the system is still partially operational, some components may be

placed in a read-only or limited-access state to allow backup processes to run. This method is less expensive than a hot backup while offering faster failover times compared to a cold backup. Organizations that require moderate availability and cost-effective backup solutions—such as medium-sized enterprises and businesses with flexible service-level agreements—often use warm backups. However, they are not as instantly accessible as hot backups, which may cause slight delays in restoration.

Choosing the Backup Location

Selecting the appropriate backup location is crucial for ensuring data availability, security, and disaster recovery readiness. Organizations typically choose from onsite, offsite, and cloud-based backup solutions based on their business needs, budget, and risk tolerance.

Onsite Data Backup

Onsite data backup refers to storing backup copies within the organization's premises, using local storage solutions such as external hard drives, Network-Attached Storage (NAS), or dedicated backup servers. This approach ensures that data can be accessed and restored quickly, reducing downtime in case of data loss. Additionally, onsite backups are generally more cost-effective since they do not require ongoing subscription fees. However, the major drawback is that they are susceptible to physical threats, including hardware failures, theft, fire, and natural disasters. If a catastrophic event occurs at the primary site, both the original and backup data may be lost, making onsite backup alone an insufficient strategy for disaster recovery.

Offsite Data Backup

Offsite data backup involves storing data in a remote location, separate from the primary site. Organizations often use fireproof and disaster-resistant facilities to protect backup data from physical security threats such as fires, floods, and theft. This method ensures that data remains available even if the primary site is compromised. However, one of the challenges of offsite backups is maintaining a consistent backup schedule, as transferring data to a remote location may require additional planning, infrastructure, and bandwidth. If backups are not updated regularly, the organization risks losing recent data in the event of a disaster.

Cloud Data Backup

Cloud data backup stores backup copies on remote servers maintained by third-party cloud providers. This method offers scalability, flexibility, and accessibility, allowing organizations to backup and retrieve their data from anywhere with an internet connection. Cloud backups are typically encrypted, protecting data from

cyber threats and unauthorized access. Additionally, cloud storage eliminates the risk of physical damage since the data is stored offsite. However, cloud backups have some disadvantages, including longer recovery times due to internet dependency and lack of direct control over the backup infrastructure. Organizations relying on cloud backups must ensure they have strong service agreements in place to address data security, compliance, and uptime guarantees.

Data Recovery

Data recovery is the process of restoring lost, deleted, corrupted, or inaccessible data from various storage media. This process is essential for organizations and individuals who experience accidental deletions, hardware failures, cyberattacks, or other data loss incidents. The recovery process involves using specialized tools and techniques to retrieve and reconstruct lost files while maintaining data integrity. Depending on the severity of data loss, recovery may be straightforward or require advanced forensic methods.

Data loss can occur due to several factors, including accidental deletions, software corruption, malware infections, hardware malfunctions, and intentional data destruction. Storage media such as hard drives, USB flash drives, SD cards, optical discs, and cloud storage platforms can all experience data loss. While most lost data is recoverable, certain cases, such as overwritten data or severe physical damage to storage devices, may result in permanent loss.

The data recovery process depends on the nature of data loss. Logical data recovery involves using specialized software to restore deleted or corrupted files, while physical data recovery requires repairing damaged storage devices in controlled environments like cleanrooms. Advanced recovery methods, such as disk imaging and forensic recovery, allow professionals to extract data even from highly damaged media.

There are various data recovery tools available, ranging from commercial software like EaseUS, Recuva, and R-Studio to forensic-grade tools such as Autopsy and FTK Imager. These tools help scan storage media, recover deleted files, and rebuild corrupted partitions. Organizations and individuals must choose the appropriate tool based on their specific data recovery needs.

To minimize the risk of data loss, it is crucial to implement strong backup strategies, use reliable storage devices, and follow best practices for data protection. Regular backups and proactive security measures help reduce reliance on complex data recovery efforts.

Domain 09: Risk Management and Disaster Recovery

Introduction

Risk management and disaster recovery are essential for protecting organizations from potential threats and ensuring business continuity. Effective risk management identifies, assesses, and mitigates risks that could disrupt operations, safeguarding assets, data, and reputation. Organizations follow structured frameworks to manage risks systematically and enhance resilience.

Disaster recovery focuses on minimizing downtime and restoring critical functions after unexpected disruptions. A well-defined business continuity plan ensures that organizations can continue operations with minimal impact. This domain explores key risk management concepts, common frameworks, and the processes involved in business continuity and disaster recovery. By understanding these principles, organizations can proactively prepare for uncertainties and maintain stability.

Risk Management Concepts and Frameworks

Risk Management

Risk management is a structured process aimed at reducing and maintaining risk at an acceptable level through a well-defined and actively implemented security program. Organizations adopt risk management strategies to safeguard their assets, data, and overall business operations from potential threats. This process involves identifying, assessing, and responding to various risks by implementing effective control measures to minimize potential negative effects. Risk management plays a critical role throughout the system's security life cycle, ensuring that organizations can proactively address vulnerabilities and maintain operational resilience.

Risk Management Benefits

Focus on Risk Impact Areas

Risk management helps organizations identify and assess critical risk areas that could significantly impact operations. By understanding these areas, businesses can prioritize resources and strategies to mitigate potential threats effectively.

Risk-Based Approach to Threats

Organizations can address risks according to their severity levels, ensuring that higher-risk threats receive immediate attention while lower-risk issues are managed appropriately. This structured approach enhances overall security and operational stability.

Improved Risk Handling Process

Implementing risk management practices streamlines the process of identifying, assessing, and mitigating risks. This leads to faster decision-making, reduced response time, and better-prepared teams to handle uncertainties.

Effective Response to Adverse Situations

With a well-defined risk management framework, security officers and key personnel can act swiftly and effectively in crisis. This proactive approach minimizes damage and ensures business continuity.

Efficient Use of Resources

Risk management enables organizations to allocate security resources efficiently, reducing waste and ensuring optimal utilization. This helps in strengthening defenses without unnecessary expenditure.

Minimized Financial Impact

By identifying and mitigating risks early, organizations can prevent potential financial losses caused by security breaches, operational failures, or business disruptions. This protects revenue and ensures long-term financial stability.

Enhanced Security Controls

A structured risk management approach helps organizations implement suitable security controls that align with business needs. This ensures that vulnerabilities are addressed with the most effective solutions, enhancing overall protection.

Enterprise Risk Management (ERM) Framework

Enterprise Risk Management (ERM) is a structured approach that organizations adopt to identify, assess, and mitigate risks effectively. It integrates various processes and activities to ensure that risks are managed systematically, reducing potential threats and enhancing operational efficiency.

Implementation of Activities

ERM defines specific implementation activities that guide an organization in handling risks. These activities are designed to proactively identify potential threats and implement measures to mitigate their impact. By establishing clear guidelines, organizations can systematically assess risks and apply necessary actions to minimize disruptions.

Structured Risk Management Process

One of the core benefits of ERM is its ability to provide a well-defined and structured process for integrating information security with risk management

activities. A structured approach ensures that risk assessment, mitigation, and monitoring are conducted in a standardized manner, reducing uncertainties and enabling organizations to make informed decisions.

Key Risk Management Actions

ERM focuses on three fundamental actions to manage risks efficiently:

1. **Risk Avoidance**

Organizations can prevent unnecessary risks by avoiding actions that may lead to vulnerabilities. This proactive approach helps eliminate threats before they materialize, ensuring a secure and stable business environment.

2. **Risk Reduction**

ERM emphasizes risk reduction by minimizing both the likelihood and impact of potential threats. By implementing preventive controls, companies can significantly lower their exposure to risks, making operations more resilient.

3. **Standardized Risk Management Practices**

A crucial aspect of ERM is the establishment of standardized risk management processes. These standards provide a consistent framework for evaluating and addressing risks across different departments, ensuring alignment with industry best practices.

Goals of the ERM Framework

Below are the key goals of implementing an ERM framework:

1. Integration with Performance Management

A key objective of ERM is to seamlessly integrate risk management practices with the organization's performance management system. By aligning risk considerations with business goals and objectives, organizations can ensure that risks are proactively managed while maintaining operational efficiency and growth.

2. Communicating the Benefits of Risk Management

For ERM to be effective, it is crucial to create awareness about the advantages of structured risk management. Communicating these benefits enables employees, stakeholders, and decision-makers to understand how risk management enhances organizational resilience, improves decision-making, and supports long-term success.

3. Defining Roles and Responsibilities

A well-defined ERM framework clarifies the roles and responsibilities of individuals involved in risk management. By assigning clear duties to employees at various

levels, organizations can ensure accountability, enhance coordination, and streamline risk mitigation efforts.

4. Standardizing Risk Reporting and Escalation Processes

Consistency in risk reporting is essential for identifying and addressing potential threats efficiently. ERM establishes a standardized approach for documenting, tracking, and escalating risks, enabling organizations to take timely actions and prevent operational disruptions.

5. Establishing a Standardized Risk Management Approach

To effectively manage risks, organizations must adopt a systematic approach that applies across all departments. ERM sets a standard methodology for assessing, prioritizing, and mitigating risks, ensuring that all teams follow a unified process to handle uncertainties.

6. Supporting Resources in Managing Risks

ERM provides guidance, tools, and resources to help employees and departments manage risks effectively. By offering training and support, organizations empower their teams to identify risks proactively and take appropriate measures to reduce their impact.

7. Defining the Scope of Risk Management

A comprehensive ERM framework establishes clear boundaries for risk management activities. It outlines the scope of risk assessments, policies, and mitigation strategies, ensuring that all risks whether operational, financial, or strategic are addressed systematically.

8. Ensuring Periodic Review and Continuous Improvement

Risk management is an ongoing process that requires continuous assessment and refinement. ERM mandates periodic reviews and verification processes to evaluate the effectiveness of risk management strategies. By analyzing past incidents and assessing emerging risks, organizations can enhance their ERM framework and improve overall resilience.

Risk Management Framework (RMF)

The Risk Management Framework serves as a template and guideline for organizations to identify, eliminate, and minimize risks. It was originally developed by the National Institute of Standards and Technology (NIST) to protect the information systems of the United States government.

The RMF was initially designed for federal agencies; however, it can be readily adopted by private sector organizations. Businesses inherently face risks, including

IT issues, litigation, and capital loss. Although it is impossible to eliminate every risk associated with operating a business, these risks can be minimized.

Here is a list of some of the most widely used Risk Management Frameworks:

1. **NIST Risk Management Framework (RMF):** Developed by the National Institute of Standards and Technology, it provides a structured process for integrating security, privacy, and risk management into the system development lifecycle.
2. **COSO Enterprise Risk Management (ERM):** Developed by the Committee of Sponsoring Organizations (COSO), this framework is widely used for comprehensive risk management in enterprise environments, focusing on strategy, performance, and compliance.
3. **COBIT:** Primarily an IT governance framework, Control Objectives for Information and Related Technologies (COBIT) also integrates risk management practices, ensuring that IT risks are managed in alignment with overall business objectives.

NIST Risk Management Framework

The NIST Risk Management Framework (RMF) is a structured and continuous process that integrates information security and risk management activities into the System Development Life Cycle (SDLC). It ensures that security risks are effectively identified, assessed, and managed to protect organizational operations, assets, and individuals. The framework consists of six key steps, each playing a crucial role in securing information systems.

1. Categorize

The first step in the RMF is categorizing the information system based on its sensitivity and potential impact on the organization. This involves defining the system's criticality and assessing the worst-case adverse effects on the organization's mission or business objectives. Proper categorization helps in determining the level of security controls required.

2. Select

Once the system is categorized, the next step is selecting baseline security controls. This includes applying guidance on tailoring these controls and making necessary modifications based on a thorough risk assessment. The goal is to ensure that security controls are aligned with organizational security policies and compliance requirements.

3. Implement

After selecting appropriate security controls, they must be implemented within the enterprise architecture. This involves integrating security measures using well-established system engineering practices. Configuration changes are also applied to enhance security posture and reduce vulnerabilities within the system.

4. Assess

To ensure that security controls are functioning as intended, they must be assessed. This involves evaluating whether the controls are correctly implemented, operating as expected, and meeting the defined security requirements. The assessment process helps in identifying weaknesses and making improvements where necessary.

5. Authorize

Once the security controls are assessed, the next step is to determine the risk level posed to the organization, its assets, individuals, and other entities. If the risks are within acceptable limits, the system is authorized for operation. This step ensures that security risks are well-documented and understood before approving the system for operation.

6. Monitor

Risk management is an ongoing process. Therefore, the final step involves continuously monitoring the information system for any changes that might impact security. This includes tracking system updates, detecting emerging threats, and reassessing control effectiveness regularly. By maintaining continuous monitoring, organizations can adapt to evolving security challenges and maintain compliance with security standards.

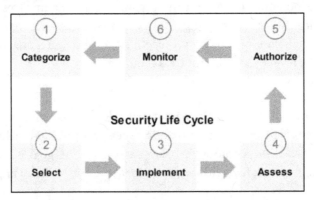

Figure 09-076: NIST Risk Management Framework

COSO ERM Framework

The COSO Enterprise Risk Management (ERM) framework defines essential components, establishes a common language, and provides clear direction and guidance for enterprise risk management. It ensures that organizations incorporate risk considerations into their decision-making processes.

Key Principle: Risk-Based Decision Making

The framework emphasizes that ERM involves elements of the management process that enable organizations to make genuine risk-based decisions. By integrating risk management into strategic planning and operational execution, organizations can enhance resilience and long-term value.

Key Stages of the COSO ERM Framework

Mission, Vision, and Core Values

This stage establishes the foundation of an organization's purpose and guiding principles. It ensures that risk management is aligned with the organization's overall objectives, creating a strong basis for decision-making and long-term sustainability.

Strategy Development

Risk assessment is integrated into the strategic planning process to ensure that business strategies account for potential risks and uncertainties. This enables organizations to proactively address challenges while pursuing growth and innovation.

Business Objective Formulation

At this stage, organizations define specific objectives that balance risk and reward. Risk considerations are aligned with performance targets to ensure that business goals remain achievable while minimizing potential disruptions.

Implementation and Performance

Strategies are translated into action while continuously monitoring risks to ensure effective execution. Performance metrics are designed to reflect risk-adjusted outcomes, enabling organizations to track progress while maintaining resilience.

Enhanced Value

By strengthening decision-making processes, organizations can drive sustainable value and long-term success. Proactive risk management enhances business resilience, allowing companies to adapt to changes and maintain stability in uncertain environments.

Supporting Components of the COSO ERM Framework

- **Governance and Culture:** Establishes ethical standards and risk-aware leadership
- **Strategy and Objective-Setting:** Aligns risk considerations with strategic goals
- **Performance:** Tracks risk-adjusted performance indicators
- **Review and Revision:** Ensures continuous improvement in risk management practices
- **Information, Communication, and Reporting:** Facilitates transparency and accountability in risk-related decision-making

By following the COSO ERM framework, organizations can integrate risk management into their core processes, leading to more informed decision-making and long-term business success.

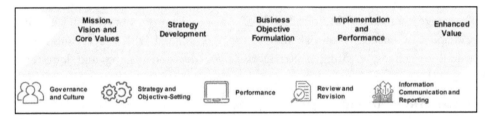

Figure 09-077: COSO ERM Framework

COBIT Framework

The Control Objectives for Information and Related Technologies (COBIT) framework is an essential IT governance framework and toolset that helps organizations effectively manage and control their IT resources. It provides a structured approach for aligning IT processes with business goals while ensuring that risks are managed efficiently. By bridging the gap between control requirements, technical complexities, and business risks, COBIT enables organizations to establish a robust IT governance structure that supports business objectives.

Regulatory Compliance and Business Value

One of the core strengths of the COBIT framework is its emphasis on regulatory compliance. It helps organizations meet industry regulations and standards while ensuring that IT processes remain transparent and auditable. Additionally, COBIT aids in maximizing the value derived from IT investments by aligning IT functions with business strategies. This alignment not only enhances operational efficiency but also simplifies the implementation of enterprise-wide IT governance and

control frameworks, ensuring a seamless and effective approach to risk management.

COBIT Implementation Lifecycle

Figure 09-03 represents a structured approach to organizational improvement and transformation, integrating three interconnected layers:

1. Outer Ring: Program Management

The outermost ring outlines the high-level stages of a program management cycle, guiding organizations through a structured process of change.

2. Middle Ring: Change Enablement

The middle layer focuses on change management, ensuring the successful adoption and integration of improvements.

3. Inner Ring: Continual Improvement Lifecycle

The innermost ring represents a continual improvement lifecycle, emphasizing an iterative approach to process enhancement.

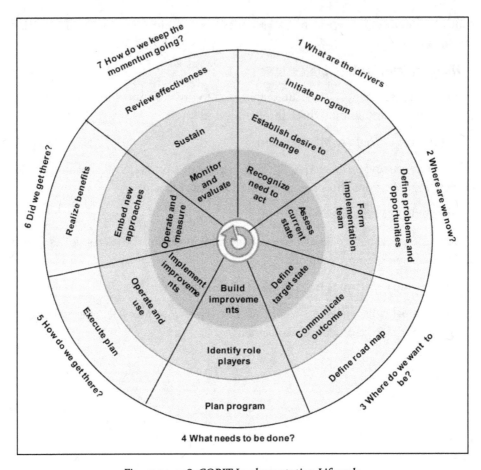

Figure 09-078: COBIT Implementation Lifecycle

COBIT adopts a lifecycle approach that enables organizations to leverage its framework to address challenges that commonly arise during different implementations. The implementation process consists of seven structured phases, ensuring a smooth transition:

1. Analyze Drivers of Change

Organizations begin by identifying pain points, risk scenarios, and triggers that necessitate change. This phase focuses on recognizing the required transformations, understanding their root causes, and determining key success factors.

2. Determine the Current State

This phase involves assessing the organization's current standing by defining the implementation scope. COBIT's enterprise goal mapping is used to align business objectives with IT-related goals, ensuring a structured approach.

3. Define the Target State

Organizations establish a target state and conduct a detailed COBIT analysis to identify existing gaps and potential solutions. While some solutions provide immediate benefits, others require a more strategic approach to implementation.

4. Identify Areas for Improvement

This phase focuses on planning actionable solutions. Organizations identify necessary projects backed by real-time business cases to implement meaningful changes that align with business goals.

5. Develop and Visualize Plans

Business plans are formulated based on defined objectives and key performance metrics. Organizations use these plans to create a roadmap for implementation and ensure alignment with strategic goals.

6. Evaluate Results

The effectiveness of the implemented business plan is assessed by comparing actual outcomes with expected benefits. This phase ensures that the transformation delivers the intended value and aligns with organizational objectives.

7. Sustain Progress and Drive Continuous Improvement

Organizations review overall progress and success, identify additional enterprise management needs, and reinforce the necessity of continuous improvement. This phase ensures long-term sustainability and ongoing enhancements.

By following these seven phases, organizations can effectively implement COBIT and achieve their IT governance and business transformation goals.

Enterprise Network Risk Management Policy

A well-defined enterprise network risk management policy plays a crucial role in establishing structured processes and procedures to mitigate information security risks. This policy provides a comprehensive framework to address different aspects of risk while designating key personnel responsible for managing these risks within the organization. By implementing a robust risk management policy, organizations can proactively identify, assess, and minimize potential security threats.

Objectives of the Risk Management Policy

1. Enhancing Risk Identification and Treatment

The policy equips the organization with the necessary skills to effectively identify and address risks. By fostering awareness and preparedness, it enables teams to assess vulnerabilities and implement appropriate countermeasures.

2. Establishing a Consistent Risk Management Framework

A standardized framework ensures a systematic approach to managing risks. By defining clear processes, organizations can maintain uniformity in risk assessment, mitigation, and response strategies.

3. Providing Direction and Purpose for Risk Management

The policy serves as a guiding principle, outlining the overall direction for managing risks. It ensures that risk management efforts align with the organization's objectives and contribute to long-term resilience.

4. Implementing Adequate Risk Mitigation Techniques

Managing risks effectively requires implementing suitable mitigation strategies. The policy facilitates the adoption of robust techniques to minimize threats and protect critical business operations.

5. Addressing Existing and Emerging Risks

The evolving nature of cyber threats and operational risks necessitates continuous monitoring and proactive responses. This policy enables organizations to combat both existing and emerging risks by staying ahead of potential security challenges.

6. Integrating Operational Risks into the Risk Management Process

Operational risks must be incorporated into the broader risk management framework to ensure comprehensive coverage. By aligning operational risks with strategic risk management initiatives, organizations can enhance resilience and decision-making.

7. Supporting Strategic and Operational Goals

An effective risk management policy contributes to achieving the organization's strategic and operational objectives. By minimizing disruptions and uncertainties, it ensures business continuity and long-term growth.

8. Facilitating Strategic Decision-Making

Risk management plays a vital role in supporting key management decisions. By providing insights into potential risks and their impact, the policy aids leadership in making informed and strategic choices.

9. Ensuring Compliance with Legal and Regulatory Requirements

Meeting legal and regulatory standards is a fundamental aspect of risk management. The policy helps organizations comply with industry regulations, avoiding legal repercussions and safeguarding reputation.

By implementing a structured enterprise network risk management policy, organizations can strengthen their security posture, enhance resilience, and align risk management strategies with their long-term business objectives.

Risk Mitigation

Risk mitigation involves implementing various strategies to minimize the likelihood of risks occurring and reducing their impact if they do materialize. A well-structured risk mitigation plan helps organizations proactively manage potential threats by identifying appropriate solutions. This process ensures that risks falling outside the department's risk tolerance are addressed through effective controls and treatments. Additionally, risk mitigation prioritizes individual risks, determining the order in which they should be mitigated, monitored, and reviewed to ensure business continuity and operational stability.

Key Risk Mitigation Strategies

1. Risk Assumption

This strategy involves accepting the risk and its potential consequences if the cost of mitigation outweighs the impact. Organizations use this approach when the risk is minimal or unavoidable but manageable within acceptable limits.

2. Risk Avoidance

Risk avoidance focuses on eliminating the risk by modifying or discontinuing certain activities. For example, an organization may decide to stop using outdated software to avoid cybersecurity threats.

3. Risk Limitation

Risk limitation is a balanced approach where organizations take measures to reduce the impact and likelihood of risks while still engaging in the activity. This strategy may include implementing security protocols, redundancy measures, or contingency planning.

4. Risk Planning

Through proactive risk planning, organizations develop structured strategies to anticipate and respond to potential risks. This includes setting up risk management policies, defining roles and responsibilities, and establishing response procedures.

5. Research and Acknowledgment

Conducting in-depth research helps organizations gain a better understanding of risks before taking action. Acknowledging potential risks allows decision-makers to make informed choices about how to handle uncertainties effectively.

6. Risk Transference

This strategy involves shifting the risk to a third party, such as outsourcing specific functions or obtaining insurance. By transferring risk, organizations protect themselves from financial or operational setbacks associated with certain threats.

By incorporating these risk mitigation strategies, organizations can enhance their resilience, improve decision-making, and ensure a well-balanced approach to risk management.

Control the Risks

Effectively managing security risks requires a structured approach that identifies existing security controls and determines additional measures needed to enhance protection. Organizations must assess their current security landscape, evaluate potential vulnerabilities, and implement necessary safeguards to reduce risk exposure. Security risks are directly linked to identified vulnerabilities and threats, making it essential to utilize the results of risk assessments to develop mitigation strategies.

Key Security Controls for Risk Reduction

1. Security Awareness for Employees

Educating employees about security best practices is one of the most critical steps in risk management. Organizations should conduct regular training sessions to inform staff about common cyber threats, phishing attacks, and safe online behaviors. Awareness programs help employees recognize risks and take proactive measures to prevent security breaches.

2. Implementation of Advanced Security Solutions

Deploying up-to-date security hardware and software solutions is essential in strengthening an organization's defense mechanisms. Security tools such as Intrusion Detection Systems (IDS), firewalls, honeypots, and Demilitarized Zones (DMZs) provide multiple layers of protection against unauthorized access and cyber threats.

3. Strengthening Network and System Security

Organizations must ensure comprehensive security measures across networks, user accounts, applications, and physical devices. Strengthening security includes

enforcing strong password policies, enabling Multi-Factor Authentication (MFA), and regularly updating software to patch vulnerabilities.

4. Enforcing Strict Access Controls

Strict access controls and security policies prevent unauthorized users from gaining access to sensitive data and systems. Role-Based Access Control (RBAC), privilege management, and continuous monitoring help restrict access to only those who need it, minimizing insider threats and external breaches.

5. Deploying Encryption for Data Transfers

Data encryption ensures that sensitive information remains protected during transmission and storage. Organizations should implement encryption protocols such as TLS for data in transit and AES encryption for stored data to safeguard confidential information from unauthorized access.

6. Establishing an Incident Handling and Response Plan

Having a well-defined incident response plan allows organizations to react swiftly to security breaches. An effective plan outlines procedures for identifying, containing, eradicating, and recovering from security incidents. Regular testing and updates to the response plan ensure that organizations can mitigate risks efficiently when faced with cyber threats.

By integrating these security controls, organizations can build a strong risk management framework that minimizes vulnerabilities, enhances cybersecurity posture, and protects critical assets from potential threats.

Risk Calculation Formulas

Risk calculation formulas help security professionals quantify potential risks and determine appropriate mitigation strategies. Various types of risk calculations exist, and not all risks warrant the same level of investment. Organizations should allocate resources based on the value of assets at risk, ensuring that risk treatments align with their significance. By using risk formulas, professionals can assess potential threats and estimate financial losses, helping organizations make informed security decisions.

Key Risk Calculation Components

1. Asset Value (AV)

Asset Value (AV) represents the monetary worth of an asset within an organization. Determining the value of assets is crucial in assessing the potential impact of a risk event and prioritizing security measures accordingly.

2. Exposure Factor (EF)

Exposure Factor (EF) is the estimated percentage of damage or impact a realized threat could have on an asset. It provides insight into how severely an asset would be affected if a specific risk materializes.

3. Single Loss Expectancy (SLE)

Single Loss Expectancy (SLE) calculates the financial loss that would occur from a single risk event. It is determined using the formula:

SLE = Asset Value (AV) × Exposure Factor (EF)

This helps organizations estimate the direct impact of a single occurrence of a threat.

4. Annual Rate of Occurrence (ARO)

Annual Rate of Occurrence (ARO) estimates how frequently a particular risk is expected to materialize within a year. It is based on historical data and industry trends, providing an approximation of risk likelihood over time.

5. Annualized Loss Expectancy (ALE)

Annualized Loss Expectancy (ALE) determines the expected financial loss due to a specific risk occurring over a year. It is calculated using the formula:

ALE = Single Loss Expectancy (SLE) × Annual Rate of Occurrence (ARO)

This metric helps organizations assess long-term financial risks and develop appropriate risk management strategies.

By leveraging these risk calculation formulas, organizations can better understand potential threats, estimate financial losses, and implement effective risk mitigation strategies.

Quantitative Risk vs. Qualitative Risk

Risk analysis plays a crucial role in assessing potential threats and their impact on an organization. There are two primary approaches to risk analysis: qualitative and quantitative. Each method provides a unique perspective on risk assessment, helping organizations make informed decisions regarding security measures and mitigation strategies.

Qualitative Risk Analysis

Qualitative risk analysis is a subjective assessment that focuses on evaluating the perceived impact of a specific risk event. This approach relies on expert judgment, industry experience, and organizational consensus to assign risk ratings. Instead of

using numerical values, qualitative analysis categorizes risks based on their severity, likelihood, and potential impact.

Most qualitative risk assessment methodologies involve interrelated elements such as threats, vulnerabilities, and controls to determine risk exposure. Organizations typically use predefined scales such as low, medium, or high risk to assess and prioritize security concerns. This method is widely used when numerical data is scarce or when a quick risk evaluation is required.

Quantitative Risk Analysis

In contrast, quantitative risk analysis takes a numeric approach, assigning measurable values to risk factors. It focuses on calculating the probability of a specific event occurring and estimating the financial cost of its impact. This data-driven approach provides a more objective view of risks, allowing organizations to make precise financial decisions regarding risk mitigation.

Quantitative analysis relies on two key factors:

- The probability of an event occurring
- The potential financial loss if the event occurs

One of the most commonly used formulas in quantitative risk analysis is:

Annual Rate of Occurrence (ARO) × Single Loss Expectancy (SLE) = Annualized Loss Expectancy (ALE)

This formula helps organizations determine the expected annual financial loss associated with a particular risk. By using numerical assessments, decision-makers can prioritize investments in security measures based on cost-benefit analysis.

Both qualitative and quantitative risk analysis methods play essential roles in risk management. While qualitative analysis provides a broad, experience-based understanding of risks, quantitative analysis offers precise, data-driven insights. Organizations often use a combination of both approaches to develop a comprehensive risk management strategy.

Business Continuity and Disaster Recovery Process

Business Continuity (BC)

Business Continuity (BC) refers to the processes and procedures organizations implement to ensure that mission-critical functions continue operating during and after a disruptive incident. It focuses on maintaining essential business operations rather than just protecting IT infrastructure. According to the ISO standard, business continuity is defined as an organization's capability to deliver products or services at predefined acceptable levels following a disaster or disruption.

Unlike traditional disaster recovery strategies that emphasize restoring IT systems, business continuity takes a broader, business-centric approach by ensuring that the organization can sustain its core activities regardless of disruptions. This approach includes planning for various scenarios, from natural disasters to cyberattacks, and developing strategies to mitigate risks and ensure smooth operations.

Objectives of Business Continuity

The primary goal of business continuity is to maintain operational stability despite unforeseen challenges. To achieve this, organizations focus on several key objectives:

- **Ensuring Operational Continuity:** A well-structured business continuity plan helps organizations maintain essential operations during and after a disruptive incident, preventing major downtime.

- **Protecting Organizational Reputation:** By ensuring uninterrupted services, organizations can maintain customer trust and safeguard their reputation, even in challenging circumstances.

- **Preparing for Disasters:** Business continuity planning involves proactive measures to anticipate potential disasters and minimize their impact, reducing recovery time and costs.

- **Enhancing Compliance Benefits:** Many industries require organizations to have a business continuity plan in place to comply with regulatory and legal standards related to risk management and operational resilience.

- **Mitigating Risks and Financial Losses:** A strong business continuity plan minimizes financial losses by reducing operational disruptions, enabling faster recovery, and ensuring that critical business functions remain unaffected.

By implementing a well-defined business continuity strategy, organizations can safeguard their operations, reduce downtime, and enhance their ability to withstand unforeseen disruptions.

Disaster Recovery (DR)

Disaster Recovery (DR) refers to an organization's ability to restore critical business data and applications following a disruptive incident. It is a data-centric strategy focused on quickly rebuilding IT infrastructure, including data centers, servers, and other essential systems, to ensure business continuity. Unlike business continuity, which emphasizes maintaining operations, disaster recovery is more technical, prioritizing the restoration of IT resources to minimize downtime.

A well-defined disaster recovery plan includes identifying potential threats, implementing backup solutions, and establishing recovery procedures to restore

lost or damaged data efficiently. Organizations must have dedicated teams responsible for executing the recovery process, ensuring minimal disruption to business operations.

Objectives of Disaster Recovery

The primary goal of disaster recovery is to restore IT infrastructure and minimize downtime following a disaster. The key objectives include:

- **Reducing Downtime:** A disaster recovery plan ensures that organizations can resume operations as quickly as possible after an incident, preventing prolonged disruptions.

- **Minimizing Financial Losses:** Downtime can lead to significant financial losses due to halted operations, missed opportunities, and reputational damage. Effective DR strategies help mitigate these risks.

- **Recovering Critical Data:** Organizations rely on disaster recovery plans to restore lost or damaged data, particularly in cases of hardware failures, cyberattacks, or natural disasters. Regular backups and redundant storage solutions play a crucial role in safeguarding business-critical information.

By implementing a robust disaster recovery strategy, organizations can ensure resilience, maintain data integrity, and minimize operational risks in the face of unexpected disruptions.

Business Impact Analysis (BIA)

Business Impact Analysis (BIA) is a systematic process used to assess and evaluate the potential impact of disruptions to critical business operations due to disasters, accidents, or emergencies. It helps organizations understand the consequences of operational interruptions and develop strategies to mitigate risks.

One of the key aspects of BIA is determining the Recovery Time Objectives (RTO) and recovery requirements for different disaster scenarios. By identifying which functions are most critical, organizations can allocate resources effectively and ensure that essential operations resume as quickly as possible.

BIA operates on the assumption that while every business component is interdependent, some functions are more crucial than others. Given that resources are often limited, organizations must prioritize recovery efforts to protect their most vital processes.

It is important to note that BIA serves primarily as an analysis tool rather than a recovery plan. It does not focus on designing or implementing recovery solutions but instead provides insights that guide decision-making in business continuity and disaster recovery planning.

Recovery Time Objective (RTO)

Recovery Time Objective (RTO) refers to the maximum allowable downtime for a computer, system, network, or application following a failure or disaster. It establishes the timeframe within which IT operations must be restored to minimize the impact on business continuity.

RTO plays a crucial role in business continuity planning as it helps organizations determine the extent to which an interruption affects normal operations and the potential revenue loss resulting from downtime. The shorter the RTO, the faster systems must be restored to maintain operational efficiency.

Typically, RTO is expressed in minutes or hours. For instance, if an organization sets an RTO of 45 minutes, it means that IT operations must resume within 45 minutes of a system failure to prevent significant disruptions to business processes.

Recovery Point Objective (RPO)

Recovery Point Objective (RPO) defines the maximum acceptable data loss an organization can tolerate in the event of a major IT outage. It establishes the timeframe for which data may be lost due to a system failure, disaster, or cyberattack, ensuring that backup and disaster recovery strategies align with business needs.

RPO plays a critical role in disaster recovery planning, helping organizations determine how frequently data should be backed up. A shorter RPO means more frequent backups and minimal data loss, whereas a longer RPO may result in higher data loss but lower backup costs.

Every organization must evaluate how long it can function without access to critical data before business operations are severely impacted. By setting an appropriate RPO, businesses can balance cost, recovery speed, and risk tolerance in their disaster recovery strategies.

Business Continuity Plan (BCP)

A Business Continuity Plan (BCP) is a comprehensive strategy designed to ensure that an organization can maintain essential operations despite potential threats or disruptions. It provides a structured approach to resilience and recovery, allowing businesses to function effectively under adverse conditions and swiftly resume normal operations after a crisis.

Goals of a Business Continuity Plan

The primary goal of a BCP is to analyze potential risks and losses, ensuring that the organization can mitigate disruptions efficiently. It plays a crucial role in the risk

management process, reducing the likelihood of severe operational failures and preventing a worst-case scenario where the business ceases operations entirely.

A well-structured BCP prioritizes the safety, health, and well-being of employees while minimizing infrastructural damage in the event of a disaster. It also ensures a smooth recovery process, helping organizations return to normal operating conditions as quickly as possible.

In addition, a BCP focuses on maintaining vital business information, including employee records, vendor contacts, client details, and other critical documents. It also emphasizes the importance of staff training and awareness, ensuring that employees understand their roles and responsibilities during a crisis. This proactive approach enhances preparedness and strengthens the organization's ability to adapt and respond to unexpected disruptions.

Disaster Recovery Plan (DRP)

A Disaster Recovery Plan (DRP) is a structured strategy developed to help specific departments within an organization recover from disasters efficiently. It focuses on restoring critical systems, applications, and data to ensure business continuity with minimal downtime. A well-defined DRP outlines the necessary steps for mitigating the impact of disruptions, helping organizations resume operations as quickly as possible.

Goals of a Disaster Recovery Plan

The primary goal of a DRP is to reduce overall organizational risk by implementing proactive measures that safeguard essential assets and infrastructure. It also aims to alleviate senior management concerns by providing a clear framework for disaster recovery, ensuring that the organization is well-prepared to handle unexpected incidents.

Additionally, a DRP ensures compliance with industry regulations and legal requirements, reinforcing the organization's commitment to maintaining security and operational integrity. Another crucial objective is to enable a rapid response to incidents, minimizing downtime and financial losses while ensuring that recovery efforts are executed efficiently.

Domain 10: Cyber Threat Intelligence

Introduction

Cyber Threat Intelligence (CTI) is a critical component of modern cybersecurity, enabling organizations to proactively detect, analyze, and mitigate threats. By gathering and processing threat data from various sources, CTI helps security teams understand attacker Tactics, Techniques, and Procedures (TTPs), ultimately strengthening an organization's defense posture.

This domain covers key aspects of Cyber Threat Intelligence, including frameworks for analyzing threats, methods for collecting and managing intelligence, and gathering Indicators of Compromise (IoCs). It highlights the importance of an accessible threat knowledge base, effective reporting, and dissemination strategies. Additionally, it explores threat modeling methodologies for risk assessment and threat profiling for identifying adversaries. Understanding these concepts enables organizations to proactively detect, analyze, and respond to cyber threats.

Threat Intelligence Frameworks

Threat intelligence frameworks are structured methodologies and systems designed to collect, analyze, and share threat intelligence to enhance cybersecurity. They help organizations understand adversary tactics, detect threats, and improve incident response by providing standardized models for threat analysis and mitigation.

CIF is a cyber threat intelligence management system that gathers, processes, and shares threat data from both public and private sources. It enables security teams to query indexed feeds for analysis and push threat intelligence to mitigation tools like firewalls, IDS, and DNS sinkholes for proactive defense.

Collective Intelligence Framework (CIF)

The Collective Intelligence Framework (CIF) is an open-source cyber threat intelligence management system designed to aggregate, process, and utilize threat intelligence from multiple sources. By integrating known malicious threat information, CIF enables organizations to enhance their incident detection, response, and mitigation capabilities. One of its key features is the ability to ingest data from both public and private threat intelligence feeds, allowing security teams to incorporate their proprietary threat data for more customized analysis.

CIF is particularly effective in handling large volumes of threat intelligence by parsing, normalizing, storing, post-processing, querying, and sharing structured data. The framework can process Indicators of Compromise (IoCs) such as IP addresses, domain names, URLs, and file hashes, categorizing them based on risk levels and enabling automated or manual security enforcement.

Additionally, CIF supports interoperability with other security tools and intelligence-sharing platforms, ensuring that organizations can distribute actionable threat intelligence efficiently. By centralizing and streamlining threat data management, CIF helps security teams make informed decisions, improve threat-hunting efforts, and strengthen overall cybersecurity defenses.

CIF Architecture

Figure 10-01 illustrates the architecture of the Collective Intelligence Framework (CIF) and how it processes threat intelligence from multiple sources.

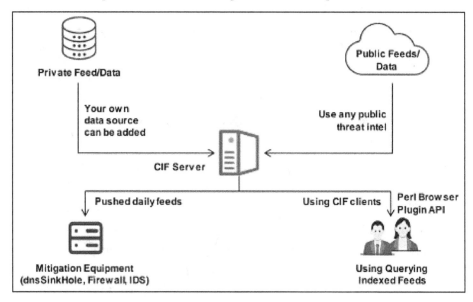

Figure 10-01: CIF Architecture

The CIF server acts as the central component, aggregating and managing both private feeds/data (proprietary intelligence from an organization) and public feeds/data (open-source or third-party threat intelligence). This aggregated intelligence can then be utilized in two key ways.

First, the CIF server pushes daily feeds to mitigation equipment such as DNS sinkholes, firewalls, and Intrusion Detection Systems (IDS) to automate proactive threat blocking. Second, security analysts can query indexed feeds using CIF clients or a Perl browser plugin API for threat hunting, forensic investigations, and incident response. This framework enables organizations to normalize, store, and operationalize threat intelligence efficiently, enhancing their ability to detect, analyze, and mitigate cyber threats.

Threat Intelligence Data Collection

Threat Intelligence Data Collection is the foundational process of gathering relevant and reliable data for cybersecurity analysis. High-quality data collection is essential for producing actionable threat intelligence, enabling organizations to detect, assess, and mitigate threats effectively.

Threat data can be sourced from multiple intelligence disciplines, including:

- **Human Intelligence (HUMINT):** Information obtained from human sources, such as security researchers, informants, or insider threat reports.

- **Imagery Intelligence (IMINT):** Visual intelligence derived from images, satellite surveillance, or network topology mapping.

- **Signals Intelligence (SIGINT):** Data collected from intercepted communications, network traffic, or encrypted signals.

- **Open Source Intelligence (OSINT):** Publicly available information from news sources, websites, forums, and reports.

- **Social Media Intelligence (SOCMINT):** Data from social media platforms, can indicate emerging threats, attack coordination, or adversary behavior.

Organizations can gather threat intelligence data through automated feeds, security tools, or manual investigations conducted by analysts. Security teams across different departments may contribute to the collection process by reporting incidents, analyzing logs, or monitoring threat actor activities. A robust data collection strategy ensures comprehensive threat visibility, improving an organization's ability to respond to cyber threats efficiently.

Threat Intelligence Sources

Threat Intelligence Sources are the origins of data used to identify and analyze cybersecurity threats. These sources provide valuable insights into adversary Tactics, Techniques, and Procedures (TTPs), enabling proactive defense strategies.

Some common threat intelligence sources include:

Open-Source Intelligence (OSINT)

OSINT involves collecting and analyzing publicly available information to derive meaningful insights for threat intelligence and cybersecurity. This data is gathered from various open sources, including media (news, blogs, and online forums), the internet (social media, websites, and search engines), public government data (official reports, regulatory filings, and transparency disclosures), and corporate or academic publications (research papers, patents, and whitepapers). OSINT is widely

used in cybersecurity, law enforcement, and intelligence operations to monitor emerging threats, track adversaries, and identify vulnerabilities without requiring privileged access.

Human Intelligence (HUMINT)

HUMINT is intelligence collected from human sources through direct interaction, interviews, or covert operations. It is commonly used in military, defense, and law enforcement to gather insights on adversary strategies, geopolitical developments, and security threats. HUMINT sources include foreign defense personnel and advisors, accredited diplomats, Non-Governmental Organizations (NGOs), Prisoners of War (POWs), refugees, and travelers who provide debriefing reports. Unlike automated intelligence collection methods, HUMINT relies on interpersonal skills and strategic questioning to extract valuable information that may not be accessible through digital or technical means.

Signals Intelligence (SIGINT)

SIGINT is intelligence obtained by intercepting and analyzing electronic signals to monitor communications, detect cyber threats, and support military or security operations. It is categorized into three main types:

1. **Communication Intelligence (COMINT):** It captures communication signals such as phone calls, emails, and radio transmissions.

2. **Electronic Intelligence (ELINT):** It gathers intelligence from electronic sensors like radar, lidar, and tracking systems.

3. **Foreign Instrumentation Signals Intelligence (FISINT):** It monitors non-human communication signals, such as telemetry from missile tests or satellite communications.

SIGINT is a critical component of national security, cyber defense, and counterintelligence efforts, enabling governments and organizations to detect potential threats and adversarial activities.

Technical Intelligence (TECHINT)

Technical Intelligence (TECHINT) involves gathering and analyzing information from an adversary's equipment, technologies, or Captured Enemy Material (CEM) to assess their capabilities and develop countermeasures. This type of intelligence is crucial in military and cybersecurity contexts, where understanding foreign technologies can provide a strategic advantage. TECHINT sources include foreign equipment, weapon systems, satellite communications, technical research papers, foreign media, and human contacts with knowledge of adversarial technology. By

studying these elements, organizations and governments can enhance their defensive capabilities, reverse-engineer threats, and improve situational awareness.

Geospatial Intelligence (GEOINT)

Geospatial Intelligence (GEOINT) involves collecting and analyzing geospatial data to monitor and assess human activities on Earth. It is used in military operations, disaster response, urban planning, and cybersecurity to track adversary movements, detect infrastructure vulnerabilities, and analyze terrain for strategic purposes. GEOINT sources include satellite imagery, Unmanned Aerial Vehicles (UAV) imagery, maps, GPS waypoints, Imagery Intelligence (IMINT), and data from the National Geospatial-Intelligence Agency (NGA). By leveraging geospatial data, analysts can create actionable intelligence to support decision-making in security, defense, and emergency response.

Imagery Intelligence (IMINT)

Imagery Intelligence (IMINT) focuses on collecting and analyzing visual data from various electronic media and devices to recreate real-world scenarios. It is widely used in surveillance, reconnaissance, and intelligence-gathering operations. IMINT sources include visual photography, infrared sensors, Synthetic Aperture Radar (SAR), Measurement and Signature Intelligence (MASINT), LASER imaging, and electro-optical systems. These tools provide high-resolution imagery for monitoring enemy movements, infrastructure, and potential threats, supporting military and security operations with accurate visual intelligence.

Measurement and Signature Intelligence (MASINT)

Measurement and Signature Intelligence (MASINT) is a specialized intelligence discipline that collects and analyzes unique signatures from fixed or dynamic targets using advanced sensor technologies. MASINT is used to detect hidden threats, verify missile launches, and assess nuclear activities. Its sources include electro-optical sensors, radar sensors, acoustic sensors like sonars, LASER detection, infrared scanning, and spectroscopic sensors. These technologies help in identifying the material composition, movement patterns, and electromagnetic signatures of adversarial assets.

Covert Human Intelligence Sources (CHIS)

Covert Human Intelligence Sources (CHIS) involve the collection of intelligence through personal or professional relationships with a target individual. This method is commonly used in law enforcement, counterterrorism, and espionage to extract critical information without alerting the target. CHIS agents, who may be informants, undercover officers, or recruited assets, operate under strict regulations such as the Regulation of Investigatory Powers Act 2000 (RIPA), UK. The

intelligence gathered through CHIS provides insights into criminal organizations, terrorist activities, and geopolitical threats.

Financial Intelligence (FININT)

Financial Intelligence (FININT) focuses on analyzing financial transactions and economic activities to uncover illicit practices such as money laundering, tax evasion, and terrorism financing. By tracking financial flows, organizations can gain insights into an adversary's nature, capabilities, and intentions. Key FININT sources include Financial Intelligence Units (FIUs), banks, Society for Worldwide Interbank Financial Telecommunication (SWIFT), and Informal Value Transfer Systems (IVTS). These financial networks help analysts identify suspicious transactions, detect fraud, and prevent the misuse of financial systems for illegal activities.

Social Media Intelligence (SOCMINT)

Social Media Intelligence (SOCMINT) involves collecting and analyzing information from social networking platforms to gain insights into emerging threats, cybercrime activities, and adversarial behavior. It is widely used for threat monitoring, law enforcement investigations, and cybersecurity risk assessments. SOCMINT sources include platforms like Facebook, LinkedIn, Twitter, WhatsApp, Instagram, and Telegram, where individuals and organizations share information, communicate, and conduct business. Cybersecurity analysts use SOCMINT to track threat actors, monitor public sentiment, and detect potential cyber threats based on social media activity.

Cyber Counterintelligence (CCI)

Cyber Counterintelligence (CCI) focuses on proactively identifying and mitigating cyber threats through deception techniques and security infrastructure. It involves setting up honeypots, passive DNS monitors, and online web trackers to detect and study potential attackers. Additionally, analysts use sock puppets (fake profiles) on online forums and publish false reports to mislead adversaries and gather intelligence on their Tactics, Techniques, and Procedures (TTPs). CCI helps organizations anticipate cyberattacks, disrupt adversarial operations, and strengthen their cybersecurity defenses.

Indicators of Compromise (IoCs)

Indicators of Compromise (IoCs) are forensic artifacts that signal potential cyber intrusions, breaches, or malicious activities within an organization's network. IoCs provide valuable intelligence by identifying security incidents early, allowing for a rapid response. Sources of IoCs include commercial and industrial sources, free IoC-specific databases, online security-related platforms, social media, news feeds, and IoC repositories (IoC buckets). Analysts use these sources to detect malware

signatures, suspicious IP addresses, and anomalous network traffic that indicate a cyber threat.

Industry Associations and Vertical Communities

Industry associations and vertical communities serve as collaborative platforms where organizations share threat intelligence to enhance collective security. These communities provide access to real-time threat data, best practices, and incident reports. Examples of such vertical community sources include the Financial Services Information Sharing and Analysis Center (FS-ISAC) for the financial sector, the Malware Information Sharing Platform (MISP) for malware intelligence, and the Information Technology—Information Sharing and Analysis Center (IT-ISAC) for IT-related security. By participating in these communities, organizations can improve their threat detection and response capabilities.

Commercial Sources

Commercial sources provide cybersecurity threat intelligence through private security vendors and research firms that specialize in detecting and analyzing cyber threats. These sources offer proprietary threat intelligence feeds, malware analysis, and security reports. Leading commercial threat intelligence providers include Kaspersky Threat Intelligence, McAfee, Avast, FortiGuard, SecureWorks, and Cisco, which supply real-time data on malware, vulnerabilities, and attack trends. Organizations rely on these sources to stay ahead of evolving cyber threats and enhance their security posture.

Government and Law Enforcement Sources

Government and law enforcement agencies play a crucial role in providing cybersecurity threat intelligence and risk mitigation guidelines. These agencies track cybercriminal activities, issue security advisories, and collaborate with private organizations to combat cyber threats. Key government sources include the US Computer Emergency Response Team (US-CERT), the European Union Agency for Network and Information Security (ENISA), the FBI Cyber Crime division, the StopThinkConnect initiative, and the CERIAS Blog from Purdue University. Organizations leverage intelligence from these sources to improve incident response strategies and comply with regulatory cybersecurity frameworks.

Threat Intelligence Collection Management

Threat Intelligence Collection Management is the systematic process of gathering, organizing, and prioritizing threat data intelligence from multiple sources to support cybersecurity operations. It involves defining collection requirements, identifying relevant intelligence sources, ensuring data reliability, and managing the storage and retrieval of collected intelligence for analysis. Effective collection

management ensures security teams obtain actionable insights to detect, respond to, and mitigate cyber threats efficiently.

Understanding Data Reliability

Ensuring the reliability of collected data is crucial in threat intelligence, as inaccurate or manipulated information can lead to misguided security decisions. Analysts must assess the trustworthiness of the data they gather, considering various factors such as authenticity, accuracy, and completeness. By evaluating source reliability, analysts can filter out misleading or irrelevant data and focus on actionable intelligence to enhance cybersecurity defense strategies.

Assessing the Relevance of Intelligence Sources

To maximize the effectiveness of threat intelligence, analysts must ensure that the collected data comes from reliable sources that provide relevant and accurate information. Data integrity must be maintained during the collection process, ensuring that it is not altered or tampered with before analysis. Organizations rely on well-established sources, such as government security agencies, industry threat-sharing communities, and vetted cybersecurity vendors, to obtain credible intelligence. Proper validation methods help analysts confirm the authenticity of the data and prevent the use of misleading or manipulated information.

Factors Affecting the Credibility of an Intelligence Source

The credibility of an intelligence source depends on factors, such as data authenticity, accuracy, and completeness. If the source lacks verification mechanisms, the collected data may be unreliable or even deceptive. Inaccurate intelligence can lead to false positives, misallocation of security resources, and ineffective responses to threats. Additionally, incomplete or insufficient data may limit an organization's ability to detect and mitigate security incidents. Analysts must critically evaluate each source and cross-check information from multiple channels to ensure the highest level of reliability.

Data Collection Methods Affecting Data Availability

The method used to collect intelligence significantly impacts the volume and type of data obtained. Different collection approaches offer varying levels of access and insights.

1. A passive method gathers internal and openly shared data, making it useful for monitoring existing threats without direct engagement with adversaries.

2. An active method allows authorized access to specific data sources, enabling deeper analysis but often requiring compliance with legal and ethical considerations.

3. A hybrid method combines passive and active techniques and includes deception-based tactics such as honeypots and traps to lure attackers and collect intelligence on their tactics.

By choosing the appropriate collection method, analysts can optimize data gathering while maintaining security and ethical integrity.

Produce Actionable Threat Intelligence

Actionable threat intelligence refers to security insights that organizations can use to prevent, detect, and respond to cyber threats effectively. The quality of intelligence directly impacts an organization's security posture, making it essential for analysts to rely on accurate, timely, and relevant data. While free or low-cost intelligence sources can provide useful insights, they may also introduce risks such as outdated information, false positives, or manipulated data from unreliable sources. Therefore, analysts must carefully evaluate and select intelligence sources that align with the organization's security needs and operational goals.

To ensure actionable threat intelligence, analysts must prioritize sources that provide comprehensive coverage of relevant threats while maintaining data integrity. The intelligence should be relevant to the organization's industry, geographical location, and operational environment. Timeliness is also a critical factor—delayed intelligence may result in missed opportunities to mitigate threats before they cause harm. Analysts should assess each intelligence source based on its historical accuracy, credibility, and the depth of its coverage regarding cyber threat actors, Indicators of Compromise (IoCs), and Tactics, Techniques, and Procedures (TTPs).

Key Considerations for Actionable Threat Intelligence

To evaluate the usefulness of intelligence data, analysts should ask the following questions:

1. Does the intelligence belong to the same geographical location as the organization?

Understanding regional threats is crucial, as cyber threats often vary by location. Localized threat intelligence can help organizations anticipate region-specific cyberattacks, regulatory concerns, and adversary tactics targeting their geographic sector.

2. Does the intelligence support the strategic business requirements of the organization?

Threat intelligence must align with the organization's business objectives and risk tolerance. If an organization operates in the financial sector, intelligence on banking malware, fraud tactics, and ransomware threats will be more relevant than generic cybercrime reports.

3. To what extent is the information about threat actors, IoCs, and TTPs useful to the organization?

Detailed intelligence on adversaries, such as their known IoCs, preferred attack vectors, and operational methods, enables organizations to strengthen their defenses proactively. Analysts must assess whether the provided intelligence can be integrated into security tools such as SIEMs, firewalls, and endpoint detection systems.

4. What are the broader effects of intelligence on the organization?

Beyond immediate cybersecurity defenses, organizations must consider how threat intelligence affects compliance, risk management, and overall business continuity. Understanding the long-term impact of threats helps in formulating strategic mitigation plans and ensuring resilience against evolving cyber risks.

By addressing these factors, organizations can transform raw data into actionable intelligence, enabling them to detect and mitigate threats proactively while improving overall cybersecurity resilience.

Collecting IoCs

Indicators of Compromise (IoCs) are critical technical artifacts used in cybersecurity to detect and analyze potential security breaches. These artifacts serve as forensic evidence that indicates an intrusion or malicious activity within an organization's network. IoCs are fundamental in building tactical threat intelligence, enabling security teams to identify ongoing or past cyberattacks by recognizing suspicious patterns or anomalies.

IoCs consist of various data points that highlight unauthorized or malicious activities within a network. These may include unusual network traffic, abnormal system behavior, unauthorized access attempts, file hash changes, and communications with known malicious domains or IP addresses. The data used to identify IoCs is gathered from multiple security sources, such as firewalls, Intrusion Detection and Prevention Systems (IDS/IPS), SIEM solutions, endpoint security tools, and external threat intelligence feeds.

The primary role of IoCs is to help analysts understand the nature of an attack by providing insights into how malware behaves, how an intrusion is executed, and what vulnerabilities are exploited. By analyzing these indicators, security teams can trace attack timelines, detect persistent threats, and strengthen defenses against similar future attacks. Additionally, IoCs are often shared among organizations, cybersecurity communities, and law enforcement agencies to enhance collective threat intelligence and improve cybersecurity resilience.

IoC Data Collection Sources

IoC data collection sources can be categorized into external and internal sources.

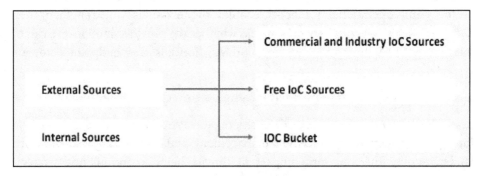

Figure 10-02: IoC Data Collection Sources

External Sources

- **Commercial and Industry IoC Sources:** Paid threat intelligence services from security vendors that provide high-quality, curated IoCs (e.g., Kaspersky, FireEye, Palo Alto Networks).

- **Free IoC Sources:** Open-source and publicly available threat intelligence feeds, such as AlienVault OTX, Abuse.ch, and VirusTotal, provide IoCs at no cost.

Internal Sources

- **IoC Bucket:** Internally collected threat intelligence based on logs, security tools, and previous attack patterns within an organization. This includes data from firewalls, IDS/IPS, SIEM platforms, and endpoint security solutions.

Combining external and internal sources help organizations improve detection, threat hunting, and incident response capabilities by leveraging a broader intelligence pool.

Accessible Threat Knowledge Base

Creating an accessible threat knowledge base is essential for effective threat intelligence management. A threat knowledge repository serves as a centralized platform where analysts can document, store, and share intelligence related to cybersecurity threats. This repository enables organizations to collaborate, analyze trends, and improve response strategies by maintaining a structured database of past incidents, attack techniques, Indicators of Compromise (IoCs), and mitigation strategies.

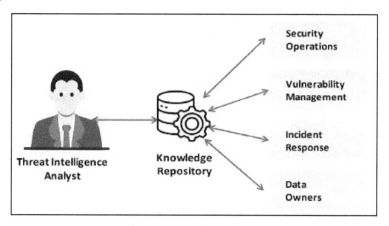

Figure 10-03: Threat Knowledge Repository

Figure 10-03 illustrates the role of a Threat Knowledge Repository in cybersecurity. A Threat Intelligence Analyst gathers and inputs threat intelligence into the repository, which serves as a centralized database for security data. This intelligence is then utilized by various cybersecurity functions, including Security Operations, Vulnerability Management, Incident Response, and Data Owners. The repository enables these teams to enhance threat detection, improve incident handling, prioritize vulnerabilities, and ensure data protection, ultimately strengthening the organization's security posture.

Features of Threat Knowledge Repository

A threat knowledge repository must include key features to effectively support cybersecurity operations. These features help security teams collect, analyze, store, and share threat intelligence in a structured and efficient manner.

Pivoting

The repository should provide the capability to contextualize threat data by correlating related activities. Analysts should be able to trace an attacker's Tactics, Techniques, and Procedures (TTPs) across multiple incidents, enabling deeper investigation and enhancing threat hunting.

Content Structuring

Threat intelligence must be stored in a structured format, following industry standards such as Structured Threat Information Expression (STIX). Proper structuring ensures that data can be easily retrieved, analyzed, and shared across security teams and automated security tools.

Data Management

The repository must allow analysts to modify or delete outdated, irrelevant, or incorrect threat data. This ensures that intelligence remains accurate, relevant, and actionable, preventing security teams from making decisions based on obsolete information.

Protection Ranking

Sensitive threat intelligence must be classified and ranked based on its confidentiality and importance. Protection ranking ensures that highly critical data is only shared with trusted partners while limiting exposure to external sources that may not have proper security clearance.

News Feeds

Real-time news, alerts, briefings, and reports should be integrated into the repository. This helps security teams stay updated on emerging threats, vulnerabilities, and cyber incidents, enabling quick adaption to evolving attack techniques.

Evaluating Performance

The ability to assess past security metrics is crucial for continuous improvement. By analyzing past incidents, attack patterns, and response effectiveness, organizations can identify gaps in their security posture and optimize their threat intelligence strategies.

Searchable Functionality

The repository should support advanced search and enrichment capabilities. Analysts must be able to query IoCs, threat actors, malware signatures, and attack campaigns to quickly retrieve relevant intelligence and enrich security investigations.

Organize and Store Cyber Threat Information in the Knowledge Base

Organizations collect cyber threat information from a diverse range of sources, including Open-Source Intelligence (OSINT), external reports, commercial threat feeds, and proprietary security data. Given the vast amount of threat data available, it is crucial to systematically store and organize this information in a knowledge

base. A well-structured knowledge base allows security teams to categorize, retrieve, and analyze threat indicators efficiently. By centralizing threat intelligence, organizations can ensure consistency, facilitate collaboration among security teams, and enhance their ability to detect and mitigate emerging threats. Properly organizing and indexing threat indicators also enables automated threat correlation, real-time monitoring, and faster incident response, strengthening an organization's cybersecurity posture.

Information stored in the knowledge base includes the following:

- The source of a threat indicator

- The established rules for using and sharing a threat indicator

- The date and time an indicator were collected

- The lifetime of validity for a threat indicator

- Whether the attacks that are related to a threat indicator have targeted specific organizations or industry sectors

- Whether an indicator is associated with Common Weakness Enumeration (CWE), Common Vulnerability Enumeration (CVE), Common Configuration Enumeration (CCE), or Common Platform Enumeration (CPE) records

- Threat actors or threat actor groups associated with an indicator

- Threat actor aliases if any exist

- The TTPs used by a threat actor

- The associated threat actor's motives and intent

- The different types of individuals targeted by the associated attacks

- The systems targeted in the associated attacks

Threat Intelligence Reports

Threat intelligence reports are structured documents that provide comprehensive details about various cybersecurity threats, including attack methods, Tactics, Techniques, and Procedures (TTPs) used by threat actors. These reports serve as a critical resource for organizations to understand potential risks, vulnerabilities, and the nature of attacks targeting their systems and data. By compiling insights on emerging and ongoing threats, intelligence reports help security teams anticipate, detect, and mitigate cyber threats effectively.

These reports are created by collecting and aggregating raw threat data from multiple sources, such as Open-Source Intelligence (OSINT), dark web monitoring,

commercial threat feeds, and internal security logs. The collected data is then transformed, analyzed, and enriched with contextual information to provide actionable intelligence. This intelligence enables organizations to make informed decisions regarding cybersecurity strategies, incident response, and risk management.

A well-structured threat intelligence report typically includes details about specific threat actors, their motives, and the industries they target. It also highlights the systems and information at risk, offering recommendations on mitigation strategies. By leveraging these reports, organizations can proactively enhance their security posture, improve threat detection, and strengthen defenses against cyber adversaries.

Generating Concise Reports

Generating concise threat intelligence reports is essential for effectively communicating relevant security insights within an organization. Regular dissemination of timely and actionable intelligence enhances internal awareness and enables proactive defense against emerging threats.

A well-structured report includes the following key elements to ensure clarity and usefulness:

- Report Details provide the basic information about the report, such as the title, date, and author
- Client Details specify the intended audience or stakeholders
- Test Details outline the scope of analysis, data sources, and methodologies used
- Executive Summary gives a high-level overview of the findings, highlighting critical threats and risks
- Traffic Light Protocol (TLP) sets restrictions on data distribution
- The Analysis Methodology explains how the data was processed and assessed
- Threat Details cover specific attack vectors, threat actors, and potential risks
- Indicators of Compromise (IoCs) provide forensic evidence of malicious activity
- Recommended Actions offer mitigation steps and security improvements to address identified threats

Threat Intelligence Dissemination

Threat intelligence dissemination is a vital for providing organizations with insights into potential threats. By sharing intelligence effectively, organizations can proactively enhance their security posture and mitigate risks. This process can be manual, with analysts compiling and distributing reports, or automated, integrating intelligence feeds into security tools for real-time decision-making. To fully leverage the advantages of threat intelligence, certain essential criteria must be met.

1. Right Content

The right content is fundamental—intelligence must be high-quality, relevant, and provide a clear understanding of the threats, their impact, and possible mitigation strategies. Poorly structured or vague intelligence can hinder response efforts and lead to ineffective decision-making.

2. Right Presentation

The right presentation is equally important. Intelligence must be delivered in a format that is easy to interpret and act upon. A well-balanced mix of text, tables, numbers, graphics, and multimedia ensures clarity and accessibility for different stakeholders. Security teams, executives, and decision-makers must all be able to extract key insights without unnecessary complexity.

3. Right Time

The right time is critical. Intelligence loses value if not shared on time. Organizations must receive information fast enough to take preventive actions before an attack occurs or mitigate damage if an incident has already taken place. Timely intelligence dissemination enables security teams to make informed and swift decisions, ensuring a proactive approach to cybersecurity threats.

Threat Modeling Methodologies

Threat modeling methodologies are systematic approaches used to identify, assess, and mitigate security threats within a system, application, or network. These methodologies help security teams anticipate potential attack scenarios, understand vulnerabilities, and implement appropriate countermeasures. Different methodologies cater to various security needs, risk levels, and organizational structures. Below are some widely used threat modeling methodologies:

STRIDE

STRIDE is a widely used threat modeling framework designed to help security analysts classify and address potential threats in a system. STRIDE stands for Spoofing, Tampering, Repudiation, Information Disclosure, Denial-of-Service

(DoS), and Elevation of Privilege. This methodology is particularly useful when analyzing a system's architecture using Data Flow Diagrams (DFDs) to identify security vulnerabilities at different interaction points. By applying it, security teams can proactively assess how each component of an application may be susceptible to attacks and implement appropriate mitigation strategies.

PASTA

The Process for Attack Simulation and Threat Analysis (PASTA) is a risk-centric threat modeling framework that focuses on simulating real-world attacks to identify security risks. PASTA follows a seven-stage methodology:

1. **Definition of Objectives (DO):** Establishes the business and security goals for the threat modeling process.

2. **Definition of Technical Scope (DTS):** Defines the system boundaries, assets, and technologies involved.

3. **Application Decomposition and Analysis (ADA):** Breaks down the application to identify its components, data flows, and interactions.

4. **Threat Analysis (TA):** Identifies and categorizes potential threats based on the system's architecture and attack surface.

5. **Weakness and Vulnerability Analysis (WVA):** Assesses existing security gaps, misconfigurations, and known vulnerabilities.

6. **Attack Modeling and Simulation (AMS):** Simulates real-world attack scenarios to understand how threats can exploit vulnerabilities.

7. **Risk and Analysis Management (RAM):** Evaluates risks based on impact and likelihood, helping prioritize mitigation efforts.

This structured approach aligns business objectives with security needs, ensuring that security measures are tailored to the most relevant threats. By emphasizing attack simulation, PASTA helps organizations proactively assess their security posture and prepare for emerging threats.

TRIKE

TRIKE is an open-source threat modeling methodology that adopts a risk management approach to assess and mitigate security threats. It consists of four key models:

1. **Requirements Model:** It defines security expectations based on user roles and access controls.

2. **Implementation Model:** It examines how these security policies are enforced within the system.

3. **Threat Model:** It identifies potential threats based on system design and user interactions.

4. **Risk Model:** It quantifies and prioritizes risks based on impact and likelihood.

TRIKE's structured approach enables organizations to integrate threat modeling into their overall risk management processes effectively.

Visual, Agile, and Simple Threat Modeling (VAST)

VAST is a threat modeling methodology designed to scale across an entire infrastructure and DevOps portfolio. Unlike traditional threat modeling methods that may not be practical for large-scale environments, VAST provides a streamlined, visually intuitive, and agile approach.

It focuses on two main types of threat models:

1. **Application Threat Model:** It identifies security threats in application architecture and workflows

2. **Operational Threat Model:** It assesses risks in the infrastructure, network, and DevOps processes.

This approach ensures security is embedded throughout the software development lifecycle while remaining efficient and scalable.

Damage, Reproducibility, Exploitability, Affected Users, and Discoverability (DREAD)

DREAD is a risk assessment model used to quantify and prioritize threats by assigning numerical values to five key factors:

1. **Damage:** Measures the potential impact of an attack.

2. **Reproducibility:** Assess how easily the attack can be repeated.

3. **Exploitability:** Determining the difficulty of exploiting a vulnerability.

4. **Affected Users:** Evaluating the number of people impacted.

5. **Discoverability:** Measures how easy it is for an attacker to find the vulnerability.

The DREAD risk formula calculates risk as the average of these five factors, helping organizations prioritize security efforts by ranking threats based on their severity.

The DREAD risk formula is as follows:

Risk = (Damage + Reproducibility + Exploitability + Affected Users + Discoverability)/5

Operationally Critical Threat, Asset, and Vulnerability Evaluation (OCTAVE)

OCTAVE is a strategic risk assessment methodology that focuses on identifying and managing security risks at an organizational level. It is divided into three key stages:

1. **Building Asset-Based Threat Profiles**: Critical assets are identified, and threats specific to them are evaluated

2. **Identifying Infrastructure Vulnerabilities**: Involves analyzing weaknesses in the organization's IT infrastructure

3. **Developing Security Strategy and Plans**: Ensures that the organization creates a comprehensive security roadmap to mitigate identified risks.

Unlike technical threat models, OCTAVE takes a more business-focused approach, emphasizing the alignment of security strategies with organizational objectives.

Threat Profiling and Attribution

Threat profiling and attribution is the process of gathering intelligence about threat actors and developing an analytical profile that helps organizations understand and mitigate cyber threats. By analyzing an adversary's Tactics, Techniques, and Procedures (TTPs), organizations can anticipate future attacks and strengthen their security defenses. This approach involves identifying the technological details, goals, and motives of threat actors, enabling cybersecurity teams to craft targeted countermeasures that effectively disrupt or neutralize threats before they escalate.

A threat profile typically includes the following attributes:

- **Description:** A detailed overview of the threat actor, including their background, affiliations, and known cyber activities.

- **Motive:** The underlying reason behind the attack, may include financial gain, espionage, activism, disruption, or political agendas.

- **Intent:** The specific objective of the attacker, such as stealing sensitive data, causing operational downtime, or damaging an organization's reputation.

- **Capability:** The level of technical expertise, resources, and tools that the threat actor possesses to execute an attack successfully.

- **Ownership Detail:** Information about the adversary's control over the attack infrastructure, such as botnets, malware, or command-and-control servers.

- **Target Detail:** The industries, organizations, or specific individuals that the attacker aims to compromise, which helps in assessing potential risks.

- **Operating Methods:** The Tactics, Techniques, and Procedures (TTPs) employed by the threat actor, such as phishing, malware deployment, zero-day exploits, or social engineering.

- **Objective:** The final goal of the attack, whether it is data exfiltration, sabotage, ransomware deployment, or persistent access to a network.

Domain 11: Penetration Testing

Introduction

In today's digital landscape, organizations face constant threats from cybercriminals seeking to exploit vulnerabilities in systems, networks, and applications. To proactively defend against such attacks, businesses employ penetration testing—a controlled security evaluation process where ethical hackers simulate real-world attacks to identify weaknesses before malicious actors can exploit them .

This domain explores the different types, phases, and methodologies involved in penetration testing, providing a structured approach to assessing security posture. We will also compare penetration testing with other security assessment techniques like security audits and vulnerability assessments, discuss the roles of Red and Blue Teams, and highlight the risks associated with penetration testing.

Additionally, we will cover pre-engagement activities, such as defining clear objectives and establishing the Rules of Engagement (ROE), to ensure ethical, legal, and effective security testing. By the end of this domain, you will have a clear understanding of penetration testing goals, methodologies, and best practices to enhance cybersecurity resilience.

Different Types of Penetration Testing and its Phases

Penetration Testing

Penetration testing is a security assessment method used to evaluate the defenses of an information system or network. It involves simulating an attack to identify vulnerabilities that malicious actors could exploit. By actively analyzing security measures, penetration testers uncover design weaknesses, technical flaws, and potential vulnerabilities within the system.

Beyond identifying weaknesses, penetration testing also documents how these vulnerabilities can be exploited, offering a detailed analysis of the potential risks. This documentation is crucial for organizations, as it helps them understand the severity of security gaps and how to address them.

Finally, the findings from penetration testing are compiled into a comprehensive report, which is then presented to both executive management and technical teams. This report helps stakeholders make informed decisions about security improvements and risk mitigation strategies, ensuring a more robust cybersecurity posture.

Why Perform Penetration Testing?

Penetration testing plays a crucial role in strengthening an organization's security posture by proactively identifying vulnerabilities and assessing the effectiveness of security controls. Here are the key reasons why organizations conduct penetration testing:

1. Identify Security Threats

Penetration testing helps organizations detect threats that could compromise their information assets. By simulating real-world attacks, security teams can uncover weak points before cybercriminals exploit them.

2. Reduce Security Costs and Enhance ROSI

By identifying vulnerabilities early, organizations can reduce IT security expenditures and improve their Return on Security Investment (ROSI). Proactively addressing weaknesses helps prevent costly security breaches and data leaks.

3. Provide a Comprehensive Security Assessment

A penetration test offers a detailed evaluation of an organization's security measures, including policies, procedures, system design, and implementation. This ensures all aspects of security are thoroughly reviewed and improved.

4. Meet Industry Compliance and Certifications

Many organizations conduct penetration testing to comply with industry regulations and obtain certifications such as BS7799, HIPAA, PCI-DSS, and GDPR. Regular security assessments help businesses meet legal and industry requirements.

5. Implement Best Security Practices

Penetration testing enables organizations to adopt and maintain security best practices in line with legal and regulatory standards, ensuring long-term security resilience.

6. Validate Security Protections and Controls

Testing helps verify the effectiveness of security measures, including firewalls, intrusion detection systems, and access controls. It ensures that security controls function as intended to defend against cyber threats.

7. Upgrade or Modify IT Infrastructure Securely

Before making changes to software, hardware, or network architecture, penetration testing ensures that the new infrastructure does not introduce security vulnerabilities.

8. Focus on High-Severity Vulnerabilities

Penetration testing helps prioritize critical security flaws by focusing on application-level security issues, ensuring that development teams and management address the most pressing risks first.

9. Prevent Future Exploits

A well-executed penetration test provides insights into potential attack vectors, allowing organizations to take preventative measures to strengthen their defenses against future cyberattacks.

10. Evaluate Network Security Devices

Penetration testing assesses the security of firewalls, routers, web servers, and other network devices to ensure they provide adequate protection and do not introduce security weaknesses.

By conducting regular penetration tests, organizations can proactively strengthen their security posture, mitigate risks, and ensure compliance with industry standards.

Comparing Security Audit, Vulnerability Assessment, and Penetration Testing

Organizations employ different security measures to protect their systems, and three common approaches are security audits, vulnerability assessments, and penetration testing. Each of these serves a unique purpose in strengthening cybersecurity.

Security Audit

A security audit focuses primarily on ensuring that an organization adheres to industry-standard security policies and procedures. It checks compliance with frameworks such as ISO 27001, HIPAA, or other regulations but does not actively test for vulnerabilities. Instead, it ensures that security measures are properly documented, implemented, and aligned with industry best practices.

Vulnerability Assessment

A vulnerability assessment goes a step further by scanning and identifying weaknesses in an organization's information systems. However, while it highlights vulnerabilities, it does not determine whether they can be exploited by an attacker. It provides a detailed report on potential security gaps but does not simulate real-world attack scenarios.

Penetration Test

A penetration test, on the other hand, combines elements of both security audits and vulnerability assessments, taking a more practical approach. It involves simulating an actual cyberattack to test how vulnerabilities can be exploited. Unlike a vulnerability assessment, penetration testing demonstrates the real impact of security flaws by actively attempting to break into the system, mimicking the tactics of malicious attackers.

In summary, a security audit ensures compliance, a vulnerability assessment identifies weaknesses, and penetration testing actively tests the exploitability of those weaknesses. Organizations often use a combination of these methods to build a comprehensive cybersecurity strategy.

Blue and Red Teaming

In cybersecurity, organizations employ Blue Teaming and Red Teaming as two distinct yet complementary approaches to evaluate and strengthen their security defenses.

Blue Teaming

Blue Teaming refers to a defensive security approach where a dedicated group of security professionals analyzes an organization's information systems to assess the effectiveness and efficiency of its security controls. The Blue Team has complete access to organizational resources, internal systems, and security configurations, allowing them to monitor, detect, and respond to security threats. Their primary role is to anticipate attacks, detect malicious activities, and mitigate threats in real-time. They also work proactively to strengthen security by implementing best practices, enhancing defensive measures, and simulating possible cyberattacks to improve the organization's security posture.

Red Teaming

Red Teaming, on the other hand, is an offensive security approach where ethical hackers conduct simulated cyberattacks on an organization's systems, often with little to no prior access to internal resources. Unlike Blue Teams, Red Teams operate from an attacker's perspective, attempting to exploit vulnerabilities and bypass security defenses to test how well an organization can withstand real-world threats. These penetration tests may be conducted with or without prior warning to the security team, ensuring an authentic evaluation of the organization's detection and response capabilities. The primary goal of Red Teaming is to identify weaknesses in network security, applications, and internal processes and provide actionable insights to improve defenses.

Both Blue Teaming and Red Teaming play crucial roles in cybersecurity. While Blue Teams focus on defense and incident response, Red Teams simulate real threats to uncover vulnerabilities. By working together in a structured Red versus Blue security exercise, organizations can create a more resilient security framework, improving both attack detection and prevention strategies.

Types of Penetration Testing

Penetration testing can be categorized into three main types based on the level of knowledge the pen tester has about the target system: black-box, white-box, and grey-box testing. Each type serves a unique purpose in assessing an organization's security posture.

Black-Box Penetration Testing

In black-box testing, the pen tester has no prior knowledge of the target infrastructure. This method closely mimics an external attack by a hacker who has no internal access to the system. The pen tester must gather intelligence and find vulnerabilities from scratch, just as a real attacker would. There are two specific approaches to black-box testing:

- **Blind Testing**: The penetration tester is provided with minimal information, such as only the organization's name. This helps simulate a real-world cyberattack scenario.
- **Double Blind Testing**: Neither the security team nor the penetration tester is aware of when the test will take place. This approach assesses how well an organization can detect and respond to unexpected threats.

Black-box testing is effective for evaluating external security defenses, such as firewalls and intrusion detection systems.

White-Box Penetration Testing

White-box testing, also known as clear-box or transparent testing, provides the pen tester with complete knowledge of the infrastructure, including network architecture, source code, and system configurations. This approach allows for a deep and thorough assessment of security vulnerabilities since the pen tester has full insight into the system's inner workings.

White-box testing is beneficial for identifying logical flaws, misconfigurations, and vulnerabilities that may not be easily detectable in black-box testing. It is commonly used for code reviews, security audits, and compliance testing.

Grey-Box Penetration Testing

Grey-box testing falls between black-box and white-box testing, where the pen tester has limited knowledge of the infrastructure. They may have partial access to

internal documentation, network architecture, or login credentials but do not possess full system details.

This type of testing balances the realism of black-box testing with the depth of White-box testing, making it effective for simulating insider threats or attacks by hackers already gained partial access to the system. It provides a more targeted approach, focusing on areas most likely to be exploited while reducing the time needed for reconnaissance.

Each type of penetration testing serves a different purpose, and organizations often use a combination of them to ensure a comprehensive security assessment.

Phases of Penetration Testing

Penetration testing is a structured security assessment that follows a defined set of phases to evaluate an organization's security posture. These phases ensure that the testing process is thorough, controlled, and does not cause unintended harm to the system. The penetration testing process is divided into three main phases: pre-attack phase, attack phase, and post-attack phase.

Pre-Attack Phase

The pre-attack phase is the planning and preparation stage where penetration testers define the scope, goals, and methodology for the test. This phase includes planning and preparation, which involves determining the rules of engagement, obtaining necessary permissions, and ensuring that the test aligns with business objectives. Penetration testers then move on to designing their methodology, selecting the tools, techniques, and frameworks they will use. Finally, they conduct network information gathering, collecting details about the target system, including domain names, IP addresses, network architecture, and other publicly available information that may aid in exploitation. This phase is crucial for understanding the target environment and laying the groundwork for the attack.

Attack Phase

The attack phase is where the actual penetration testing takes place. It begins with penetrating the perimeter, where pen testers attempt to bypass security controls such as firewalls and intrusion detection systems. Once inside the network, they proceed to acquire the target, which involves identifying critical systems, applications, and data that could be exploited. The next step is escalating privileges, where pen testers attempt to gain higher levels of access to move deeper into the system. After successfully infiltrating, they proceed with execution, implementing, and retracting, where they simulate real-world attack scenarios, execute payloads, and then carefully remove any traces of their activities to avoid unnecessary

disruption. This phase determines how vulnerable an organization is to different attack techniques and helps uncover security weaknesses.

Post-Attack Phase

The post-attack phase focuses on documentation, cleanup, and mitigation of vulnerabilities. The pen testers begin with reporting, where they document their findings, including vulnerabilities discovered, methods used, and recommendations for remediation. This report is crucial for organizations to improve their security measures. Next, they perform clean-up, ensuring that any changes made during testing such as new user accounts, modified configurations, or deployed scripts are removed. Finally, they conduct artifact destruction, eliminating any logs, files, or evidence of testing that could mislead security teams or impact normal operations.

By following these three phases, penetration testing provides organizations with a comprehensive evaluation of their security defenses, helping them identify vulnerabilities, improve security controls, and strengthen their overall security posture.

Security Testing Methodology

Security testing methodology is a structured approach designed to identify, assess, and verify vulnerabilities in an information system's security mechanisms. The goal of this methodology is to help organizations to detect weaknesses and implement appropriate security controls to protect sensitive data and critical business functions. Various security testing methodologies exist to standardize and enhance penetration testing practices.

Examples of Security Testing Methodologies

Open Web Application Security Project (OWASP)

OWASP is an open-source initiative focused on improving software security, particularly in web applications. It provides organizations with tools, software applications, and knowledge-based documentation to help them develop, purchase, and maintain secure applications. OWASP's widely recognized security guidelines, such as the OWASP Top 10, assist organizations in identifying and mitigating common security risks in web applications.

Open Source Security Testing Methodology Manual (OSSTMM)

OSSTMM is a peer-reviewed security testing methodology that ensures high-quality security assessments. It covers various aspects of security, including data controls, fraud prevention, social engineering, network security, wireless security, mobile devices, physical security, and access control mechanisms. OSSTMM is widely used

by security professionals to conduct comprehensive security evaluations based on standardized testing methods.

Information Systems Security Assessment Framework (ISSAF)

ISSAF is an open-source project designed to assist security professionals in conducting thorough security assessments. Its mission is to research, develop, publish, and promote a practical and widely accepted information systems security assessment framework. ISSAF provides detailed guidelines for penetration testing, security audits, and vulnerability assessments, making it a valuable resource for security professionals.

Licensed Penetration Tester (EC-Council LPT) Methodology

The EC-Council LPT Methodology is an industry-recognized penetration testing framework developed for advanced security professionals. It offers a structured and comprehensive approach to security auditing, covering areas such as ethical hacking, vulnerability assessments, and risk analysis. This methodology helps organizations identify and mitigate security threats by following a well-defined and systematic testing approach.

Each of these methodologies plays a crucial role in enhancing cybersecurity practices by providing organizations with a structured framework for identifying vulnerabilities and implementing effective security measures. By leveraging these methodologies, businesses can improve their security posture, reduce risks, and safeguard their critical assets from potential cyber threats.

Risks Associated with Penetration Testing

Penetration testing is a critical security practice, but it comes with certain risks that must be carefully managed. A successful penetration test requires meticulous planning, engagement, and execution to avoid unintended consequences. Organizations should be aware of the potential risks before conducting a penetration test.

Potential Risks of Penetration Testing

1. **Exposure of Sensitive Data**

During a penetration test, pen testers may gain access to sensitive or protected data if a vulnerability is successfully exploited. If not properly managed, this could lead to data leaks or unauthorized access, even by ethical hackers.

2. Knowledge of Organizational Vulnerabilities

Pen testers who conduct a penetration test will have access to detailed information about the security weaknesses of the organization's infrastructure. If this information is mishandled or leaked, it could pose a serious security threat.

3. Disruption of Services (Denial-of-Service Testing)

Certain types of penetration tests, such as Denial-of-Service (DoS) testing, can temporarily or permanently disrupt critical services within an organization. If not properly controlled, such tests may cause downtime, impacting operations and revenue.

4. Impact on Employee Morale (Social Engineering Attacks)

When penetration tests involve social engineering techniques, such as phishing or impersonation, employees may feel deceived or uncomfortable. This could lead to trust issues or dissatisfaction among the workforce if not handled appropriately.

Mitigating the Risks

Organizations can reduce these risks by implementing proper security measures and legal agreements before conducting penetration tests. Signing a Non-Disclosure Agreement (NDA) and other legal documents ensures that pen testers:

- Follow predefined guidelines and ethical standards
- Limit their access and actions to approved boundaries
- Do not misuse or disclose sensitive information

By taking these precautions, organizations can successfully conduct penetration tests while ensuring that the process remains secure, ethical, and minimally disruptive.

Types of Risks Arising During Penetration Testing

Penetration testing can introduce various risks to an organization, potentially leading to service disruptions, security breaches, or legal complications. Some penetration testing activities may unintentionally cause Denial-of-Service conditions, account lockouts, or critical system crashes. To mitigate these risks, organizations should carefully plan and execute penetration tests while adhering to legal and operational guidelines.

1. Technical Risks

Technical risks are directly linked to the targets within a production environment. These risks can impact system stability, data integrity, and service availability.

- **Failure of the Target:** Testing might cause unexpected crashes of applications, databases, or network infrastructure.

- **Disruption of Services:** Certain tests, like Denial-of-Service (DoS) attacks, can overload systems, making them temporarily or permanently unavailable.
- **Loss or Exposure of Sensitive Data:** If data protection measures are not in place, penetration tests might lead to data leaks, corruption, or unauthorized access to sensitive information.

2. *Organizational Risks*

Organizational risks are side effects of penetration testing that impact operations, incident response, and business continuity.

- **Unwanted Triggering of Incident Response Procedures:** Continuous security testing may lead to false alarms, straining security teams and diverting attention from actual threats.
- **Negligence in Monitoring and Response:** If an organization fails to properly monitor systems during and after a penetration test, real security breaches might go undetected.
- **Disruption of Business Continuity:** Testing may inadvertently affect critical business processes, leading to downtime and revenue loss.
- **Damage to Reputation:** A failed or mishandled penetration test exposing vulnerabilities can harm an organization's credibility among customers and stakeholders.

3. *Legal Risks*

Legal risks arise when penetration testing violates regulatory requirements or contractual agreements.

- **Violation of Laws and Regulations:** Unauthorized or improperly conducted penetration tests can violate privacy laws (such as GDPR, HIPAA) and result in legal penalties.
- **Violation of Rules of Engagement (ROE):** If pen testers exceed agreed-upon boundaries, they may inadvertently violate contracts or access information beyond their authorization.

Mitigating Risks in Penetration Testing

To prevent these risks, organizations should:

- Define clear Rules of Engagement (ROE) outlining what is allowed and restricted
- Use secure testing environments for high-risk scenarios to avoid disrupting production systems
- Ensure compliance with legal requirements by consulting with legal teams before testing
- Monitor tests in real-time and have an incident response plan ready

By addressing these risks, organizations can conduct effective penetration tests while safeguarding their systems, reputation, and compliance obligations.

Pre-Engagement Activities

Pre-engagement activities play a crucial role in ensuring the successful execution of a penetration testing engagement. These activities lay the foundation for effectively managing the test, setting clear expectations, and preventing potential misunderstandings between the penetration tester and the client.

One of the key aspects of pre-engagement activities is defining the scope, limitations, and objectives of the penetration test. Failing to properly follow these activities can lead to various challenges such as scope creep, client dissatisfaction, or even legal complications. Without a well-defined pre-engagement plan, penetration testers might test areas outside the agreed scope, causing disruptions or security risks.

To ensure a smooth penetration testing process, pre-engagement activities should begin with determining the goal of the test. This includes clarifying the testing approach, identifying key assets to be assessed, and outlining the legal and compliance requirements. A structured pre-engagement phase helps align expectations, reduce risks, and ensures a smooth and organized penetration testing process.

Goals of Penetration Testing

The goals of penetration testing are established based on the organization's security needs, ensuring that the test aligns with both business objectives and compliance requirements. These goals are typically derived from the purpose section of the Rules of Engagement (ROE) and the Preliminary Information Request Document, which outline the key expectations of the penetration test.

One of the primary objectives is to identify what the target organization wants to be tested. This could include specific applications, networks, or security controls that need assessment. Additionally, penetration testing aims to define both primary and secondary goals for the organization.

- Primary goals are usually business risk-driven, focusing on identifying and mitigating security vulnerabilities that could lead to financial loss, reputational damage, or operational disruptions.

- Secondary goals are often compliance-driven, ensuring the organization meets industry regulations and standards such as ISO 27001, HIPAA, PCI-DSS, or GDPR.

By clearly outlining these goals, penetration testing helps organizations enhance their security posture, address potential threats, and ensure compliance with legal and industry standards.

Goal	Primary or Secondary?
Protecting the stakeholder's data	
Reducing financial liability for noncompliance with regulation (for example, GDPR)	
Protecting the company's intellectual property	
Ensuring a high level of trust in regard to customers	
Reduce the likelihood of a breach to protect brand reputation	
Safeguard the organization from failure	
Prevent financial loss through fraud	
Identify the key vulnerabilities	
Improve the security of the technical systems	

Table 11-017: Goals of Penetration Testing

Rules of Engagement (ROE)

The Rules of Engagement (ROE) serve as a formal agreement between the penetration testers and the organization, providing explicit permission to conduct security assessments. This document outlines the scope, objectives, limitations, and legal considerations associated with the penetration testing process.

Top-Level Guidance

ROE provides high-level instructions on how the penetration test should be conducted. It defines the boundaries of testing, ensuring that pen testers stay within ethical and legal limits while performing security assessments. The document also clarifies what systems can be tested, what methods can be used, and any restrictions that must be followed.

ROE's Assistance in Overcoming Legal and Policy Barriers

A well-defined ROE helps penetration testers navigate legal and policy-related restrictions, allowing them to use various penetration testing tools and techniques without violating organizational policies or industry regulations. It ensures the test is carried out in a controlled and authorized way, avoiding unnecessary risks like data breaches, service disruptions, or legal issues.

By establishing clear Rules of Engagement, organizations and pen testers can ensure a structured, ethical, and effective penetration testing process while maintaining compliance with security policies and industry standards.

Domain 12: Security Operations Center (SOC)

Introduction

In today's evolving cybersecurity landscape, organizations must be equipped with the right tools and strategies to detect, respond to, and mitigate security threats effectively. A Security Operations Center (SOC) serves as the central hub for monitoring, analyzing, and defending against cyber threats in real-time. This domain explores the fundamental concepts of security operations, the role of a SOC, its key operational functions, and the structured workflow that enables proactive threat management.

Security Operations Concepts

Security Operations

Security operations refer to the continuous practice of maintaining and managing a secure IT environment. This is achieved through the implementation and execution of specific services and processes designed to protect an organization's digital assets. These operations involve a predefined set of processes that guide daily security tasks, ensuring alignment with the organization's security baselines. By following these standardized procedures, organizations can establish a structured approach to cybersecurity, minimizing risks and responding efficiently to potential threats.

Traditionally, security operations have been centered around two key aspects: security monitoring and security incident management. However, in modern security frameworks, organizations have introduced a third essential component— situational awareness. This addition enhances an organization's ability to anticipate and respond to cyber threats proactively.

The following key components are fundamental to modern security operations, ensuring a comprehensive and proactive approach to cybersecurity.

- **Situational Awareness**: This involves leveraging threat intelligence to gain insights into emerging cyber threats. By staying informed about the evolving threat landscape, organizations can make data-driven security decisions and adapt their cyber defenses accordingly.
- **Security Monitoring**: This process involves collecting, storing, and analyzing security logs and data from various sources, including firewalls, intrusion detection systems, and endpoint security tools. Effective security monitoring helps identify potential threats before they escalate into major incidents.
- **Security Incident Management**: This aspect focuses on promptly addressing security incidents to minimize damage and restore normal operations with

minimal impact. Incident response teams follow predefined protocols to contain and mitigate security breaches efficiently.

To manage these operations effectively, organizations establish a dedicated Security Operations Center (SOC). A SOC functions as a centralized unit responsible for monitoring, analyzing, and responding to security threats in real-time. It plays a critical role in ensuring continuous security by leveraging advanced tools, security professionals, and automated systems to detect and mitigate cyber risks efficiently.

By incorporating structured security operations, organizations can strengthen their overall cybersecurity posture, enhance threat detection capabilities, and ensure swift incident response to protect their digital environment.

Security Operations Center (SOC)

A Security Operations Center (SOC) is a centralized unit responsible for the continuous monitoring and analysis of an organization's information systems. It oversees various components, including networks, servers, endpoints, databases, applications, and websites, to effectively detect and respond to security threats. By maintaining constant vigilance, a SOC helps organizations identify potential vulnerabilities and mitigate security risks before they escalate into major incidents.

One of the key functions of a SOC is to provide a single point of control and visibility for an organization's security operations. This centralized approach ensures that all assets are continuously monitored, assessed, and defended against cyber threats. By consolidating security data from multiple sources, SOC analysts gain a comprehensive view of an organization's security posture, enabling efficient detection and response to anomalies.

Additionally, a SOC plays a crucial role in evaluating an organization's security posture by identifying suspicious activities or deviations from normal behavior within its information systems. Advanced monitoring tools, such as Security Information and Event Management (SIEM) systems, help detect unusual patterns that may indicate potential cyber threats.

Another vital function of a SOC is to facilitate situational awareness and real-time threat detection. If an intrusion attempt or cyberattack is detected, the SOC triggers real-time alerts, allowing security teams to take immediate action. By leveraging threat intelligence and automated response mechanisms, a SOC helps organizations strengthen their defense mechanisms and minimize the impact of security incidents.

In essence, a well-established SOC enhances an organization's ability to protect its digital assets through proactive monitoring, rapid incident response, and continuous improvement in security operations. It acts as the frontline defense

against cyber threats, ensuring the organization's resilience in an evolving cybersecurity landscape.

Understanding the Security Operations Center (SOC) Workflow

The workflow and key components of a Security Operations Center (SOC) by showcasing the data sources, data processing stages, and the final security insights that help organizations monitor and protect their IT infrastructure as illustrated in Figure 12-01.

1. Data Sources (Input to SOC)

The left side of the diagram represents various data sources that feed security-related information into the SOC. These include:

- **Firewall:** Monitors and controls network traffic
- **Database:** Stores critical data that needs protection
- **Endpoints:** Devices such as computers and mobile phones
- **Web Applications (WWW):** Online platforms exposed to potential cyber threats
- **File Server:** Repositories of sensitive organizational data
- **Email:** A common vector for phishing and malware attacks
- **Management Server:** Centralized control for IT resources
- **Routers & Switches:** Network devices that control data flow
- **Intrusion Prevention/Detection Systems (IPS/IDS):** Security tools for identifying threats

2. Data Ingestion Process

Once data is collected from these sources, it goes through the data ingestion process, where information is processed and prepared for further analysis. This process includes:

- **Collection:** Gathering security event logs and alerts from different sources
- **Normalization:** Standardizing data formats for uniform analysis
- **Indexing:** Organizing data to make it searchable and accessible
- **Database Storage:** Storing the processed data for future reference
- **Correlation:** Connecting different security events to identify potential threats

3. SOC Modules (Security Analysis and Actions)

The processed security data is then analyzed using SOC modules, which include:

- **Alerting:** Notifying security teams of potential threats in real-time
- **Reporting:** Generating security reports to assess threats and vulnerabilities
- **Query:** Searching and analyzing security logs for deeper investigation
- **Archiving:** Storing historical security data for compliance and future reference

- **Workflow Management:** Streamlining security processes and incident handling

4. SOC Views (Security Insights and Monitoring)

Finally, SOC analysts and security teams use various visualization tools to monitor security status and respond to threats. These views include:

- **Dashboard Monitoring:** Real-time security status overview

- **Threat Trend Analysis:** Tracking security incidents over time

- **Incident Reports:** Documenting security breaches and their resolutions

- **Data Insights & Analytics:** Using graphical representations to detect patterns

The Security Operations Center (SOC) acts as the central command for cybersecurity, allowing organizations to detect, analyze, and respond to threats in real-time, ensuring the security of their IT infrastructure.

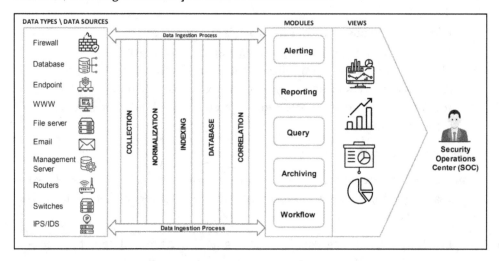

Figure 12-079: Security Operations Center (SOC) Workflow

SOC Operations

A Security Operations Center (SOC) plays a crucial role in managing and securing an organization's IT infrastructure. One of the key functions of a SOC is handling log data, which provides valuable insights into system activities, security incidents, and potential threats. The log management process consists of three essential steps: log collection, log retention and archiving, and log analysis.

Log Collection

The first step in SOC operations is log collection, where logs are gathered from various devices and systems within a network. These logs come from firewalls, servers, endpoints, routers, Intrusion Detection Systems (IDS), and other security devices that can impact the organization's security posture. By systematically collecting logs, SOC teams ensure that all activities—whether normal or suspicious—are recorded, enabling proactive threat detection and incident response.

Log Retention and Archiving

Once collected, logs are centrally stored and archived to ensure their availability for future use. These records are crucial for forensic investigations, helping security teams analyze past incidents and determine the root causes of security breaches. Additionally, retained logs help prevent threats by revealing attack patterns and enabling organizations to implement preventive measures. Proper archival practices also help organizations meet compliance requirements and industry regulations.

Log Analysis

The final step in the process is log analysis, where SOC technologies and tools extract meaningful insights from the vast amount of raw log data. Advanced analytics techniques help identify anomalies, detect suspicious activities, and track key security metrics. By analyzing these logs in real-time, SOC teams can detect cyber threats, generate alerts, and respond to incidents before they escalate. Effective log analysis improves situational awareness and strengthens an organization's overall security posture.

Monitoring of Security Environments for Security Events

Once logs are analyzed, the extracted security insights are transferred to the SOC team for continuous monitoring. This enables security professionals to assess the organization's current security posture and promptly detect any suspicious activities. By analyzing security events in real-time, SOC teams can identify anomalies, detect potential breaches, and initiate appropriate responses before an incident escalates.

Event Correlation

Security incidents rarely occur in isolation. Therefore, SOC teams use event correlation techniques to connect data from multiple sources, such as firewalls, Intrusion Detection Systems (IDS), and endpoints. These events are analyzed and contextualized using predefined correlation rules, allowing SOC teams to distinguish between routine activities and potential threats. Correlating events

helps security analysts identify patterns, detect sophisticated attacks, and eliminate false positives, ensuring a more effective security response.

Incident Management

Effective incident management is essential for minimizing security risks and optimizing SOC resources. SOC teams follow a structured approach to prioritize security incidents based on predefined rules and objectives. High-priority incidents, such as data breaches or malware attacks, are addressed immediately, while lower-risk events are monitored for further escalation. By classifying and addressing threats efficiently, organizations enhance their response capabilities and reduce the impact of cyber incidents.

Threat Identification

Identifying threats in real-time is critical to preventing security breaches. SOC teams use advanced research, analytics, and security tools to detect potential vulnerabilities within the organization's IT infrastructure. This involves assessing the likelihood of exploitation, identifying weak security controls, and taking proactive measures to mitigate risks before attackers can exploit them.

Threat Reaction

Once a threat is identified, the SOC team determines whether a reactive or proactive approach should be taken:

- **Reactive Threat Response:** If an active security threat is detected, SOC teams take immediate action to contain and remediate the issue. This could involve isolating compromised systems, blocking malicious IPs, or deploying patches to vulnerable assets.
- **Proactive Threat Response:** Instead of waiting for an attack to occur, SOC teams proactively analyze infrastructure weaknesses and implement security improvements before cybercriminals can exploit vulnerabilities. This approach strengthens defenses and minimizes potential risks.

Reporting

A critical aspect of SOC operations is generating detailed security reports for clients and stakeholders. These reports provide insights into detected threats, security incidents, system vulnerabilities, and response actions taken. SOC reporting supports real-time security management, compliance audits, and long-term security strategy planning.

SOC Workflow

Figure 12-02 illustrates the Security Operations Center (SOC) workflow, outlining the process of security event monitoring, analysis, and incident response. The

workflow follows a structured sequence of steps, ensuring effective threat detection and mitigation.

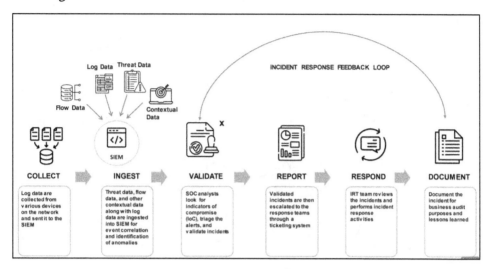

Figure 12-02: SOC Threat Detection and Response Workflow

Breakdown of the SOC Workflow

1. *Collect*

   o Log data is collected from various devices on the network, including firewalls, endpoints, and servers

   o This data is sent to a Security Information and Event Management (SIEM) system for further processing

2. *Ingest*

   o Multiple data sources are ingested into the SIEM, including:

     ▪ **Log Data:** Raw security logs from network devices

     ▪ **Threat Data:** Indicators of Compromise (IoCs) and known malicious activity

     ▪ **Contextual Data:** Additional information to enrich analysis (e.g., asset details, geolocation)

   o The SIEM correlates events and identifies anomalies to detect potential security threats

3. *Validate*

   o SOC analysts review alerts, looking for Indicators of Compromise (IoC)

o   They triage and validate incidents to confirm whether they are true security threats

4. *<u>Report</u>*

o   Validated incidents are escalated to the Incident Response Team (IRT) via a ticketing system for further investigation and mitigation

5. *<u>Respond</u>*

o   The IRT team reviews the incident and performs incident response activities, such as:

  ▪   Containing and mitigating threats

  ▪   Blocking malicious IPs or isolating affected systems

  ▪   Deploying security patches

6. *<u>Document</u>*

o   The incident is documented for:

  ▪   Business audits and compliance

  ▪   Lessons learned to improve security posture

Incident Response Feedback Loop

- After an incident is documented, its findings and lessons learned are fed back into the SIEM system

- This feedback loop helps improve detection rules, refine security policies, and enhance future threat detection capabilities

Domain 13: Computer Forensics and Software Security

Introduction

Computer forensics and software security are critical aspects of cybersecurity, focusing on the protection and investigation of digital systems. Computer forensics involves the identification, preservation, analysis, and presentation of digital evidence to investigate cybercrimes, data breaches, and unauthorized access. It plays a vital role in legal proceedings by ensuring that digital evidence is collected and analyzed in a forensically sound manner.

Software security, on the other hand, deals with securing applications from vulnerabilities and threats through secure coding practices, encryption, access controls, and security testing. By integrating security measures throughout the Software Development Lifecycle (SDLC), organizations can mitigate risks such as malware infections, exploitation of software flaws, and unauthorized access. Together, computer forensics and software security help in preventing cyber threats, ensuring data integrity, and strengthening the overall security posture of digital systems.

Computer Forensics

Computer forensics, also known as digital forensics, involves the identification, preservation, analysis, and presentation of digital evidence from electronic devices. This field is crucial for investigating and preventing cybercrimes, ensuring that digital evidence is handled in a manner admissible in court.

Objectives of Computer Forensics

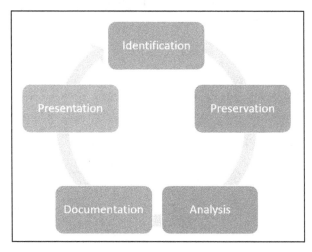

Figure 13-01: Objectives of Computer Forensics

1. Identifying, Gathering, and Preserving Evidence of Cybercrime

The primary goal is to systematically collect and protect digital evidence related to cyber incidents. This process must maintain the integrity of the evidence to ensure its admissibility in legal proceedings.

2. Tracking and Prosecuting Perpetrators

By analyzing digital footprints, computer forensics aids in tracing cybercriminals and providing evidence for their prosecution. Techniques such as examining metadata and network logs are employed to pinpoint the sources of malicious activities.

3. Estimating the Impact of Malicious Activities and Understanding Intent

Forensic analysis helps assess the extent of damage caused by cyberattacks, including financial losses and data breaches. Understanding the attacker's intent—whether for financial gain, espionage, or other motives—assists organizations in strengthening their security measures.

4. Finding Vulnerabilities and Security Loopholes

Through a detailed examination of attack vectors, computer forensics identifies exploited vulnerabilities, enabling organizations to address security weaknesses and prevent future incidents.

5. Recovering Deleted, Hidden, and Temporary Files for Evidence

Utilizing specialized tools, forensic experts can retrieve data that perpetrators may have attempted to conceal or delete. This includes recovering deleted files, uncovering hidden data, and analyzing temporary files to gather crucial evidence.

Phases Involved in the Computer Forensics Investigation Process

The computer forensics investigation process is typically structured into several key phases, each with specific objectives and tasks. While different sources may outline varying numbers of phases, the core components generally include:

1. **Pre-Investigation Phase (Preparation)**

This initial phase focuses on preparing for the investigation. Tasks include establishing a computer forensics lab, assembling an investigation team, obtaining necessary approvals, and ensuring all tools and resources are in place. Proper preparation is crucial for maintaining the integrity and efficiency of the subsequent investigation.

2. **Investigation Phase**

This central phase involves acquiring, preserving, and analyzing digital evidence. Investigators collect data from relevant devices, ensure its integrity, and analyze it to identify the source of the incident and the individuals involved. Techniques such as data recovery, log analysis, and cross-drive analysis are commonly employed.

3. Post-Investigation Phase

In this final phase, all actions taken and findings uncovered during the investigation are thoroughly documented. The final report should be clear and comprehensible to the intended audience, providing adequate and acceptable evidence. This documentation is essential for legal proceedings and for informing future security measures.

Pre-Investigation Phase

1. Setting Up a Computer Forensics Lab

A computer forensics lab serves as a designated space for conducting investigations. It is equipped with specialized tools and technologies to analyze collected evidence, helping investigators solve cases and identify culprits.

2. Building the Investigation Team

A well-structured team is essential for evaluating the crime, analyzing evidence, and identifying potential suspects. Each member contributes in ensuring a thorough and effective forensic investigation.

3. Reviewing Policies and Laws

Understanding applicable federal, state, and local laws is necessary to ensure compliance throughout the investigation. This step helps investigators operate within legal boundaries and maintain the admissibility of evidence in court.

4. Establishing Quality Assurance Processes

Implementing a systematic and well-documented process ensures accuracy, reliability, and credibility in handling evidence. Quality assurance measures help maintain the integrity of forensic findings.

5. Implementing Data Destruction Standards

Proper data destruction methods are crucial for securely disposing of sensitive information. Industry-approved techniques prevent unauthorized access and protect confidential data from being misused.

6. Conducting a Risk Assessment

Assessing potential security risks within an organization helps identify vulnerabilities and their impact. This step enables businesses to implement necessary measures to mitigate risks and enhance cybersecurity.

Investigation Phase

1. Initiating the Investigation Process

Before beginning the investigation, incident responders must have a clear understanding of the objectives of the examination. Establishing clear goals ensures that the investigation follows a structured and effective approach.

2. Performing Computer Forensics Investigation

First Response

The initial response is crucial in handling the incident. Investigators must act swiftly to assess the situation, prevent further damage, and document critical details about the crime scene.

Search and Seizure

Law enforcement and forensic experts conduct searches to locate and seize digital evidence. This process must adhere to legal guidelines to ensure that evidence remains admissible in court.

Collecting the Evidence

All relevant digital artifacts, such as files, logs, and metadata, are systematically collected. Proper documentation and chain of custody records are maintained to preserve the integrity of the evidence.

Securing the Evidence

Evidence must be stored in tamper-proof forensic methods to prevent tampering or corruption. Secure storage methods and encryption techniques help maintain the authenticity of digital data.

Data Acquisition

Forensic experts extract data from various digital devices while preserving the integrity of the original evidence. Imaging techniques, such as disk cloning, are commonly used to create accurate duplicates of data for analysis.

Data Analysis

Investigators examine the acquired data to identify suspicious activities, recover deleted files, and trace digital footprints. This phase helps establish connections between evidence and the suspected crime.

Post-Investigation Phase

The Post-Investigation Phase in computer forensics is essential for synthesizing findings and ensuring their effective presentation in legal contexts. This phase encompasses three critical components: Evidence Assessment, Documentation and Reporting, and Testifying as an Expert Witness.

1. Evidence Assessment

This process involves correlating the obtained evidential data to reconstruct the sequence of events and understand the full scope of the incident. Analyzing how each piece of evidence interconnects is crucial to forming a comprehensive narrative of the crime. This assessment is key to understanding the incident's dynamics and the involved entities.

2. Documentation and Reporting

Thorough documentation entails recording all actions performed during the investigation, including methodologies employed, tools used, and findings uncovered. The resulting report should be detailed, presenting evidence clearly and systematically, often supplemented with visual aids like charts and timelines to highlight critical activities. This meticulous documentation ensures that the investigative process is transparent and that the findings are communicated effectively to stakeholders.

3. Testifying as an Expert Witness

In legal proceedings, forensic investigators may be called upon to testify as expert witnesses to elucidate technical aspects of the evidence for the court. This role requires a deep understanding of the evidence, as well as the ability to present complex information in an accessible manner to those without technical backgrounds. The expert witness must also affirm the accuracy of the investigative process and the integrity of the evidence presented.

Integrating Security in the Software Development Life Cycle (SDLC)

Integrating security into the Software Development Life Cycle (SDLC) is essential to ensure that applications are developed with robust protection against potential threats. This approach, known as the Secure Software Development Life Cycle (SSDLC), embeds security practices at each phase of development, proactively addressing vulnerabilities and reducing the risk of security breaches.

Phases of Software Development Life Cycle

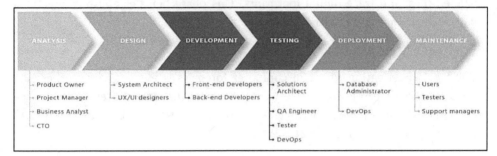

Figure 13-02: Phases of the Software Development Life Cycle

1. **Planning and Requirement Analysis:** This initial phase involves defining the project's scope and gathering comprehensive requirements, including explicit security considerations. Identifying potential security risks early enables the development of strategies to address them throughout the project.

2. **Design:** In this phase, the software architecture is designed with a focus on security. This includes implementing secure coding standards, threat modeling, and establishing security controls to protect against identified risks.

3. **Development:** Developers write code adhering to secure coding practices to prevent common vulnerabilities such as SQL injection and cross-site scripting. Regular code reviews and static analysis tools are employed to detect and rectify security issues during this stage.

4. **Testing:** Security testing, including vulnerability assessments and penetration testing, is conducted to identify and address security flaws. This ensures the software functions as intended without exposing users to security risks.

5. **Deployment:** Secure deployment practices are implemented to maintain the integrity of the software in the production environment. This involves configuring security settings appropriately and ensuring the deployment process does not introduce new vulnerabilities.

6. **Maintenance and Continuous Improvement:** Post-deployment, ongoing maintenance is crucial to address emerging threats and apply necessary updates or patches. Continuous monitoring and improvement of security measures help in adapting to the evolving threat landscape.

Functional vs. Security Activities in the SDLC

SDLC Phase	Functional Activities	Security Activities
Requirement	- Define functional requirements - Define non-functional requirements - Determine technology requirements	- Define security requirements
Design	- Establish guidelines and architectural design	- Create a secure design - Set secure coding standards - Perform threat modeling - Secure the architecture
Development	- Implement functional programming logic - Conduct unit testing	- Implement security requirements - Follow secure coding standards - Adopt secure coding practices
Testing	- Perform functional testing (black-box, grey-box, and white-box testing)	- Conduct security testing
Deployment	- Deploy the software	- Ensure secure deployment
Maintenance	- Update functionality	- Apply security patches and updates

Table 13-01: Functional vs. Security Activities in the SDL

Advantages of Integrating Security in the SDLC

Integrating security into the Software Development Life Cycle (SDLC) provides numerous benefits that enhance software quality, reduce risks, and improve overall efficiency. Here are some key advantages:

Reduction of Software Vulnerabilities

Incorporating security measures throughout the development process significantly minimize the presence of software vulnerabilities resulting in more robust and secure applications.

Regulatory Compliance

Secure development practices help organizations comply with industry regulations, standards, and legal requirements, ensuring that software meets necessary security guidelines.

Minimized Costly Rework

Identifying and eliminating security flaws early in the SDLC prevents expensive rework, reducing costs associated with fixing vulnerabilities post-deployment.

Enhanced Developer Job Satisfaction

A security-focused approach equips developers with the tools and knowledge to build safer software, leading to increased job satisfaction and confidence in their work.

Improved Customer Satisfaction

Secure software enhances user trust, ensuring better customer experience and satisfaction by protecting sensitive data and ensuring reliable system performance.

Embedded Security Culture

Integrating security from the start fosters a strong security culture within development teams, promoting quality, reliability, and long-term resilience against cyber threats.

Reuse of Trusted Software Components

Secure coding practices allow organizations to safely reuse verified and trusted software components, accelerating development and ensuring consistent security standards.

Reduced Maintenance Costs

By addressing security early, organizations save on long-term maintenance costs, as fewer vulnerabilities mean fewer patches, updates, and emergency fixes.

Security Requirements

Security requirements are a critical aspect of software development, ensuring that applications maintain confidentiality, integrity, and availability throughout their lifecycle. Addressing security from the beginning helps prevent vulnerabilities and strengthens the overall system.

Non-Functional Security Requirements

Security requirements are often categorized as non-functional aspects of software development. They focus on maintaining data confidentiality, ensuring system integrity, and guaranteeing availability against cyber threats.

Overlooked by Stakeholders

Many stakeholders tend to overlook security requirements during the initial inception phase of software development. This oversight can lead to security gaps, making the system susceptible to potential threats.

Impact of Negligence

Ignoring security requirements can expose the application to various cyberattacks, data breaches, or system abuses. Negligence in defining security needs may result in costly fixes and reputational damage for organizations.

Security as a Strategic Process

To build resilient software, security requirements should be an integral part of the strategic application development process. This ensures that security measures are proactively defined, implemented, and maintained throughout the development cycle.

Gathering Security Requirements

Effective security in software development starts with properly gathering and defining security requirements. This process ensures that security considerations are incorporated early, reducing vulnerabilities and strengthening the overall system.

1. Eliciting Security Requirements

Gathering security requirements involves various approaches, such as stakeholder discussions, risk assessments, and threat modeling. Identifying security needs early in the development process helps prevent future security flaws.

2. Separating Security and Functional Requirements

Security requirements should be enumerated separately from functional requirements. This separation enables independent review and testing, ensuring that security measures are thoroughly validated without being overshadowed by functional objectives.

3. Avoiding Complexity and Inaccuracy

Mixing security requirements with functional requirements can make the security gathering process more complicated and less accurate. Separating these aspects ensures that security is given the attention it deserves, leading to better-defined and well-implemented protections.

Why We Need Different Approaches for Security Requirement Gathering

Security requirement gathering demands a distinct approach from functional requirement gathering because it focuses on preventing potential threats rather than enabling intended functionalities. Understanding this difference is crucial for building secure systems.

Functional vs. Security Requirements

Functional requirements define what a system should do. These are considered positive requirements because they specify expected system behavior, ensuring the software performs its intended tasks correctly. Functional requirements focus on usability, performance, and efficiency.

In contrast, security requirements define what a system should not do. These are known as negative requirements because they impose restrictions that prevent unauthorized actions, security breaches, and malicious exploits. Security requirements focus on protecting the system from vulnerabilities and external threats.

Challenges in Identifying Security Requirements

People often find it easier to specify what they want from a system, but they struggle to define what they do not want. This is because users and developers primarily focus on expected outcomes rather than potential security risks. Identifying security requirements requires considering misuse cases, possible attack vectors, and system weaknesses, which may not be apparent during standard requirement gathering.

The Need for a Critical and Adversarial Approach

Security requirements cannot be gathered through a purely constructive approach. Instead, the system must be examined from a negative, critical, and destructive perspective to uncover hidden vulnerabilities. This involves thinking like an attacker, analyzing how the system could be exploited, and identifying security loopholes before they can be misused. Unlike functional testing, which validates expected behavior, security assessment requires anticipating and mitigating unintended behaviors.

Key Benefits of Addressing Security at the Requirement Phase

Incorporating security considerations at the requirement phase of software development is crucial for building robust and resilient applications. Addressing security early in the development lifecycle helps prevent costly vulnerabilities and ensures compliance with industry standards. The key benefits of security at requirement phase include:

- Addressing security at the requirement phase can save billions of dollars compared to dealing with security issues at later stages of software development.

- It defines the security mechanisms that must be implemented to meet regulations, standards, and best practices for secure application development, ensuring protection against attacks.

- Security requirements provide developers with an overview of the key security controls needed to build a secure application.

- Properly understood security requirements aid in implementing security during the design, development, and testing stages, reducing risks and vulnerabilities early in the software lifecycle.

Secure Application Design and Architecture

The design and architecture phase of software development plays a crucial role in ensuring the security of an application. A well-structured security approach at this stage helps prevent vulnerabilities, reducing long-term risks and costs.

1. Impact of Security Negligence: If security is neglected during the design and architecture phase, vulnerabilities may go undetected until later stages. These security gaps become difficult to identify and expensive to fix once the application is in production.

2. Early Detection of Security Flaws: Incorporating security vigilance in the design phase allows for the early detection of security flaws, minimizing risks before they become major threats. This proactive approach strengthens the overall security posture of the application.

3. Security-Driven Application Design: A secure design is built upon the security requirements defined in earlier phases of the Software Development Life Cycle (SDLC). Ensuring that these requirements are properly addressed helps create a more resilient and robust application.

4. Challenges in Secure Design: Designing security controls can be challenging, as implementing strict security measures may sometimes conflict with business functionality requirements. Achieving the right balance between security and usability is essential to maintain both protection and operational efficiency.

Goals of the Secure Design Process

The secure design process is essential for building robust and resilient software. By integrating security into the early stages of development, organizations can proactively mitigate risks and strengthen application security. The key goals of this process include:

1. **Threat Identification for Developers**: One of the primary objectives of secure design is to identify potential threats in sufficient detail. This ensures that developers have a clear understanding of security risks and can implement appropriate safeguards in their code to mitigate associated vulnerabilities.

2. **Threat-Resilient Architecture:** The software architecture should be designed to mitigate as many security threats as possible. A well-structured architecture minimizes attack surfaces and ensures that security mechanisms are embedded at every layer of the application.

3. **Enforcing Secure Design Principles:** Secure design principles should be enforced throughout the development lifecycle, compelling developers to consider security from the beginning. By integrating security best practices into coding standards, organizations can proactively prevent vulnerabilities rather than reactively addressing them.

Secure Design Principles

Secure Design Principles are a set of best practices that guide developers in building secure applications. These principles ensure that security is an integral part of the development process, helping to create robust software architectures that resist cyber threats.

1. **Enforcing Security Practices in Development:** Secure design principles provide clear guidelines for developers, ensuring that security is incorporated throughout the development phase. By following these principles, developers can proactively address potential security risks.

2. **Driving Secure Architectural Decisions:** These principles aid in making secure architectural decisions, ensuring that security is a foundational element rather than an afterthought. A well-designed architecture reduces vulnerabilities and strengthens the overall security posture of an application.

3. **Eliminating Design and Architecture Flaws:** Secure design principles help identify and eliminate weaknesses in an application's design and architecture. By proactively addressing potential security flaws, developers can mitigate common vulnerabilities such as injection attacks, insecure authentication, and data leaks.

Common Security Vulnerabilities

To prevent common security vulnerabilities, developers should follow a set of secure design principles throughout the software development lifecycle. These

principles ensure that applications are built with security in mind from the ground up.

Core Secure Design Principles:

- Security through obscurity
- Secure the weakest link
- Use least privilege principle
- Secure by default
- Fail securely
- Apply defense in depth
- Do not trust user input
- Reduce attack surface
- Enable auditing and logging
- Keep security simple
- Maintain a separation of duties
- Correctly fix security issues
- Apply security in the design phase

Advanced Secure Design Considerations:

- Protect sensitive data
- Exception handling
- Secure memory management
- Protect memory or storage secrets
- Fundamentals of control granularity
- Fault tolerance
- Fault detection
- Fault removal
- Fault avoidance
- Loose coupling
- High cohesion
- Change management and version control

Design Secure Application Architecture

A well-structured application architecture is crucial for ensuring security, especially in web applications that handle sensitive data and user interactions. Secure architecture follows a layered security approach, protecting each tier of the system from potential threats.

Three-Tier Web Application Architecture

A typical web application consists of three main tiers:

- Web Tier: Handles user requests and serves web pages

- Application Tier: Processes business logic and interacts with the database

- Database Tier: Stores and manages data securely

Security at One Tier is Not Enough

Securing only one layer of the architecture is insufficient. If an attacker bypasses security at one tier, they may still exploit vulnerabilities in another layer to compromise the entire application.

Defense-in-Depth Approach

A secure web application should follow the defense-in-depth principle, ensuring security controls at each tier. This multi-layered defense strategy reduces the risk of breaches by adding redundancy to security measures.

Multi-Tiered Security Approach

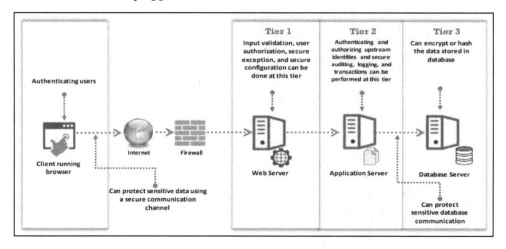

Figure 13-03: Multi-Tier Security Architecture

Figure 13-03 illustrates a multi-tier security architecture, which is a structured approach to securing web applications. This design ensures that security is implemented at different levels, providing multiple layers of protection. By segmenting security controls across tiers, organizations can reduce the risk of breaches, safeguard sensitive data, and enhance overall system integrity.

1. Client Layer: User Authentication and Secure Communication

The process starts with a client running a web browser. The user interacts with the application, and authentication is performed to verify credentials before granting access. Secure communication channels, such as SSL/TLS encryption, protect sensitive data transmitted over the internet. This prevents eavesdropping and man-in-the-middle attacks, ensuring the confidentiality and integrity of data.

2. Firewall Protection: Network Security Barrier

A firewall serves as a security barrier between the client and the internal network, filtering incoming and outgoing traffic. It helps prevent unauthorized access, blocks malicious requests, and acts as the first line of defense against cyber threats. By enforcing security rules, the firewall ensures only legitimate requests reach the web server.

3. Three-Tier Security Architecture

The application architecture is structured into three tiers, each performing distinct security functions to enhance overall protection.

Tier 1: Web Server – Input Validation and Access Control

The web server plays a critical role in securing the application by implementing input validation to prevent vulnerabilities like SQL injection and Cross-Site Scripting (XSS). It also manages user authorization, ensuring that only authenticated users can access specific resources. Additional security measures at this layer include secure exception handling to prevent attackers from exploiting application errors and secure configuration to eliminate security misconfigurations.

Tier 2: Application Server – Authentication and Secure Transactions

The application server is responsible for authenticating and authorizing upstream identities, ensuring that user roles and permissions are verified before executing requests. It also enforces security auditing and logging, which helps track user activities and detect anomalies. Additionally, secure transactions are managed at this tier, ensuring the integrity and confidentiality of data during operations.

Tier 3: Database Server – Data Encryption and Secure Storage

The database server focuses on protecting stored data by implementing encryption or hashing techniques. This ensures that even if the data is compromised, it remains unreadable without proper decryption keys. Secure database communication is enforced to preventing unauthorized access, ensuring that sensitive information remains protected during interactions between the application and database.

Key Components of Multi-Tier Architecture

The layered security approach provides several benefits, including enhanced data protection, controlled access, and improved monitoring. Authentication and authorization mechanisms prevent unauthorized access; while logging and auditing ensure better tracking of security incidents. By implementing encryption and secure configurations at each tier, organizations can significantly reduce security risks.

Key components of a multi-tiered security approach include:

- **Input Validation:** Ensuring that all user inputs are properly validated to prevent injection attacks and other malicious inputs

- **Database Layer Abstraction:** Implementing abstraction layers to prevent direct access to the database, reducing exposure to SQL injection attacks

- **Server Configuration:** Properly configuring servers to minimize vulnerabilities and disable unnecessary services

- **Proxies and Web Application Firewalls (WAFs):** Utilizing proxies and WAFs to filter and monitor incoming traffic, blocking malicious requests

- **Data Encryption:** Encrypting sensitive data both in transit and at rest to protect it from unauthorized access

- **Operating System Hardening:** Applying security patches and configuring operating systems to enhance security

About Our Products

Other products from IPSpecialist LTD regarding CSP technology are:

- AWS Certified Cloud Practitioner Study guide
- AWS Certified SysOps Admin - Associate Study guide
- AWS Certified Solution Architect - Associate Study guide
- AWS Certified Developer Associate Study guide
- AWS Certified Advanced Networking – Specialty Study guide
- AWS Certified Security – Specialty Study guide
- AWS Certified Big Data – Specialty Study guide
- Microsoft Certified: Azure Fundamentals
- Microsoft Certified: Azure Administrator
- Microsoft Certified: Azure Solution Architect
- Microsoft Certified: Azure DevOps Engineer
- Microsoft Certified: Azure Developer Associate
- Microsoft Certified: Azure Security Engineer
- Microsoft Certified: Azure Data Engineer Associate
- Microsoft Certified: Azure Data Scientist
- Microsoft Certified: Azure Network Engineer
- Oracle Certified: Foundations Associate
- Microsoft Certified: Security, Compliance, and Identity Fundamentals
- Terraform Associate Certification Study Guide
- Docker Certified Associate Study Guide
- Certified Kubernetes Administrator Study Guide

Other Network & Security related products from IPSpecialist LTD are:

- CCNA
- CCDA Study Guide
- CCDP Study Guide
- CCNP Security SCOR Study Guide
- CCNP Enterprise ENCOR Study Guide
- CCNP Service Provider SPCOR Study Guide
- CompTIA Network+ Study Guide
- CompTIA Security+ Study Guide
- Ethical Hacking Certification v 12 First Edition Study Guide
- Ethical Hacking Exam – AI Edition
- Certified Blockchain Expert v2 Study Guide
- Fortinet Professional Certification Study Guide

- Palo Alto Certified Network Security Administrator
- Palo Alto Certified Network Security Engineer

www.ingramcontent.com/pod-product-compliance
Lightning Source LLC
LaVergne TN
LVHW062302060326
832902LV00013B/2006